Subsidies in I

Subsidies in India

Rishi Muni Dwivedi
Assistant General Manager
Indian Overseas Bank
Regional Office
Ludhiana, India

New Century Publications
New Delhi, India

NEW CENTURY PUBLICATIONS
4800/24, Bharat Ram Road,
Ansari Road, Daryaganj,
New Delhi - 110 002
Tel.: 23247798, 65396605
Telefax: 011- 41017798
E-mail: indiatax@vsnl.com
www.newcenturypublications.com

Editorial office:
34, Gujranwala Town, Part-2,
Delhi - 110 009
Tel.: 27247805, 27464774

First Published 2006

ISBN: 81-7708-117-9

Published by New Century Publications and printed at Singhal Print Media, New Delhi -110 005

PRINTED IN INDIA

About the Book

A subsidy is a grant of money from an outside third party to either the buyer or the seller of a commodity. The effect of a subsidy is opposite of the effect of a tax. A cash subsidy is the opposite of a direct tax while a subsidised commodity is the opposite of a taxed commodity. Hence, subsidies are sometimes called negative taxation.

Providing minimum consumption entitlement to the poor by subsidising the items consumed by them is an extremely important welfare dimension of fiscal policy. However, subsidies can generate negative effects also. Once received, people become dependent on the subsidies. Hence, subsidies are sometimes termed as sweet poison.

This book explains and examines the whole gamut of subsidies, both explicit and implicit, in India at the level of Central and State Governments. There are 46 chapters in all which have been categorized into the following 12 theme parts. Some overlapping in categorisation is possible because a subsidy programme/scheme may have multiple objectives.

Part I: Economics of Subsidies
Part II: Subsidies for Agriculture and Allied Sectors
Part III: Subsidies for Food Security
Part IV: Subsidies for Industrial Development and Export Promotion
Part V: Subsidies for Employment and Labour Welfare
Part VI: Subsidies for Energy and Transport Development
Part VII: Subsidies for Health and Education
Part VIII: Subsidies for Housing and Urban Development
Part IX: Subsidies for Rural Infrastructure and Development
Part X: Subsidies for Welfare of Women, Children and Disadvantaged Groups
Part XI: Subsidies for Development of Special Problem Regions
Part XII: Subsidies for Cinema, Art and Culture

Author's profile

Dr. Rishi Muni Dwivedi is B.Sc. (Agriculture), M.Sc. (Agriculture) and Ph.D. His professional qualifications include CA.I.I.B., CRB (Indian Institute of Banking and Finance, Mumbai) and CPPM, Development and Project Planning Centre, University of Bradford, UK. He has 25 years of experience in Indian Overseas Bank as officer in various capacities in rural credit and development. He has to his credit 160 articles, mainly on agriculture and rural development finance. Presently, he is Assistant General Manager, Indian Overseas Bank (Regional Office), Ludhiana.

Preface

A subsidy is a grant of money from an outside third party to either the buyer or the seller of a commodity. Subsidies allow a buyer to procure a commodity/service at a lower price than would otherwise have been necessary. Similarly, a business firm will not stay in operation unless revenue is sufficient enough to cover cost plus some return on investment. If revenue from buyers is insufficient, a subsidy from an outside agency may keep the firm in operation.

The effect of a subsidy is opposite of the effect of a tax. A cash subsidy is the opposite of a direct tax while a subsidised commodity is the opposite of a taxed commodity. Hence, subsidies are sometimes called negative taxation.

Providing minimum consumption entitlement to the poor by subsidising the items consumed by them is an extremely important welfare dimension of fiscal policy. Subsidies can correct for the under-consumption of goods with positive externalities. With the social benefits of a particular service or commodity exceeding the aggregate of private benefits to individual consumers, market solutions result in under-consumption and subsidies can make the necessary correction. However, the benefits can be maximised only when the subsidies are transparent, well targeted, and suitably designed for effective implementation without any leakages.

However, subsidies can generate negative effects also. Once received, people become dependent on the subsidies. Hence, subsidies are sometimes termed as sweet poison. Misuse of subsidies for political purpose is known worldwide. Subsidies support one industry at the expense of the other. When a person is given subsidy benefit, it imposes burden on some other person in the country. Subsidies interfere in the free working of the economy in the following ways.

- Through subsidies, free money circulates in the economy without increase in actual income/production.
- Subsidies make the beneficiaries lethargic.

- Subsidies lead to misallocation of resources.
- Malpractices have often been noticed in the administration of subsidies.
- Subsidies are often misused by politicians.

Subsidies represent a sizable item of the non-Plan revenue expenditure of the Government of India. In the 2006-07 budget, they accounted for Rs. 46,213 crore (13.4 per cent) out of a total non-Plan revenue expenditure of Rs. 3,44,430 crore. Food and fertilisers are the two main items subsidised by the Government through budgetary support.

Of late, drastic changes have occurred in Government's policy towards subsidies. The crux of this policy is to roll back subsidies and thus curb the growth of non-Plan expenditure. Another dimension of the present policy is to restrict the availability of subsidised items to vulnerable sections of society.

Three reasons account for the increase in the Central Government subsidies in recent years:

- moving the petroleum sector to a transparent system of budgetary subsidies and delay in the announced phasing out of the subsidies on PDS, kerosene and domestic LPG;
- increase in explicit budgetary subsidies on food and fertilizer; and
- increase in input costs unaccompanied by any improvement in recovery rates resulting in escalation of implicit subsidies on a variety of economic and social services.

The reforms programme initiated in 1991 aimed at, among other things, reducing fiscal imbalances and improving allocative efficiency by minimizing the distortions in relative prices arising from budgetary and fiscal imprudence. Containing and targeting subsidies constituted an important element of reforms. Containment and targeting of subsidies can serve the following objectives:

- remove economic distortions, thereby improving economic efficiency and growth.
- achieve redistributive objective.

- reduce budgetary burden and release precious resources.

National Common Minimum Programme (NCMP) of the Government of India pledges: "All subsidies will be targeted sharply at the poor and the truly needy like small and marginal farmers, farm labour and urban poor."

Government showed its seriousness about targeting subsidies at the poor and the truly needy in the budget speech for 2006-07. Extensive discussions with stakeholders on three major subsidies, namely food, fertilizer and petroleum were held for the purpose. Views of the general public were also sought. Working groups/committees have gone into the question of fertilizer and petroleum subsidies. The latest committee formed in this regard is Dr. C. Rangarajan Committee. Government is trying to evolve a consensus on the issue of subsidies. However, the Government has pledged that all subsidies will be targeted sharply at the poor and the truly needy the small and marginal farmers, farm labour and urban poor.

This book explains and examines the whole gamut of subsidies, both explicit and implicit, in India at the level of Central and State Governments. There are 46 chapters in all which have been categorized into the following 12 theme parts. Some overlapping in categorisation is possible because a subsidy programme/scheme may have multiple objectives.

Part I: Economics of Subsidies
Part II: Subsidies for Agriculture and Allied Sectors
Part III: Subsidies for Food Security
Part IV: Subsidies for Industrial Development and Export Promotion
Part V: Subsidies for Employment and Labour Welfare
Part VI: Subsidies for Energy and Transport Development
Part VII: Subsidies for Health and Education
Part VIII: Subsidies for Housing and Urban Development
Part IX: Subsidies for Rural Infrastructure and Development
Part X: Subsidies for Welfare of Women, Children and Disadvantaged Groups
Part XI: Subsidies for Development of Special Problem Regions

Part XII: Subsidies for Cinema, Art and Culture

I take this opportunity to thank the management of Indian Overseas Bank for giving me the permission to write this book. The support and encouragement given by my father Shri Surendra Narain Dwivedi, Mother Shrimati Savitri Devi, brothers Dr. Kanti Swarup, Ravindra, Rajesh and Manoj to complete this mammoth task is deeply appreciated.

Ludhiana
July 2, 2006

Rishi Muni Dwivedi

Contents

Part VII Subsidies for Health and Education

Part XII Subsidies for Cinema, Art and Culture

Dedicated to
My Wife
Dr. Sushma Dwivedi
and Daughters
Divya, Deepika and Shruti

Part I
Economics of Subsidies

1. **Provision for Public Goods**
2. **Nature and Role of Subsidies**

1

Provision for Public Goods

The government is big and important in our times. We depend on the government to protect ourselves against external aggression, internal disorders, pollution, epidemics, social injustice, exploitation, unemployment and poverty. Furthermore, government is expected to

- provide educational, medical and housing facilities,
- build roads, bridges and communication networks,
- ensure personal freedom and enforcement of contracts and
- maintain our democratic institutions and cordial relations with foreign countries.

Though the list is not exhaustive, it does provide an idea of the amplitude of the multifarious activities of modern governments.

1.1 Market for Private Goods

Market mechanism operates almost successfully in the case of private goods. The two chief characteristics of private goods are:

- benefits derived are internalised, and
- consumption is rival.

In other words, market for private goods functions on the basis of exclusion principle. According to this principle, he who pays the price gets the commodity, and he who does not pay the price is denied the same. The principle applies in the case of private goods like food, furniture, houses, cycles, and hundreds of other marketable goods. As we see in our daily life, the nature of these goods is such that the exclusion principle can be readily applied. When A pays the price, he is handed over the shirt but B is refused the same if he fails to make the payment. This is so because benefits derived are internalised and consumption is rival.

1.2 Limitations of Market Mechanism

Left to itself, market mechanism cannot perform all economic functions optimally. The premise that market mechanism leads to efficient use of resources, i.e. it produces in the cheapest way what consumers want the most, is based on the following assumptions:

- There is perfect competition in the factor market as well as in the commodity market.
- Individuals can be excluded from consuming goods if they do not pay for them.

These conditions are rarely fulfilled in practice. Monopolistic and oligopolistic tendencies replace competitive forces to rob capitalism of its virtues. To quote, "In reality, various difficulties arise. Markets may be imperfectly competitive, production may be subject to decreasing cost, consumers may lack sufficient information or be misled by advertising, and so forth. For these reasons, market mechanism is not as ideal a provider of private goods as it might be." [1]

State intervention becomes necessary to curb such tendencies to protect consumers' interests. Even if it is assumed that competition is assured in the factor and commodity markets, still certain goods, because of their peculiar production and consumption characteristics, cannot be provided through market mechanism. In view of the problem of externalities, certain services (like defence, and street lighting) have to be provided through the public sector. This leads us to the discussion of public or social goods.

1.3 Public (or Social) Goods [2]

According to Richard Musgrave, "Social goods are goods the consumption of which is non-rival. That is, they are goods where A's partaking of the consumption benefits does not reduce the benefits derived by all others." [3] Two appropriate examples of non-rival consumption are: (a) defence services and (b) internal security.

Market mechanism fails in the case of public goods. The production and consumption characteristics of social goods are such that they cannot be provided through the market economy.

It would be inefficient to apply exclusion principle in the case of above two services. Efficient resource use requires that price should equal marginal cost. Since the marginal cost in this case is zero, the additional consumer should be admitted even if he pays zero price. It is noteworthy that exclusion, even if desired, is not possible in the above mentioned two cases.

In short, market may fail due to non-rival consumption or due to non-excludability or both of these reasons.

Notes

1. Richard Musgrave and Peggy Musgrave, *Public Finance in Theory and Practice* (New York: McGraw-Hill Book Company, 1985), p. 48.

2. The terms public goods and social goods are used interchangeably here. For niceties of the distinction between the two, see *ibid*, pp. 50-51.

3. *Ibid*, p. 49.

2

Nature and Role of Subsidies

2.1 What is a Subsidy?

A subsidy is a grant of money from an outside third party to either the buyer or the seller of a commodity. Subsidies allow a buyer to procure a commodity/service at a lower price than would otherwise have been necessary. Similarly, a business firm will not stay in operation unless revenue is sufficient enough to cover cost plus some return on investment. If revenue from buyers is insufficient, a subsidy from an outside agency may keep the firm in operation.

The effect of a subsidy is opposite of the effect of a tax. A cash subsidy is the opposite of a direct tax while a subsidised commodity is the opposite of a taxed commodity. Hence, subsidies are sometimes called negative taxation.

2.2 Are Tax Concessions Subsidies?

These are provisions in tax laws which encourage individuals and corporations to undertake activities desired by the government. Almost all tax systems incorporate provisions which exclude certain items and deduct others from the tax base. These provisions may take the form of exemptions, deductions, allowances, and tax credits. Tax incentives (or tax preferences) reduce the amount of tax which would otherwise be payable by a taxable entity. These tax preferences are referred to as tax incentives. Broadly speaking, items which erode the normally accepted base of a tax may be treated as tax incentives.

Tax incentives, an integral part of tax systems the world over, are designed to promote a wide spectrum of socio-economic objectives. If judiciously used, they can become an effective tool of economic change on desired lines.

Tax incentives involve sacrifice of tax revenue and hence need to be devised carefully. The revenue foregone is similar to a subsidy or a grant to a taxable entity and hence akin to government expenditure. For example, there is no fundamental difference between an outright subsidy payment to a new industrial undertaking set up in a backward area and foregoing tax revenue on account of tax concession to it. However, outright subsidy payments attract public attention more readily than tax concessions (hidden subsidies) which lie scattered in the cobwebs of frequently changing tax laws. Thus, activities which deserve budgetary support should preferably be encouraged through expenditure programmes rather than the nebulous medium of tax incentives. The alternatives to tax incentives are: direct subsidies, government loans at subsidised interest rates, and foreign exchange facilities.

However, when support through tax concessions becomes necessary, their economic effects should be properly evaluated, i.e. whether the cost in terms of revenue foregone is justified by the likely benefits. In other words, a tax incentive should be appraised in the same way as any other item of public expenditure. The loss of revenue must be estimated on net basis because some increase in revenue may be attributable to stepped up economic activities due to tax favour. To what extent the intended positive effects (increased savings, investments, production etc.) of tax concessions are realised and to what degree they offset the negative effects (loss of revenue, equity distortions), are complex questions requiring rigorous empirical analysis.

2.3 Subsidies in National Income Calculation

The value of goods and services produced in a country are ordinarily measured at prices at which these are traded in the market. When we buy a tube of toothpaste the price we pay includes an element of tax like excise duty or sales tax (indirect taxes). Thus, the payment we make does not go wholly to the people who produce the goods. A part of the payment goes to the government in the form of taxes. This payment to government does not reflect the true cost of producing the goods concerned.

Contrarily, when the government pays subsidies (say to handloom weavers) the money incomes of factors exceed the market value of their output. Valuation of goods at market prices violates the basic principle that the value of goods produced is equal to the sum of the money income received by the factors of production.

In order to get a total of national income which corresponds to the income payments actually received by factors of production, we must subtract the total of indirect taxes from and add the value of subsidies to national income measured at market prices. Hence,

National income at factor cost = National income at market prices − Indirect taxes + Subsidies

2.4 Targeting of Subsidies

Subsidies may be categorised in terms of the target in view.

2.4.1 Subsidies for a Product: Such subsidies are used to promote a product in various ways as, for example,

- Product development including research for quality improvement
- Sales promotion
- Product storage
- Export

2.4.2 Subsidies to a Person: Subsidies targeted to a person are specific subsidies. These are provided to a person under special circumstances. Thus, monetary assistance received by widows, handicapped and other needy persons from the social welfare departments of governments falls under this category.

2.4.3 Subsidies to a Group of Persons: These are provided to a group or category of persons such as landless labourers, freedom fighters and displaced persons.

2.4.4 Subsidies for a Region: To ensure regional balanced development, governments generally provide extra funds for special problem regions of a country. These regions may include desert lands, drought prone areas, hilly terrains and tribal areas.

2.5 Classification of Subsidies (in order of preference)

Subsidies are financed either from tax or non-tax revenue, or result in a deficit. Since some subsidies are less justifiable than others, it is important to categorise services in terms of their desirability vis-à-vis subsidisation.

Subsidies are generally classified into the following three categories:

- public goods,
- merit goods and
- non-merit goods.

2.5.1 Public Goods: The best examples of public goods are defence, internal security and general administration. These services are characterised by non-rivalry and non-excludability in consumption. Such services are available to all citizens and cannot be priced. Hence, they are not included in the calculation of subsidies.

2.5.2 Merit Goods: These goods encompass a large variety of services like anti-pollution measures, malaria eradication programme, primary education and health, roads and bridges, scientific research, flood control, and soil and water conservation. The social benefits resulting from these services are much greater than the sum of private benefits to individual consumers. This is so because these services contain elements of *externality* beneficial to the society as a whole. Subsidies on these services are justified because of availability of benefits in the form of externality.

2.5.3 Non-merit Goods: These include, *inter alia*, food, fertilisers, higher education. The element of externality is either absent or limited. Social and equity objectives are generally the ground for subsidising these services. Considerable controversy exists about such subsidies.

2.6 Role of Subsidies

Subsidies play a vital role in the economy of a country. A country has various resources which are to be gainfully deployed for the benefit of the population of the whole country. Subsidies are provided to ensure equitable utilization of the resources for the people. The developed, developing and underdeveloped countries have different kinds of subsidies. Developed countries provide subsidies to their population for improving standard of living, the underdeveloped countries provide subsidies for meeting bare minimum needs of the vast majority of population.

Subsidies are the converse of indirect taxes and are specific to goods and services. Subsidies are different from transfer payments, which are straight income supplements to individuals, who are normally the poor and the vulnerable.

2.7 Effects of Subsidies

2.7.1 Positive Effects of Subsidies: Providing minimum consumption entitlement to the poor by subsidizing the items consumed by them is an extremely important welfare dimension of fiscal policy. Subsidies can correct for the under-consumption of goods with positive externalities. With the social benefits of a particular service or commodity exceeding the aggregate of private benefits to individual consumers, market solutions result in under-consumption and subsidies can make the necessary correction. However, the benefits can be maximised only when the subsidies are transparent, well targeted, and suitably designed for effective implementation without any leakages.

2.7.2 Negative Effects of Subsidies: Subsidies can generate negative effects also. Once received, people become dependent on the subsidies. Hence, subsidies are sometimes termed as sweet poison. Misuse of subsidies for political purpose is known worldwide. Subsidies support one industry at the expense of the other. When a person is given subsidy benefit, it imposes burden on some other person in the country. Subsidies interfere in the free working of the economy in the following ways.

- Trough subsidies, free money circulates in the economy without increase in actual income/production.
- Subsidies make the beneficiaries lethargic.
- Subsidies lead to misallocation of resources.

- Malpractices have often been noticed in the administration of subsidies.
- Subsidies are often misused by politicians.

2.8 Measures for Effective Utilisation of Subsidies

Operational inefficiency in the case of provision of any public good or service leads to higher cost of production and greater subsidies. There is a wedge between subsidies that are actually received by the users of the service and subsidies that are borne by the Government. Several types of inefficiencies may accompany the public provision of services. Apart from direct costs like overstaffing, poor maintenance of assets, procedural delays, and delays in taking critical decisions, there are systemic inefficiencies.

Subsidies can prove effective to achieve the desired goals if they have the following components:

1. The focus should be on physical achievements and not on financial disbursements.
2. The effects of subsidies should be monitorable and measurable in terms of quality or quantity.
3. Subsidies should be given as a one-time help or for a short period. Subsidies on continuing basis should be avoided.
4. The parameters fixed for the subsidy should be transparent.
5. Subsidies should be cost-effective. Most of the assistance should reach the intended beneficiary and very small amount should be spent on administrative arrangements.
6. Subsidies should be properly targeted, i.e. benefit should go to the really deserving.
7. Timing of subsidies should be made proper. For example, free seed distribution should be just before sowing.

2.9 Subsidies in India

Subsidies represent a sizable item of the Centre's non-Plan revenue expenditure. In the 2006-07 budget, they accounted for Rs. 46,213 crore (13.4 per cent) out of a total non-Plan revenue expenditure of Rs. 3,44,430 crore. Food and fertilisers are the two main items subsidised by the Government through budgetary support.

2.9.1 Vadilal Dagli Committee (1979): The Government of India constituted a committee in February 1978 under the chairmanship of Shri Vadilal Dagli. The Committee submitted its report in May 1979.

The Committee was set up to evaluate and review the whole gamut of controls and subsidies and make suitable recommendations. It was asked to examine

- The manner in which subsidies had actually operated and whether or not the objectives sought to be achieved had actually been achieved.
- In what manner was the system of controls connected to the system of subsidisation in the national economy?
- Are such subsidies justifiable and will it be possible to moderate or eliminate the system of subsidisation by suitable modification in the system of controls?

The Committee noted with concern the substantial growth in the magnitude and diversity of subsidies. It identified three types of subsidies:

- direct subsidies given from the budget,
- cross subsidies without any budgetary implications where one set of consumers subsidise the other and
- covert subsidies where the cost of a subsidy is borne by the budget but not shown as such.

On the basis of its findings, it made the following recommendations:

- the costs and recipients of benefits of all subsidies should be reviewed periodically, say once every three years,
- subsidies should in general be given only to sustain tiny units, decentralised production, or to support the consumption of the weaker sections of population,
- where necessary, clear-cut, overt subsidies should be given in lieu of indirect subsidies as, for example, losses of PSUs arising out of a deliberate policy decision of the Government

to keep prices below the cost of production in the interest of keeping down the general price level and
- budget of the Central Government should be restructured in terms of the above criteria.

2.9.2 Post-liberalisation Thinking on Subsidies: Of late, drastic changes have occurred in Government's policy towards subsidies. The crux of this policy is to roll back subsidies and thus curb the growth of non-Plan expenditure. Another dimension of the present policy is to restrict the availability of subsidised items to vulnerable sections of society.

Three reasons account for the increase in the Central Government subsidies in recent years:

- moving the petroleum sector to a transparent system of budgetary subsidies and delay in the announced phasing out of the subsidies on PDS kerosene and domestic LPG;
- increase in explicit budgetary subsidies on food and fertilizer; and
- increase in input costs unaccompanied by any improvement in recovery rates resulting in escalation of implicit subsidies on a variety of economic and social services.

The reforms programme initiated in 1991 aimed at, among other things, reducing fiscal imbalances and improving allocative efficiency by minimizing the distortions in relative prices arising from budgetary and fiscal imprudence. Containing and targeting subsidies constituted an important element of reforms. Containment and targeting of subsidies can serve the following objectives:

- remove economic distortions, thereby improving economic efficiency and growth;
- achieve redistributive objective;
- reduce budgetary burden and release precious resources; and

National Common Minimum Programme (NCMP) of the Government of India pledges: "All subsidies will be targeted sharply at the poor and the truly needy like small and marginal farmers, farm labour and urban poor."

As per the human Development Report, 2004 of the UNDP, India has been placed at a rank of 127th position out of 177 countries. The report measures the life expectancy, undoubtedly related to the quality and quantity of the food we consume (which in turn is impacted by the medical care that follows), educational attainment and the adjusted real income. All these measures reflect very poorly in the case of India. Out of all this food is the first thing. Hence there is a strong case for India to provide the subsidies to those poor people.

Government showed its seriousness about targeting subsidies at the poor and the truly needy in the budget speech for 2006-07. Extensive discussions with stakeholders on three major subsidies, namely, food, fertilizer and petroleum were held for the purpose. Views of the general public were also sought. Working groups/ committees have gone into the question of fertilizer and petroleum subsidies. The latest committee formed in this regard is Dr. C. Rangarajan Committee. Government is trying to evolve a consensus on the issue of subsidies. However the Government has pledged that all subsidies will be targeted sharply at the poor and the truly needy the small and marginal farmers, farm labour and urban poor.

Part II
Subsidies for Agriculture and Allied Sectors

3

Agricultural Development in General

3.1 Place of Agriculture in the Indian Economy

Agricultural sector occupies a key position in the Indian economy. It provides employment to about 65 per cent of the working population of India. Around one-quarter of India's national income originates from the agricultural sector. Agricultural products like cereals (mainly rice), tea, coffee, cashew, spices, tobacco and leather are important items of India's exports and hence foreign exchange earnings. Agriculture is also the source of raw material for agro-based industries including textiles, cigarettes, jute, sugar, paper, processed foodstuffs and *vanaspati*. Moreover, agricultural sector provides market for capital goods (tractors, pump sets and other agricultural machinery), inputs (fertilisers, insecticides), and light consumer goods. The nation has invested huge resources for the development of agriculture under various plans.

The development of the agricultural sector depends, to a large extent, on such core industries as power, petroleum, fertilisers and machine tools. Thus, there is an inter-dependence between agriculture and industry.

It is imperative that the problems of farmers are addressed with a sense of urgency. Agriculture being a State subject, the bulk of public investment in agriculture takes place at the level of States and the Central Government supports the States as a catalyst.

Two major components of agricultural development strategy in India have been: (a) subsidies on inputs and (b) minimum support price for output.

Given below are some of the schemes/programmes launched since Independence in 1947 where some kind of assistance or subsidy was provided for the purpose.

3.2 Intensive Agricultural District Programme (IADP) or Package Programme

Implemented from the year 1960 in 15 selected districts in 14 States (one district in each State and 2 districts in Kerala State) the programme was to use the improved package of practices to serve as model districts. Objectives of the programme was to find out and show a way of spectacular increase in the productivity of agricultural land by using modern technology and to identify the methods of effecting changes in the farmer's attitude with a view to motivating them to adopt improved production practices.

3.3 Intensive Agricultural Area Programme (IAAP)

Commenced in the year 1964-65, this programme emphasised intensive agricultural development of the area, as a whole and was crop oriented. Agricultural information centre was also set up to provide information to the farmers on the improved technologies. Farm and Home Unit of All India Radio owes its emergence from such self-contained agricultural information centers. The programme was launched for the intensive development of major crops like Paddy, wheat, sugarcane, millets, cotton, pulses, potato etc. In the beginning 1084 blocks in 114 districts were covered under the programme benefiting 90 lakh hectares area and 20 lakh farming families.

3.4 High Yielding Variety Programme (HYVP)

Increasing food production was the dire need of the 1960s. The production and productivity of various crops has gone up considerably due to introduction of High Yielding Varieties (HYV) launched in 1966-67. Wheat, paddy, maize, Jowar and Bajra were the main crops selected for giving more emphasis under the programme. In the beginning programme covered 100 districts only but was later on spread to other area also.

3.5 Mini-kit Programme for Rice, Wheat and Coarse Cereals

The objective of the scheme is to increase the productivity by popularize the use of newly released hybrid/high yielding varieties and spread the area coverage under location specific high yielding varieties/hybrids. This is to be done by spreading fast the coverage of area under location specific high yielding varieties/hybrids, building up of stocks of improved seed at the farm level, train the extension workers with the newly evolved technology and propagation and adoption of improved production technology.

Mini kits are distributed under the programme and State level training programmes and specialized orientation programmes are arranged. All States are eligible for the assistance. It is a Central Sector scheme started in 1972-73 for rice, 1974-75 for wheat and 1974-75for coarse cereals.

100 per cent financial assistance is provided by the Government of India.

3.6 Special Foodgrain Production Programme (SFPP)

This programme was launched in the year 1989-90 in 169 potential districts termed as thrust districts in 14 states namely Andhra Pradesh, Assam, Bihar, Gujarat, Haryana, Karnataka, Madhya Pradesh, Maharashtra, Orissa, Punjab, Rajasthan, Uttar Pradesh, West Bengal and Tamil Nadu. In the year 1990-91, the programme was extended to 311 thrust districts in 19 states and one Union Territory. Objective of the programme was to increase the agricultural production to a level of 166 million tons in 1988-89 and 175 million tons in 1989-90 by planning better and efficient input management;

- Harnessing ground water through tube wells;
- Increased fertilizer use by 20 kg nutrients/hectare;
- Better and timely control of pests and weeds;

3.7 Accelerated Maize Development Programme (AMDP)

The maize is cultivated mainly for food, fodder, feed and industrial uses. It is staple food for tribal and poor people in the country. More than 3,500 products of daily application are derived from it. Hence there is need to increase the production of maize in our country. The scheme has an objective of increasing maize production and productivity in the country from 10 million tonnes to 11.44 million tonnes and from 1.5 tonnes/hectare to 1.80 tones/hectare respectively up to the terminal year of 9th Plan i.e. 2001-2002 (revised). The scheme started during 1995-1996. It is a Centrally sponsored scheme.

The main emphasis is being given for transfer of modern crop production technology through the following components;

Components for which 100 per cent Assistance is given by Central Government.

- Front line Demonstration by ICAR;
- Training of Officers at National and State Level;
- Production of certified seed of Maize;
- Seed Mini-kit Demonstrations;
- Conference/Seminars/Workshops on Maize Development;
- Evaluation & Monitoring.

Components with 75 per cent assistance by Central Government and 25 per cent by State Governments.

- Field Demonstrations on improved crop production technology and Integrated Pest Management (IPM);
- Training of farmers on crop production technology;
- Incentives for use of certified seeds of hybrids/improved varieties (deleted since 2001 as desired by Planning Commission);
- Incentives for use of improved implements;
- Publicity through electronic media; and
- Contingencies for POL.

The programme (AMDP) is in implementation in all maize potential districts of 26 states viz; Andhra Pradesh, Assam, Arunachal Pradesh, Bihar, Chhattisgarh, Gujarat, Haryana, Himachal Pradesh, Jharkhand, J&K, M.P, Karnataka, Maharashtra, Manipur, Meghalaya, Mizoram, Nagaland, Orissa, Rajasthan, Punjab, Sikkim, Tamil Nadu, Tripura, Uttaranchal, Uttar Pradesh & West Bengal.

3.8 Technology Mission on Cotton

The scheme is being implemented since February 2000 in 9

major States viz .Punjab, Haryana, Rajasthan, Tamil Nadu, Karnataka, Andhra Pradesh, Maharashtra, Gujarat; Madhya Pradesh and 2 minor States {Viz. Uttar Pradesh and Orissa} and 2 non-Traditional States (viz. West Bengal, Tripura) of the Country. The Funds are being provided to ICAR for Establishment of Ginning & Training Centre, (Nagpur) and for Front Line Demonstrations. Apart from this, assistance is also being provided for Production of Breeder, Foundation and Certified Seeds. It is a Centrally Sponsored Scheme

Objectives of the scheme are to enhance the production, per unit area through

- technology transfer,
- supply of quality seeds,
- elevating IPM activities/ and
- providing adequate and timely supply of inputs to the farmers .

The components under the scheme include:

- assistance for production of breeder, foundation and certified seed and distribution of certified seed;
- Field and Integrated Pest Management Demonstrations; (c) Training of farmers and Extension Workers;
- Distribution of Plant Protection Equipments; water saving devices; Bio-agents and pheromone traps.

Assistance is also being provided for the establishment of bio-agents labs and seed delinting plants for adequate availability of bio-agents and quality delinting seed respectively.

3.9 National Pulses Development Project (NPDP)

The objective of this centrally sponsored scheme is to increase the production of pulses in the country to achieve self sufficiency. The scheme envisages assistance to the States for following components:

- Seed related: Purchase of Breeder seed, production of foundation and certified seed, distribution of certified seeds & mini-kits and crash programme for production of seed of pulses.

- Demonstration: Frontline, Block and IPM Demonstration
- Improved Method of irrigation: Distribution of sprinklers.
- Distribution of improved farm implements and plant protection equipment including power drawn implements.
- Distribution of Rhizobium cultures, Nutrients and Micro-nutrients, gypsum/pyrite, Nuclear Poly hedrosis Virus (NPV) & seed treatment chemical.
- Training of Farmers

3.10 Oilseeds Production Programme (OPP)

To achieve the self-sufficiency and to increase the production of oilseeds in the country is the objective of the scheme. It is a Centrally Sponsored Scheme.

The scheme envisages assistance to the States for following components:

- Production and purchase of Breeder seed, production of foundation and certified seed and distribution of certified seeds and mini-kits, crash programme for production of TL seed of soyabean & Groundnut.
- Frontline, Block and IPM Demonstration
- Distribution of sprinklers.
- Distribution of improved farm implements and plant protection equipment including power drawn implements.
- Distribution of Rhizobium cultures, Nutrients and Micro-nutrients, seed treatment chemical, weedicides, gypsum, pyrite, Root Grub Control.
- Seed storage, threshing floor and irrigation at Government farms.
- Training of Farmers.

The scheme is being implemented on 75:25 basis as Central and State share respectively.

3.11 Promoting Use of Informatics in Agriculture

It is a Central Sector Scheme run by Ministry of Agriculture - Department of Agriculture & Cooperation. The scheme was started in the year 1998-1999 for implementation during the Ninth

Plan Period. The website of this Department was launched on April 13, 1999.

Objectives of the scheme is to make available all information relating to agriculture on the website in due course of time for the use of farmers, exporters, traders, Research Institutions, State Agriculture Departments and the Central Government in order to achieve higher levels of productivity and income for the farmers. It is envisaged that extension and advisory services would be available to the farmers on a real time basis as a result of the scheme, which would enable them to plan their production, post-harvest management and marketing in a more efficient manner. The tools of IT would enable networking of the agriculture sector in the country, which will create a large reservoir of database for the use of Policy makers, farmers and their organizations.

The Scheme consists of:

- Strengthening of Information Technology apparatus in the Department of Agriculture and Cooperation (Headquarters);
- National Agriculture Informatics Centre; and
- Early Warning Information System

3.12 Research and Development in Post-Harvest Technology (PHT) Scheme

Main objective of the R&D in PHT Scheme is to develop state of the art technology for processing of oilseeds, pulses, maize and oil palm and popularize use of newly developed technology to augment availability of quality edible oils, pulses and maize products. The scheme "Research & Development in Post Harvest Technology in Oilseeds, Pulses, Oil palm & Maize consists of two major programmes:

- Research & Development Projects for Post Harvest Technology
- Popularization and Demonstration of Post Harvest Technologies.

The following programmes under popularization & demonstrations in Post Harvest Technologies are being implemented during Tenth Five Year Plan:

- Establishment of palm oil mill of 2.5 tonnes FFBs per hour with technology developed by Regional Research Laboratory, Trivendrum.
- Establishment of 1 TPD Modern Oil Expeller with the technology developed by MERADO, Ludhiana.
- Modernization of Huller Rice Mills.
- Establishment of Rice bran Oil Refineries.
- Establishment of Red palm oil & vegetable oil blend project.
- Upgradation of existing palm oil mills
- Upgradation of soybean oil refineries.
- Upgradation of Solvent Extraction Plants.
- Upgradation of Oil Milling.
- Primary processing for Maize.

Under the programme of modernization of Huller Rice Mills, State Governments are the implementing agencies for the selection of beneficiary.

3.13 Human Resource Development Training Support to Agriculture

The objectives of the scheme are:

1. To improve professional competence of Senior & middle level extension functionaries in the areas of extension management, training management and communication management and that of Subject Matter specialists in the areas of Agriculture, Horticulture, Animal Husbandry & allied disciplines – both working under States/Union Territories, though NTCs, STCs, Regional & Overseas Training Programmes.
2. To create and strengthen training infrastructure at National, Regional and State/UTs levels for organizing effective training programmes.
3. To strengthen extension & training activities of North Eastern Hilly States, Sikkim, Goa, & UTs by providing adequate financial support on priority basis.
4. To expose farmers to latest Crop Production followed by their

counter parts in progressive States through Exchange visits.

The Directorate of Extension has strengthened the network of training to senior level extension managers. The training is imparted at National Institute of Agriculture Extension Management, Hyderabad, middle level extension functionaries at Extension Education Institutes, subject matter specialists in specialized areas at centres of Excellence for Training and State Agriculture Management & Extension Training Institutes at state level who in turn disseminate the latest technology for actual implementation at the farmers field.

3.14 National Project on Development and Use of Bio-fertilizers

Bio-fertilizers are very popular now-a-days for the health conscious world. Use of bio fertilizers reduces chemical residues in the crop harvests. Bio-fertilisers are being considered important component of Integrated Plant Nutrient System (IPNS) and Organic farming for sustaining the agriculture. The scheme provides for

- Production and distribution of Bio-fertilizers (BFs)
- Develop Standards for different BFs and Quality control
- Release of grants for setting up BF units
- Training and Publicity

Under this scheme the Government provides non-recurring grants-in-aid up to Rs. 20 lakh for setting up bio-fertiliser production units of 150 MT capacity. The grant-in-aid is offered to State Departments of Agriculture/cooperatives/public sector undertakings of fertilisers, NGOs and private agencies provided their proposals are received from respective State Governments. It is a Central Sector Scheme.

One time grant-in-aid to the extent of Rs.1.50 lakh is provided for establishment of Blue-green algae sub-centre to produce 30-40 tonnes of BGA/annum provided their proposals are received from respective State Governments.

This scheme is being implemented in the country with the help of a National and 6 Regional centres for training, field demonstration and its promotion and also through Department of Agriculture & Cooperation i.e. release of one time grant-in-aid for setting up BF units. Financial assistance of 20 lakh is being provided for creating a production capacity of 150 tons of bio-fertilizers per annum and Rs.10 lakh for 75 tons capacity per annum. The grants are released through the State Governments in two instalments.

3.15 Establishment and Maintenance of Seed Bank

The objective of this central sector scheme is to make available seeds for contingent situations and also develop infrastructure for seed storage. Salient features of the scheme are:

- Establishment of seed bank for maintenance of foundation & certified seeds of different crops
- To ensure timely availability of seeds to the farmers and to take care of the special requirement of seed at the time of natural calamity
- To create infrastructure facilities for production and distribution of quality seeds

The scheme provides for revolving funds for procurement of seeds (50 per cent costs of raw seed) for keeping in the seed bank. Scheme also reimburses the maintenance cost of seed or various components like processing/packing, revalidation, transportation, storage, storage loss, insurance of seeds during storage and price differential for undistributed quantity of seeds as per norms fixed under the scheme.

3.16 Transport Subsidy for the Movement of Seeds to the North Eastern States, Sikkim, Himachal Pradesh, Jammu & Kashmir, Uttaranchal and Hill Areas of West Bengal.

Objective of the scheme is to ensure supply of seeds to the farmers in time at reasonable prices in the identified States. The scheme provides to subsidise the cost of transportation of seeds required by the farmers in the North Eastern States, Sikkim, Himachal Pradesh, Jammu & Kashmir, Uttaranchal and; Hill Areas of West Bengal so as to make seed available at reasonable rate as prevailing in other parts of the country and to make available seeds well in time before sowing season to the farmers in above areas.

Scheme provides for the reimbursement of 100 per cent difference between rail/road transport charges for seed moved from outside the state to State Capital/District HQ. of identified states and actual cost of transportation of seeds subject to maximum limit of Rs.60/quintal whichever is less is reimbursed for movement of certified seed within the states from state capital/district HQs of these States to sale outlets/sale counters.

NSC, SFCI, State seed corporations of various states and state seed certification agencies are eligible for the assistance. Physical targets of seeds for each seed corporation are fixed based on which revolving funds provided. Maintenance cost of the seeds is also reimbursed based on the proposals received from seed corporations.

The scheme is in operation since 1999-2000 and is being implemented through National Seeds Corporation, State Farms Corporation of India and seed corporations of Andhra Pradesh, Assam Orissa Gujarat, Haryana, Karnataka, Madhya Pradesh, Punjab, Rajasthan, U.P, Uttaranchal, Maharashtra & West Bengal while the benefit of the scheme is available to the entire country.

Seed of about 20 crops of various varieties which are suitable for different agro-climatic zones of the country specially for meeting any contingent situation arising out of drought/flood situation are maintained in the seed Bank.

3.17 Strengthening and Modernization of Pest Management

To reduce the injudicious and indiscriminate use of chemical pesticides, the Government of India has adopted Integrated Pest Management (IPM), encompassing cultural, mechanical and biological methods and need based use of chemical pesticides, as the cardinal principle and main plank of plant protection in the country. To achieve this objective, establishment of adequate number of bio-control laboratories in the country is essential. The Government of India has decided to involve non-governmental organization etc. in setting up of these laboratories and provide them grants-in-aid for purchase of equipment for this purpose.

3.18 Strengthening of Agricultural Marketing Infrastructure, Grading and Standardization

This scheme has been formulated to encourage the rapid development of infrastructure projects in agriculture and allied activities including dairy, meat, fisheries and minor forest produce

An investment subsidy of 25 per cent of the capital cost or Rs. 50 lakh whichever is lower is available under the scheme on each project providing direct service delivery to the producer/farming community in post harvest marketing of new produce. Investment subsidy will be 33.33 per cent up to Rs. 60 lakh in North East States, Hilly and tribal areas and to SC/ST entrepreneurs and their cooperatives.

Projects eligible for Assistance:

- Infrastructure projects like market yards, platforms for loading, assembling and auctioning, weighing and mechanical handling equipments
- Infrastructure for direct marketing from producers to consumer, processing units, bulk buyers etc.
- Infrastructure for E-trading market extension and market oriented production planning.
- Mobile infrastructure for post harvest operations, grading, packing, quality testing etc.
- Functional infrastructure for assembling, grading, standardization and quality certification, labelling, packaging, value addition facilities (without changing the product form).

3.19 Subsidies for Tea Production

Under the Small Tea Growers Protection Scheme, 60,000 tea growers (who own or manage up to 25 acres of land) will get a subsidy of Rs. 2 per Kg. on green leaf tea produced and sold by them. Subsidy will be paid for a period of 6 months from July 2005.

3.20 UNDP-funded Programme on National Food Security

Food Security of the poor nations is a matter of concern to United Nations. Hence it is assisting various nations to become self sufficient in food requirements. Objectives of the scheme are:

- Intensification of Agriculture
- Diversification of farming system
- Environmental and gender sensitive technology transfer with a focus on rain-fed and marginal lands and
- Innovative community initiatives
- Main streaming gender concerns in agriculture. The scheme has the following Sub-Programmes:
- Development of Hybrid Rice Technology for large scale adoption in India by ICAR
- Maize based cropping system in India by TMOP Division of Department of Agriculture and Cooperation.
- Strengthening Natural Resource Management and sustainable livelihoods of Women of Tribal Orissa (Orissa).
- Empowerment of Women farmers for Food Security in Uttar Pradesh (U.P.).
- Sustainable dry land agriculture by Mahila Sangam in Andhra Pradesh (A.P.).
- Management Support for Food Security.

4

Agriculture Extension Work

Agricultural Extension Work is a major requirement for providing the information to farmers about the new technologies to be used in agriculture to increase the production and productivity.

The Ministry of Agriculture has developed a broad Policy Framework for Agricultural Extension (PFAE). The Policy Framework has five major guiding elements:

- Reforming Public Sector Extension.
- Promoting private sector to effectively complement, supplement and wherever possible to substitute public extension.
- Augmenting Media and Information Technology Support for Extension.
- Mainstreaming Gender Concerns in Extension.
- Capacity Building/ Skill up-gradation of farmers and extension functionaries.

4.1 New Schemes of Extension Division of the Development of Agriculture and Cooperation (DAC)

The Tenth Five Year Plan Approach Paper called for radical overhaul of extension services and significant improvements in sophistication of technology dissemination methodologies. It highlighted the need for specific measures to ensure that research technology development and extension services meet the special needs of farmers. Accordingly, DAC, Ministry of Agriculture, Government of India is implementing the following schemes during the Tenth Plan period:

- Mass Media Support to Agriculture Extension
- Support to State Extension Programmes for Extension Reforms.

- Agri-Clinics/Agri-Business Centres
- Establishment of Kisan Call Centres
- Extension Support to Central Institutions
- Externally Aided Projects

The scheme "Support to State Extension Programmes for Extension Reforms" is the main scheme to operationalize agricultural extension reforms across the country. Under the scheme funding support shall be provided to the States/UTs for undertaking extension reforms within the broad purview of the Policy Framework for Agriculture Extension (PFAE), complying with its key areas/norms, and shall be operated based on Extension Work Plans prepared by them. Under the scheme funding shall be released to the States based on their Extension Work plans developed within the broad framework of the PFAE and areas indicated under the cafeteria of reform oriented activities. The States shall propose the new institutional arrangements, they intend to put in place in the First Work Plan, or even earlier, to be submitted by them to the DAC for approval. This agency will have the responsibility of implementing the extension reforms at district level.

4.2 Agricultural Technology Management Agency (ATMA)

It is a district level body created under the ITD component of NATP for pilot testing Agricultural extension reforms. One of the first tasks of ATMA like institutions is to facilitate the preparation of Strategic Research and Extension Plan (SREP) of the district. The SREP is prepared through participatory methodologies such as Participatory Rural Appraisal (PRA) involving all the stakeholders and farmers. The SREP contains detailed analysis of all the information on existing farming systems in the district and research – extension gaps required to be filled-up. It also prioritizes the research – extension strategies within the district.

4.3 State Extension Work Plan (SEWP)

Based on the research-extension strategies given in the SREPs, block/district level plans shall be developed by each

ATMA like institutions. The State Extension Work Plan developed at state level shall contain a consolidated activity-wise plan incorporating all the District Agriculture Action Plans (DAAPs) in the state and state level activities to be carried out with activity-wise budgetary requirement as per the norms prescribed in the cafeteria. It will also indicate all other extension activities that may be undertaken from out of resources provided under any other scheme of the Centre/State Governments. The DAAPs developed under the scheme should be processed consistent with Article 243 ZD of the Constitution.

The Cafeteria includes cost norms and ceilings applicable for each activity. Under the Cafeteria, activities to be undertaken at State and District level are categorized separately. The state level activities include support for upgrading state level training institutions such as SAMETI, HRD of extension functionaries, organization of state level Agri-Exhibitions and Monitoring and Evaluation of the Scheme.

The district level activities are further categorized in four groups namely, farmer oriented activities, farm information dissemination, research-extension-farmer (R-E-F) linkages and administrative expenses. Farmer oriented activities include development of SREP, mobilization of farmer groups, training/exposure visit of farmers, field demonstrations, all aimed at empowering the farmers and improving their participation in technology dissemination process. Under the category farm information dissemination, local level agricultural exhibitions, information dissemination through printed materials and development of technology packages in electronic form are covered. The R-E-F linkages based activities include organization of Farmer-Scientist Interaction at local level, organization of Field-days and Kisan Goshties and support for local level researchable issues emanated from the SREP. The administrative expenses under district level activities provide support for running ATMA like Institutions and a few block level Farm Information and Advisory Centres.

It has been specified in the Cafeteria that funds for 'Farm-

Information Dissemination' category can't exceed 20 per cent of total resources available for district level activities under the Scheme. These percentages for 'REF Linkage' and 'Administrative Expenses' categories are 15 per cent and 20 per cent respectively. Any savings in any of these three categories could be utilized for 'Farmer-Oriented Activities'.

The cost norms and ceilings may be exceeded by a maximum of 10 per cent of the specified amount in exceptional circumstances by a local decision. All such cases shall have to be reported in the next year's Work Plan and shall be subject to ex-post guidance. Any other deviation from the prescribed norms/ ceilings or any new activity not specified in the Cafeteria could be taken up by States with prior approval of the DAC. Limited funds are being provided under the scheme for purchase of equipments for ATMA at district level and for State level activities

The resources required for the scheme shall be shared between centre and the state in the ratio of 90:10. The 10 per cent state's share shall consist of cash contribution of the State, beneficiary contribution or the contribution of other non-governmental organizations (The actual contribution made by other than the State Government in a year may be counted for the next year's State's contribution.)

The entire Tenth Plan outlay (Rs.226.07 crore) for the scheme shall be utilized for activities to be implemented by States/ districts. The decision on use of funds will be taken at 3 levels namely – Centre, State and District.

- An amount of Rs. 167.56 crore amounting to 77.53 per cent has been allocated for district level programmes.
- An amount of Rs. 22.15 crore amounting to 10.25 per cent has been allocated for State level programmes.
- An amount of Rs. 26.41 crore amounting to 12.22 per cent shall be available under the control of the Government of India. This amount shall be utilized for innovative activities to be approved by the Government of India. However, implementation of these activities will be done by States/districts.

The scheme would cover 252 districts during the Plan period, which will include 1/3rd of the districts taken from all the States except North-eastern States and Jammu & Kashmir wherefrom 50 per cent of the districts shall be covered.

5

Irrigation Development

5.1 Irrigation in India: An Introduction

In India, as in other countries, rivers have had a powerful influence on national and local life. Successful agriculture in most parts of the country is not possible without the use of river waters. The large land resources of India cannot be put to productive use without a simultaneous development and use of the water resources. In fact, an integrated development of the land and water resources of India is of fundamental importance to the country's economy. From times immemorial, life and civilization in India have been dependent largely on rivers. The earliest civilizations developed along the banks of the Indus and the Ganga and their tributaries. In the Deccan, except for the narrow strip along the western coast, large parts of the population have depended for their existence on river waters.

Public investment in irrigation has fallen significantly over successive Plan periods. This is largely due to resource constraints faced by Governments both at the Centre and the States. However, resources are not the only problem. Potential irrigation projects are located in areas which are either very difficult or environmentally sensitive, which makes it difficult to implement them.

In India, of the 142.6 million hectares of net cultivated area, 57 million hectares (40 per cent) is irrigated. The remainder, 85.6 million hectares (60 per cent) is rainfed. Rainfed areas comprise primarily of the arid and semi-arid regions and the drought prone areas. Going by the past trend, the average expansion of irrigation is around four million hectares every five years. Extrapolating this trend, it is projected that another 20 million additional hectares may be brought under irrigation in the next 25 years. This will still leave 65 million hectares, nearly half the cultivated area, under rainfed conditions. With the Green Revolution, which remained confined to the irrigated areas, showing signs of fatigue in the irrigated areas, attention is increasingly being focused on rainfed areas to provide impetus for future agricultural growth. The Ministry of Agriculture has accorded very high priority to the holistic and sustainable development of rainfed areas through integrated watershed management approach.

5.2 Command Area Development Programme (CADP)

The programme is in operation since 1974-75 aiming at bridging the gap between potential created and its utilization. During the Ninth Plan period (1997-2002) central assistance of Rs. 764.42 crore was provided to different states under the programme. The CADP is proposed to be restructured during the Tenth Plan (2002-07) to improve existing conditions of water availability at the point of the government outlets of major and medium irrigation projects and make the stakeholders responsible for operation and upkeep of the downstream systems. The restructured CAD Programme is also to take into account the need for better water management practices within and outside the major and medium irrigation commands through inclusion of tank rehabilitation, on-farm development works in minor irrigation projects, drainage and water logging amelioration activities.

Major constraints in the implementation of the programme are

- unreliability of water supply at outlet,
- gap between available technology and its adoption, and
- lack of participation of farmers.

To overcome these constraints and to make the programme more effective, the programme was restructure by retaining only those components, which are beneficial to the farmers, and including new components for correcting deficiencies in water supply and improving drainage systems. The restructured programme is being implemented.

Major achievements of command area development programme include the following:

- 29 per cent rise in irrigation intensity from 89 per cent to 118 per cent in Chambal Command (Rajasthan).

- 56 per cent rise in water use efficiency in Eastern Yamuna Command.
- Water consumption reduced from 7.27 M3/T.ha (planned use) to 4.17 M3/T.ha in Periya-Vaigai command (Tamil Nadu).
- 32.5 per cent increase in paddy production and 16 per cent rise in wheat production in 6 years in Sharda canal command (U.P).
- 120 per cent rise in paddy in 10 years in Periyar-Vaigai Command (Tamil Nadu).
- 76 per cent increase in farm income in 21 years in Chambal Command (Rajasthan).

5.3 Accelerated Irrigation Benefits Programme (AIBP)

Country's Ultimate Irrigation Potential (UIP) has been assessed at 139.89 million hectares (m.ha). So far about 68 percent of UIP has been harnessed. Average annual growth in irrigation potential at about 1.5 m.ha per annum up to the end of Eighth Plan (1992-97) was proposed to be increased to 3.4 m.ha annually by the end of Ninth Plan (1997-2002). The slower progress in creation of irrigation potential at the rate of about 1.80–1.85 m.ha per annum during the Ninth Plan was due to varied reasons including constraint of resources with the State Governments.

As large number of river valley projects, both multipurpose and irrigation, have spilled over from plan to plan, mainly because of financial constraints being faced by the State Government, the Governments of India launched the Accelerated Irrigation Benefits Programme during 1996-97 for accelerating implementation of ongoing irrigation/multipurpose projects on which substantial progress has been made and which are beyond the resources capability of the State Governments and for other major and medium irrigation projects which are in advanced stage of construction and could yield irrigation benefits in next four agricultural seasons.

Funds under this programme are provided to the States in the form of Central Loan Assistance. A fast Track Programme for completion of major and medium irrigation projects which can be completed in one year (two working seasons) with full central assistance was introduced in February 2002. The States were categorized as reforming States if the water rates were rationalised to recover full operation and maintenance costs and such States became eligible for better ratio to avail Central Loan Assistance. With effect from 1.04.2004, the grant component has been included in AIBP with 70 per cent loan and 30 per cent grant for General Category States and 10 per cent loan and 90 per cent grant for Special Category States for projects under Fast Track Programme. For projects not under Fast Track an incentive of conversion of loan to grant criteria as mentioned above shall be given if projects are completed on schedule. The time limit for completion of Fast Track Projects has been extended to three working seasons and for projects under normal funding to 6-8 working seasons.

So far, an amount of Rs. 14,670 crore has been released as CLA under this programme for 181 major/medium and 3,810 Surface Minor Irrigation Schemes. After commencement of the programme 28 major medium projects have been completed and an irrigation potential of 2195 thousand hectares has been created under AIBP up to March 2003. The potential of 67.35 thousand hectares has been created through Surface MI Schemes under AIBP up to March 2004.

5.4 Watershed Development

A watershed (or catchment) is a geographic area that drains to a common point, which makes it an ideal planning unit for conservation of soil and water. A watershed may comprise of one or several villages, contain both arable and non-arable lands, various categories of land-holdings, and farmers whose actions may impact on each others' interests. The watershed approach enables a holistic development of agriculture and allied activities in the area taking into account land-use based on crops, horticulture, agro-forestry, silvi-pasture and forests.

The watershed development programme is being implemented

by the Ministries of Agriculture, Rural Development and Environment and Forests. The current strategy of various ongoing national, bilateral and internationally-aided projects for development of rainfed areas is based on the concept of conservation of rainwater for integrated development of watersheds, promotion of diversified and integrated farming systems, management of common property resources and augmentation of family income and nutritional levels of participating watershed communities through alternate household production systems.

While there were some visible gains, the problem of sustainability continued to plague the first generation watershed development projects as evidenced by the unwillingness of local communities to operate and maintain completed structures and plantations on community property. The beneficiaries were too often merely passive recipients rather than active participants in the development of their watersheds.

Under the 'Common Approach for Watershed Development' the watershed development programmes have been restructured by retaining the technical strengths of the older programmes and incorporating the lessons learnt from successful projects, especially on community participation. It is now mandatory for the 'watershed development' to be planned, implemented, monitored and maintained by the watershed community. The restructured, second-generation watershed projects have kept people's participation at centre-stage.

The Tenth Five Year Plan period (2002-07) has a target of treating 15 million hectares of rainfed land under the various Watershed Development Programmes.

Water-use efficiency in Indian agriculture is one of the lowest in the world. Government will have to promote micro-irrigation technology, comprising drip and sprinkler irrigation, on a large scale. The National Project for the repair, renovation and restoration of water bodies was launched in March 2005. The pilot project is planned for 16 districts in 9 States and will cover nearly 700 water bodies, and 20,000 hectares of additional land will come under irrigation. The allocation for the pilot project was increased to Rs.100 crore in the 2005-06 budget.

5.5 Ganga Kalyan Yojana (GKY)

Introduction: Good crop production needs irrigation and more production can break the vicious circle of poverty. The main concern of the Ministry of Rural Areas and Employment is upliftment of the rural poor. This can be achieved by various programmes, which include provision of new assets and upgradation of existing assets for higher income generation. With this objective, minor irrigation programmes been funded under IRDP and Million Wells and Scheme (MWS) on individual/groups. However, exploitation of ground water based asset-creation/upgradation has not received focused attention. Therefore this scheme is being launched. With the launch of this scheme Bore Well/Tube Well Scheme of IRDP and Million Wells Scheme (MWS) was subsumed under Ganga Kalyan Yojana. Such assistance will be provided under Ganga Kalyan Yojana.

To provide irrigation through exploitation of ground water through bore wells and tube wells is the objective of scheme.

The scheme was launched on February 1, 1997 as sub scheme of IRDP for 1996-97 but since April 1, 1997 the scheme is being implemented as an independent scheme.

The target group will be the individuals and groups belonging to below poverty line.

Eligibility Criteria: The eligibility criteria under the scheme are as follows:

1. The Beneficiaries will be the individuals and groups (5 to 15 small and marginal farmers) belonging to below poverty line other than those already assisted under any minor irrigation scheme of the State or Central Government.
2. The SC/ST groups would normally consist only of members of these communities. This is considered necessary in order to maintain group cohesion harmony and to retain the command and control of the assets in the hands of the members belonging to SCs/STs and ensure their uninhibited

participation. When, however, in a contiguous area owned by this group, land of non-SC/ST falls in a manner that it is not possible to form exclusive SC/ST groups, they may also be allowed to be members of the group subject to a maximum of 25 per cent of the members and 25 per cent of the total area of the project.

3. 50 per cent of the funds are earmarked for the SC/ST. It is clarified that expenditure on non-SC/ST members of a SC/ST group should be met from the non-SC/ST earmarked funds.

Selection of Beneficiaries: Gram Sabha in an open General Body Meeting in the presence of officers/staff of the block, revenue staff, bank officials and representatives of NGOs where such NGOs are involved in the formation of groups will duly approve the selection of beneficiaries. This list will then be forwarded to the Block Panchayat and through to the DRDAs/Zila Parishads. The Block Panchayat and DRDA/ZP will scrutinise the list to eliminate ineligible beneficiaries, if any.

Area of Operation: The area of operation of the scheme would be the entire country except blocks/areas declared as over exploited (level of exploitation 100 per cent), dark (between 85 per cent and 100 per cent) or grey (between 65 per cent and 85 per cent), the coastal strip, 15-20 km. from the seashore and the pockets identified by the State Governments.

Sponsorship of the Scheme: The scheme is sponsored by the Central Government. Central Government will do 80 per cent funding and the State Governments will do 20 per cent funding. The funds will be allocated to the States in the ratio of poverty.

DRDA/Zila Parishads would implement the scheme.

Loan Amount: The amount of gap between the project cost and subsidy admissible whether in respect of group or individual schemes would be funded through term credit advanced by financial institutions.

Project Cost: The project cost for the purpose of the scheme consists of the following:

- Cost of drilling
- Construction of pump shed

- Storage tanks,
- Distributory system of feeder channels or pipes to distribute water to the lands of individuals in group projects,
- Land levelling and
- Provision of lifting device.

Drip and sprinkler irrigation systems would not be funded as part of the project. Except for the drilling works, no contractor should be employed in the installation of the project. The State Governments would lay down norms for carrying out such operations.

Subsidy: The subsidy available under the scheme will be as follows:

Particulars	Subsidy
1. Group Schemes (monetary ceiling per group Rs. 40,000)	
a. SC/ST & Physically Handicapped	75 per cent
b. Others	50 per cent
2. Individual beneficiaries: (Ceiling Rs. 12,500)	Rs. 5,000 per acre

Where in non-SC/ST Groups, the SC/ST/Physically disabled beneficiaries are members, they will be eligible for 75 per cent subsidy subject to overall subsidy for the Group.

The land held jointly by two or more persons but operated as single holding would qualify as single beneficiary for the purpose of calculation of subsidy.

Margin: The applicant need not bring any margin as the subsidy will be treated as margin.

Cost of Operation and Maintenance: Part of the operation and maintenance cost subject to ceiling of 5 per cent of the project cost per annum will be admissible as additional subsidy for 3 years for the SC/ST/Physically disabled groups. It will be left to the group to decide through which agency they would like the operation and maintenance. For other groups and for individual schemes no subsidy on operation and maintenance is admissible.

Projects Approval: The procedure for approval of the projects will be the same as for IRDP. DRDAs/Zila Parishads shall prepare an Annual Plan equivalent to 125 per cent of funds allocated under the scheme in the preceding financial year. When preparing the Annual Action Plan, completion of incomplete works should be given priority over taking new works. DRDA/Zila Parishads should not take up works under the scheme, which cannot be completed within two financial years. The DRDA/ZP shall be the sole authority to accord approval to the projects.

Association of the Users and Facilitator: The availability of the Group Schemes would be to the beneficiaries who form themselves into users' associations. The assets provided under the scheme would vest in the users' association. The groups will select one from among their members as facilitator on part time basis. The facilitator may, if necessary, be paid a token honorarium by the association. The facilitator would be in-charge of the day-to-day operations of the irrigation project and would serve as a link between the implementing agency and the users association. The facilitator would be given adequate training in the operation, repairs and maintenance of pump sets, rudiments of crop husbandry and water management etc. The responsibility of providing training to the facilitators will vest with the implementing agency. Non governmental organisations (NGOs) may be involved wherever possible for motivation, group formation, identification, and training of facilitators, maintenance etc. The association may itself maintain and operate the scheme or award the maintenance and operation of the scheme on contract basis to any Government or private agency. The State Governments/DRDA/Zila Parishads would not be authorised to transfer funds directly to a Government/private agency even where operation and maintenance has been entrusted to it. This is considered necessary to ensure accountability of the operating and maintaining agency to the users' association. In SC/ST groups, the facilitator will be from either of these communities only.

With the launch of the Swarnjayanti Gram Swarojgar Yojana on April 1, 1999, the Ganga Kalyan Yojana has been subsumed with it.

5.6 Million Wells Scheme (MWS)

Introduction: During 1988-89, the Million Wells Scheme (MWS) was launched as a sub scheme of National Rural Employment Programme (NREP) and Rural Landless Employment Guarantee Programme (RLEGP). It continued as a sub-scheme of Jawahar Rozgar Yojana from April 1989 to 31-12-95. From 1-1-96, MWS was operated as an independent scheme. On 1.4.1999 the scheme was merged with the Swarnjayanti Gram Swarojgar Yojana (SGSY).

Objectives: The objective of the scheme is to provide open irrigation wells free of cost to poor, small and marginal farmers who are below the poverty line and freed bonded labourers.

Target Group: The target group for the scheme comprised of small and marginal farmers belonging to SCs/STs and freed bonded labourers up to 1992-93. From 1993-94 onwards, the scheme has been extended to include poor small and marginal farmers belonging to non-SC/ST category as well, who are below the poverty line and are listed in the IRDP register of the village. The financial assistance provided to SC/ST poor, small and marginal farmers under MWS, however, must not be less than two-thirds of the total funds utilised under the scheme in any year.

Allocation of Funds: It is a centrally sponsored scheme. Funds under the scheme are shared between the Centre and the States on 80:20 basis. State-wise allocation is arrived at on the basis of the proportion of rural poor in a State to the total rural poor in the country. State Governments fix the district-wise allocation and physical targets keeping in view the size of the unirrigated land in a district, potential for well irrigation and need for improvements of land held by the rural poor.

Works to be taken up under MWS: MWS is primarily intended to provide open wells. Tube wells and bore wells are not to be taken up under this scheme. However, where wells are not feasible due to geological factors, funds under the scheme could be utilised for other works of minor irrigation like irrigation tanks, water-harvesting structures and also for the development of lands belonging to the target group. The fund cannot be diverted for any other purpose. Each well/irrigation source constructed under the scheme has to be located in the holding of the beneficiary and an entry to that effect should be made in the revenue records. The beneficiaries themselves undertake the construction of wells through their own labour and by hiring local labour for which they are paid. Engagement of contractors is strictly prohibited under the scheme.

Cost/Area Norms: A committee comprising of Chief Secretary/Secretary (Rural Development), Secretary (Planning), Secretary (Irrigation) and Chief Engineers, Minor irrigation of the State decides the cost/area norms in regard to works under the scheme.

Implementing/Executive Agency: At the district level DRDA/ZP is the implementing agency of the scheme. But the beneficiaries themselves execute the construction of wells under MWS through their own labour for which they are paid or by hiring local labour. In no case the work should be entrusted to contractors.

Monitoring and Supervision: The DRDA/ZP is also responsible for monitoring and supervision of the scheme in the district. The state level monitoring is the responsibility of the State Level Coordination Committee of the State. At the State level, Secretary, Rural Development is the nodal agency for implementation of the scheme. Apart from the above, the implementation of the scheme is also supervised by the Monitoring and Vigilance Committees set up at the State, District and Block levels for all the programmes for the Ministry. At the Central level, the MWS is regularly monitored through monthly and annual progress reports from the district /states. The Area Officers of the Ministry of Rural Areas and Employment also provide feedback on the implementation of MWS.

Recently introduced changes in MWS: Some recently introduced changes in MWS are as follows:

1. Strict compliance to ensure 2/3rd of MWS expenditure for the benefit of SCs/STs;
2. Providing lifting device to the beneficiaries wherever needed under IRDP/SC/ST Finance Corporations etc;
3. Educating beneficiaries in improved farm practices through agricultural extension programmes;
4. Active involvement of the Panchayati Raj Institutions in planning and selection of MWS beneficiaries. The village Panchayat has to select the beneficiaries which have to be then approved by the DRDA/ZPs;
5. Reservation of 3 per cent allocation for the year for disabled persons. This reservation would be horizontal reservation i.e. disabled persons belonging to SCs/STs and others would fall in their respective categories;
6. Fixation of district-wise physical and financial targets from 1997-98 onwards which was not done earlier;
7. Priority to be given to MWS beneficiaries under the horticulture development component of Employment Assurance Scheme.

Evaluation: A regular Concurrent Evaluation of MWS by this Ministry is under process. However, some State specific Concurrent Evaluation (September-December, 1995) by the Lal Bahadur Shastri National Academy of Administration (LBSNAA), Mussoorie has revealed that the scheme is definitely a success as it has provided water sources for agriculture and other activities. Similarly, in an evaluation of Rural Development Programme in Andhra Pradesh conducted by the Institute of Resource Development and Social Management, it has been brought out that MWS has helped the farmers by providing an assured irrigation facility for agriculture. The farmers raise mostly commercial crops. The scheme has helped the farmers to enhance both crop production and productivity. As a result of this the beneficiary household income has gone up from Rs.750 to Rs. 2,500 per month. These Findings of the evaluation studies show that MWS has been useful and effective in alleviation of poverty particularly of the rural SC/ST poor, marginal/small farmers and providing income appreciation on a long term basis. These evaluations, however, also reveal some weaknesses of the scheme. In many cases, the land of the beneficiary continues to be single cropped area. Motivation to procure pump sets and use it for a second crop has been found to be inadequate.

The beneficiaries are not able to make optimal utilisation of the wells because of lack of complementary facilities like lifting devices (pump sets) and power to energize.

5.7 Conclusion

A timely and adequate supply of water is absolutely essential for securing the maximum output from the land. In India, a large part of the cultivated area is still dependent on rainfall which is seldom adequate and timely throughout the whole country. Annual failure of crops in different regions of India is, therefore, a common, feature of Indian Agriculture. The most effective way of increasing crop production in India is to provide through irrigation an additional source of water supply to cultivated land.

Situated as India is geographically, with a tropical or sub-tropical climate with practically no rainfall over a large part of the year and uncertain rains during the monsoon months, successful cultivation is not possible in many parts of the country without the aid of irrigation. In the absence of irrigation facilities, large areas produce only a catch crop depending on rainfall alone, which as explained above, is often deficient and unevenly distributed from the point of view of agricultural requirements. It is not surprising, therefore, that the average yield per acre of cultivated area is very low. With the provision of irrigation facilities the yield per acre can be increased considerably.

Apart from the rainfall, its shortage and abnormal distribution, floods, hailstorms, frosts and other vagaries of the season also affect India's agriculture. Other causes that contribute to a low yield include uneconomic units of cultivation, lack of fertilizers or manure, the use of bad seed, etc. The pattern of cultivation that has developed under these conditions is generally of an uneconomic type and does not provide adequate employment for those engaged in agricultural pursuits. Over large areas of the country only one crop per year can be grown, during or after the monsoon rains. But where adequate irrigation facilities are available, the pattern of agriculture is different. Two crops can generally be grown and in places, even three.

Irrigation is the major determining factoring agricultural production. Rainfall in India is erratic. Hence it is necessary that assured source of irrigation is available to the farmers to ensure timely field operations. Many schemes have been started for this purpose.

6

Use of Fertilisers

6.1 Fertiliser Consumption in India

Use of fertilisers is necessary to improve yield of various crops. Fertiliser consumption has been on the increase in India. In November 1977, the Government introduced the Fertiliser Retention Price and Subsidy Scheme under which fertilisers are supplied at subsidised prices to farmers throughout the country.

The issue price of fertilisers is revised from time to time. In spite of this, subsidy on fertilisers is an important item of non-plan expenditure. While it is desirable that small and marginal farmers should continue to enjoy the benefits of subsidised fertilisers, it is questionable if such benefits should continue to be extended to big farmers as well.

Manures and fertilisers play the same part in relation to the soil as food in relation to the body. Just as a well-nourished body is capable of the maximum effort, a well nourished soil will have the best fertility.

The quality of the soil varies greatly in a country of the size of India. A systematic survey of the soils of India has not yet been carried out, though it is generally known that Indian soils are deficient in organic matter, nitrogen and phosphates. Soil samples have been analysed in different areas, but their correlation into a soil-survey for the whole country has not been undertaken. Field experiments have been conducted in various regions to determine the response of crops to various combinations of organic and inorganic manures, but in most cases crops responses and soil analysis have not been linked up. A very little work in connection with the effects of trace-elements in the soil has been done hitherto.

Organic matter, nitrogen, phosphorus and potash are the chief constituents which must be supplied to the soil. Nitrogen is of the first importance in crop production. The soil has a mechanism by which it absorbs nitrogen from the atmosphere and makes it available to living beings in the form of grain and fodder; men and cattle derive energy from the consumption of these and the nitrogen taken from the soil is returned to it in the form of organic manures like farmyard manure, green manure, oilcakes, composts of various kinds, bone-meal and various types of chemical fertilizers, thus completing the nitrogen cycle.

Next in importance is phosphate. Plants absorb phosphates from the soil which are returned to it through animal and human excreta and through decayed plants and their ashes and the bones of dead animals.

Indian soils, while deficient in nitrogen and phosphates, are generally rich in potash. Lack of potash does not, therefore, present a serious problem at present but it is one that should be watched.

The consumption of fertilizers has been steadily increasing over the years. A great deal of variability is observed in fertiliser consumption between the States. Amongst States in the plains per hectare consumption is highest in Punjab, Haryana, Andhra Pradesh and Tamil Nadu. It is lowest in Madhya Pradesh and Rajasthan. *Kharif* crops account for nearly one-third of the total fertiliser consumption, whereas the *rabi* crops accounted for a much larger share. This has now changed. Consumption is more evenly spread between the two sowing seasons, reflecting perhaps more assured water availability in *kharif* season at all India level.

6.2 Urea Pricing, Control and Subsidy

Consequent to decontrol of phosphatic and potassic fertilizers on August 25, 1992, the prices of these fertilizers rose sharply resulting in a sharp fall in their consumption. A separate subsidy scheme (called concession scheme) was then introduced to stimulate the consumption of these fertilizers. The price concession (subsidy) on these fertilizers has been substantially increased in recent years.

The objective of providing fertilizers to farmers at affordable prices, while also ensuring adequate return on investment to the producing units, has been the corner stone of the fertilizer pricing policy of the government. However, it is being increasingly felt that the individual retention price scheme (RPS) for urea producers has resulted in certain aberrations over the years. RPS has led to the adoption of a cost plus approach in reimbursing cost of production to the urea units. This approach generates no compulsion for producers to improve their efficiency.

Since the selling prices of fertilizers are less than the cost of production, the difference between the selling price and the cost of production as assessed by the Government is borne as subsidy on urea.

6.3 Retention Price-cum-Subsidy on Urea: New Pricing Policy for Urea Units

Given the importance of fertilizer pricing and subsidization for the growth and viability of the fertilizer industry and agriculture, the need for streamlining the subsidy to urea units has been on the agenda of the Government for a long time. A New Pricing Scheme (NPS) for urea units for replacing the existing Retention Pricing Scheme (RPS) came into effect from April 1, 2003. The NPS is being implemented in stages. Stage-I coincided with the fiscal year 2003-04 and Stage-II covers the two years of 2004-05 and 2005-06. In respect of complex fertilizers, a more rational pricing formula has been brought into implementation.

A High Powered Fertilizer Pricing Policy Review Committee (HPC) was constituted to review the existing system of subsidization of urea, suggest an alternative broad-based, scientific and transparent methodology, and recommend measures for greater cohesiveness in the policies applicable to different segments of the industry. The Committee submitted its report to the Government on April 3, 1998. It recommended, inter-alia, that unit-wise RPS for urea may be discontinued. It recommended that instead of unit-wise RPS, a uniform Normative Referral Price (NRP) be fixed for existing gas-based urea units and also for DAP. A Feedstock Differential Cost Reimbursement (FDCR) is given for a period of five years for urea units.

6.4 Expenditure Reforms Commission on Fertiliser Subsidies

Expenditure Reforms Commission (ERC) headed by Shri K.P. Geethakrishnan had also examined the issue of rationalizing fertilizer subsidies. The Commission submitted its report on 20th September 2000. ERC has recommended inter-alia, dismantling of existing RPS and in its place introduction of a Concession Scheme for urea units based on feedstock used and the vintage of plants in respect of gas-based units. The Department of Fertilizers has examined the recommendations of ERC in consultation with the concerned Ministries/Departments. The Department has also obtained the views of the fertilizer industry and the State Governments/Union Territories, Ministry of Agriculture and economists/research institutes on the ERC report.

The Government on 19.12.2002 approved a new pricing policy keeping in view the recommendations of ERC for replacing the existing RPS. The new pricing scheme came into existence w.e.f. 1.4.2003. The new policy aims at greater transparency, uniformity and efficiency in disbursements of subsidy payments to urea units and will induce them to take cost reduction measures on their own and be competitive. A Working Group constituted by the Department of Fertilizers is now examining several issues for implementing the next stage of the New Pricing Scheme for fertilizers commencing from April 1, 2006. The fertilizer subsidy bill could be pruned if naphtha and FO/LSHS, now used as feedstock, are replaced by natural gas.

6.5 Computation of Concession

The concession rates for decontrolled phosphatic and potassic (P&K) fertilizers are based on the cost price study of DAP (indigenous and imported) and MOP conducted by the then Bureau of Industrial Costs & Prices (BICP) (now Tariff Commission) in 1998 along with the modifications proposed by an Inter Ministerial Group (IMG) consisting of representatives of Department of Agriculture and Cooperation, Department of Expenditure, Department of Fertilizers and Planning Commission. The concession rates for DAP (indigenous and imported) and

MOP are arrived at by subtracting the cost of sales from the Maximum Retail Prices (MRPs) indicated under the Concession Scheme. For indigenous DAP, the cost of sales is the sum of the normative industry price (including cost of raw materials, conversion cost and return) and the selling and distribution cost; for imported DAP and MOP, the industry cost of sales includes average C&F cost of imported material, customs duties, selling and distribution cost and reasonable return. The concession rates for complex grade fertilizers have been so far derived from the concession rates of indigenous DAP and MOP proportionate to their nutrient content. The policy of the Government is to maintain a reasonable differential in the rates of concession in favour of indigenous DAP vis-a-vis imported DAP and as the domestic industry faces certain disadvantages in the availability of raw materials used in the manufacture of DAP in the country.

The manufacturers and importers are paid concession (subsidy) to enable them to sell the fertilizers at or below the indicated MRPs. The concession is roughly the difference between the MRP and the industry average cost of production/sales for indigenous DAP; and the MRP and the cost of import/sales for imported DAP. The final rates of concession on indigenous DAP, imported DAP and MOP (correspondingly on complexes) are adjusted on quarterly basis according to fluctuations in the prices of raw materials/intermediates (ammonia and phosphoric acid) and the exchange rate as well as the prices of DAP in the international market.

6.6 Capital Investment Subsidy Scheme for Commercial Production Units of Organic Inputs under "National Project on Organic Farming"

This scheme would help in augmenting the production of quality organic inputs in order to cater to the needs of the growing demand of plant nutrients in India.

This new Capital Investment Subsidy Scheme has been introduced to be implemented by National Centre of Organic Farming (NCOF) in collaboration with NABARD/NCDC during the Tenth Plan period with an approved central assistance of Rs. 23 crore. The scheme will be implemented in all the states to encourage establishment of commercial production units of organic inputs namely bio-fertilisers, fruit & vegetable waste compost and vermiculture hatcheries. The scheme provides credit linked and back ended subsidy for the production units at the rate of 25 per cent of the capital cost of the project subject to the maximum of Rs 20 lakh for bio-fertiliser, Rs.1.5 lakh for vermiculture hatchery and Rs. 40 lakh for fruit & vegetable waste compost units.

The main objectives of the scheme are

- To promote organic farming in the country by making available the organic inputs such as bio-fertilisers, vermicompost and fruit & vegetable waste compost and thereby better return for the produce.
- To increase the agricultural productivity while maintaining the soil health and environmental safety.
- To reduce the total dependence on chemical fertilisers by increasing the quantum of quality bio-fertilisers/compost availability in the country.
- To set up hatcheries for vermiculture so that the demand of enough earthworm population for on farm production of vermicompost can be met with.
- To convert the organic waste in to plant nutrient resources.
- To prevent pollution and environment degradation by proper conversion and utilisation of organic waste.

7

Cooperatives

7.1 Cooperatives in India: An Introduction

The cooperative movement in India started in 1905. Consumer cooperatives, sugar mills, cooperative credit societies, spinning mills, brick kilns; etc. are many areas where cooperatives are helping the people. The cooperatives are as a reaction to the plight of rural people trapped by landlessness, moneylenders and the exploitative policies of private firms. Cooperatives are an agent of change in the rural areas.

The essence of the cooperative movement is that it gives the farmers the status of shareholders and assures them agricultural, educational and medical facilities. The strength of the movement is the involvement of the farmers who are shareholders in the cooperative regardless of the status and size of their holdings.

Though initially the subsidies provided to the cooperative sector did benefit farmers both rich and poor, they gradually came to benefit mainly the rich farmers as their share was more in the cooperatives. Various States are extending full support to the cooperatives.

At the Central Government level the cooperatives are being taken care of by the Ministry of Agriculture - Department of Agriculture & Cooperation. There are many schemes sponsored by the Central Government for the benefits of cooperatives. Some of the Central Sector schemes for assistance to cooperatives are given below:

7.2 Assistance to National Cooperative Federations

Objective of the scheme is to provide financial assistance to National Cooperative Federation for promotion and development of research & survey of projects. The scheme provides for the promotion of Technical & Consultancy Services, Intensification of field studies, research and statistical activities, improvement of infrastructural facilities/office buildings/premises. Federation comprising by and large of cooperative for weaker sections or predominantly with promotional role suffering from the constraints of inadequate resources are eligible for the assistance.

7.3 Assistance to National Agriculture Cooperative Marketing Federation of India (NAFED)

Objective of the scheme is to strengthen financial position of NAFED for increasing its business activities in marketing of agricultural produce through state federations, primary cooperative marketing societies etc. for providing better prices to growers. The scheme enables NAFED to undertake price support operations, market interventions, and commercial purchases. It helps NAFED to play an effective role in providing market support both internally as well as promotion of exports.

7.4 Cooperative Marketing, Processing, Storage etc. Programmes in Underdeveloped States

Objective of the scheme is to correct regional imbalances and to provide needed momentum to the pace of development of various programmes of cooperative agricultural marketing, processing, storage etc. in under/least developed States/UTs by providing financial assistance on liberal terms to augment the income of farmers and weaker sections of the community. The scheme provides for distribution of agricultural inputs, development of agro processing including storage, marketing of food grains and plantation/horticulture crops, development of weaker and tribal sections, cooperatives, in dairy, poultry and fisheries.

7.5 Share Capital Participation in Cooperative Sugar Factories

Objective of the scheme is to supplement the resources of State Governments to enable them to contribute to the share capital of cooperative sugar factories so as to expedite the project implementation. Under the scheme, assistance is extended for investment loan for share capital participation in new cooperative sugar mills, term loan assistance to the existing cooperative sugar mills for undertaking modernization, expansion and diversification projects

Financial assistance is given to NCDC as loans for passing on the same to the cooperative sugar mills through Stare Governments. Cooperative sugar factories are eligible for the assistance. Cooperative Societies and their Federations may formulate suitable proposal in the prescribed formats available with State Cooperation Department and in the Regional Offices of NCDC.

7.6 Integrated Cooperative Development Projects in Selected Districts (ICDP)

The aim of this scheme is the overall development of the selected project area through cooperative efforts in the agriculture and allied sectors including fishery, poultry, handloom, rural industries etc. in an integrated manner. The scheme aims to strengthen existing primary cooperative societies and other functional cooperatives, to develop PACS as multi purpose entities, to improve existing cooperative structure including modernization and up gradation of management of cooperatives.

Financial assistance is provided to the cooperative societies through State Governments in the form of loan as well as subsidy. Primary agricultural credit societies and other special purpose cooperative Primary societies are eligible for the assistance.

Name of the districts to be covered is decided by the State Government. The project report is finalized by the State Govt. (State Cooperation Department/independent consultant). NCDC sanctions assistance to the eligible co-operative Societies.

7.7 Share Capital Participation in Grower's Cooperative Spinning Mills

Objective of the scheme is to help cotton growers to fetch remunerative return for their produce through value addition. The scheme provides for assistance to share capital loan for new mills as well as term loan assistance to undertake expansion and modernization of growers cooperative spinning mills. Financial assistance is given to NCDC as loans and grants, which in turn will provide assistance to grower's cooperative spinning mills through State Governments. Growers cooperative spinning mills are eligible for the assistance. Eligible Cooperative Societies may formulate suitable proposal in the prescribed formats available with State Cooperation Department and in the Regional Offices of NCDC.

8

Animal Husbandry

India is having the largest number of cattle heads in the world but the yield is comparatively low. Many schemes are in operation for improvement in the yield. Some of the schemes for development of animal husbandry are given below:

8.1 Intensive Cattle Development Projects (ICDP)

The projects were started in the year 1964-65. The State sector implemented the Intensive Cattle Development Projects and Key Village Blocks (KVB) programmes. These programmes constitute major cattle development programmes in the country. The programme's objective was to induce the milk production in the areas covered by large milk collection and processing plants by all round development of cattle and attend to all aspects of cattle development. In 1971-72, 52 ICDPs and 529 Adarsh Village Blocks were covered under the scheme. Later on the scheme was operative through 131 ICDPs and 550 Key Village Blocks, which covered nearly one fifth of the breedable cattle/buffaloes in various states and Union Territories in the country. Various kind of assistance was provided to the farmers for various purposes.

8.2 Integrated Dairy Development Projects in Non-Operation Flood, Hilly and Backward Areas

The scheme was launched during the Eighth Plan. The scheme has been continued during the 9th Plan with a total outlay of Rs. 250 crore as a Centrally Sponsored Scheme. Development of milch cattle, Increase the milk production by providing technical inputs services, Procurement, processing and marketing of milk in a cost effective manner, ensure remunerative prices to the milk producers, Generate additional employment opportunities and improve social, nutritional and economic status of residents of comparatively more disadvantaged areas are the main objectives of the scheme. The scheme is to be implemented through State Dairy Development Departments/Directorates of Dairy Development/ State level Milk Cooperative Federations. Beneficiaries of the scheme are the Small, marginal and landless labourers with special attention to the farmers belonging to SC/ST categories. 100 per cent grant in aid to the concerned State Government is available.

8.3 Assistance to Cooperative Milk Unions

Under the Perspective Plan, 2010, drawn up for Cooperative Milk Unions, the National Dairy Development Board is fulfilling the objective of raising milk procurement and increase cooperative share in marketing of milk and milk products. 80 Milk Unions have submitted their Perspective Plans to NDDB with an outlay of about Rs. 900 crore. NDDB has approved Plans of about 60 Milk Unions with an investment outlay of Rs. 750 crore.

The Perspective Plan has four thrust areas:

1. Strengthening the cooperative businesses
2. Enhancing productivity
3. Managing quality
4. Building a national information network

8.4 National Project for Cattle and Buffalo Breeding (NPCBB)

The Project envisages genetic upgradation and development of indigenous breeds on priority basis. Objectives of the scheme are to arrange delivery of vastly improved artificial insemination service at the farmers' doorstep, to progressively bring under-organized breeding through artificial insemination or natural service by high quality bulls, all breedable females among cattle and buffalo within a period of 10 years and to undertake breed improvement programme for indigenous cattle and buffalo breeds so as to improve their genetic qualities as well as their availability. This is a major programme initiated by Government of India from October 2000 over a period of ten years, in two phases each of five years, with an allocation of Rs 402 crore for the 1st phase. The 1st phase of the project started in October 2000 and 26 States are participating under the project and financial assistance the tune of Rs. 233.17 crore has been released to these States till August 2005.

8.5 Assistance to States for Feed and Fodder Development

According to Working Group report of on Animal Husbandry and Dairying for Tenth Five Year Plan of Planning Commission, the available fodder can meet the demand of only 46.7 per cent of livestock. The successive drought in several States has also brought out the need to develop fodder banks in vulnerable areas and strategies for improving the efficiencies of fodder supplies from one region to the other region of the country. The department has two schemes Central Fodder Development Organization and Centrally Sponsored Scheme Assistance to States for Feed and Fodder.

The assistance is provided to the State Governments for establishment of fodder banks to preserve fodder for use during drought and scarcity period. Large areas in many States are used for growing grass, which could be preserved in the fodder banks. During Ninth Plan, assistance of Rs. 289.49 lakh was provided for establishment of fodder banks in the different States of the country.

8.6 Enrichment of Straw and Cellulosic Wastes

Under this scheme assistance is given to the farmers to enrich the quality of straw used for livestock, by treatment with urea and molasses. This help in increasing productivity and reducing the cost of milk production. During Ninth Plan, assistance of Rs. 524.30 lakh was provided to the different States.

8.7 Dairy/Poultry Venture Capital Fund

This is a Central Sector Plan Scheme. The main objective of the scheme is to create a venture capital fund for providing financial assistance to agricultural farmers/individual entrepreneurs and groups of all sections of unorganized as well as organized sector for the following purposes:

- To promote setting up of small dairy farms for milk production
- To bring structural changes in the unorganized sector; processing and marketing of pasteurized milk at village level
- To bring about upgradation of quality and traditional technology to handle milk on a commercial scale
- To boost the unorganized poultry sector in states where development is in primitive state and also to give incentive and create infrastructure facilities for export of poultry products by organized sector from advanced states
- Establishment of poultry and breeding farms with low input technology and also for other poultry species
- Setting up of poultry feed plant/ laboratory
- Setting up of egg grading, packing and storing facility for promoting export
- Marketing of poultry products (specialized transport vehicles, cold storage etc)

The funds under the scheme will be distributed among dairy and poultry activities with an overall ratio of 2:1.

8.8 Livestock Health

With the liberalization of trade after the advent of WTO's SPS agreement, the chances of ingress of exotic diseases in to the country have increased.

For ensuring the maintenance of disease free status and to be compatible with the standards and in order to control the economically important livestock diseases and to undertake the obligatory functions related to animal health in the country.

8.8.1 Assistance to States for Control of Animal Diseases (ASCAD): The 10th plan allocation for this scheme is Rs. 255.00 crore. Under this component, assistance is provided to State/Union Territory Governments for control of economically important diseases of livestock and poultry. The programme is being implemented on 75:25 sharing basis between the centre and the states; however, 100 per cent assistance is provided for training and seminar/workshops. The programmes envisage collection of information on the incidence of various livestock and poultry diseases from States and Union Territories and compile the same for the whole country.

8.8.2 National Project on Rinderpest Eradication (NPRE): The objective of the scheme is to strengthen the veterinary services and to eradicate Rinderpest and Contagious Bovine Pleuro - Pneumonia (CBPP) and to obtain freedom from Rinderpest & CBPP infection following the pathway prescribed by Office International des Epizooties (OIE), Paris. The Tenth Plan allocation for this component is Rs. 40 crore.

8.8.3 Foot & Mouth Disease Control Programme (FMD-CP): This programme is being implemented in 54 specified districts of the country in the first phase with 100 per cent central funding as cost of vaccine, maintenance of cold chain and other logistic support to undertake vaccination. The State Governments are providing other infrastructure and manpower. Five rounds of vaccinations will be done during the tenth plan and allocation for this component is Rs. 200 crore. About 1,500 lakh vaccination will be carried during the five rounds of vaccination.

8.9 Piggery Development

The Department was implementing a Centrally Sponsored Scheme "Assistance to States for Integrated Piggery Development" since 1991-92. Though it was discontinued after the 9th plan, it is being revived 2005-06 onwards as a component of the new macro-scheme "National Project for Improvement of Poultry and Small Animals. Exotic breeds of 280 pigs of Large white, Landrace and Hampshire were imported by this department for state government pig farms, from USA during 1999-2000. These pigs have now started producing piglets.

8.10 Sheep Development

The main reasons for low productivity are poor exploitation

of genetic potential of indigenous animals, low absorption of available technology, inadequate resource of feed and fodder, insufficient health cover, inadequate marketing and credit support etc. The population of some of the pure bred small ruminants, equines, pigs and pack animals has come down considerably and such breeds has come to the category of threatened breeds in the country. The farms or the farmers unit in their respective breeding tract are to be established with 100 per cent central assistance for breeds of these animals wherein their population is less than 10,000, with active participation of State Governments and NGOs etc. A centrally sponsored scheme for conservation of such threatened breeds was started during Tenth Five Year Plan. A sum of Rs. 876 lakh has been released to the States of Arunanchal Pradesh, Gujarat, Himachal Pradesh, Karnataka, Kerala, Manipur, Mizoram, Nagaland, Punjab, Rajasthan, Sikkim, Tripura and West Bengal for conservation of breeds like Pony (Spite, Bhutia and Manipuri), Horse (Kathiawadi, Grey Sindhi and Marwari), Pig (Doom, Zovawk, Angamaly, Don, Mali and Ghoongro), Yak (Yak and Hazi), Goat(Long Haired Goat, Black Bengal and Malabari) and Sheep(Bandur and Bonpala) .

8.11 Assistance to State Poultry/Duck Farms

The scheme was started during Ninth Plan period. The Scheme is to assist State Poultry/Duck Farms for strengthening them in terms of hatching, brooding and rearing of the birds with provision for feed mill and their quality monitoring and in-house disease diagnostic facilities. These farms will strictly maintain the parent stock of low input technology birds. States/UTs are the implementing agencies. State poultry farms dealing with rural poultry, backyard poultry owners through State farms are the beneficiaries under the scheme.

8.12 Assistance for Modernisation of Slaughter Houses and Carcass Utilization Plants

The scheme started in the year 1988-89 with the following objectives:

Modernization of Slaughter Houses

- To supply hygienic meat for domestic and export market
- To reduce environmental pollution
- To reduce bird-hit menace to air-crafts

Establishment of Carcass Utilization Centre

- To fully utilize animal by-products of fallen animals and waste from slaughter houses.

To reduce environmental pollution, following are the implementing agencies for the scheme.

- State Governments
- Directorates of Animal Husbandry
- Municipal Corporations
- Local Bodies
- Livestock Corporations

9

Horticulture

Horticultural Crops in India: An Introduction

The Government has identified horticultural crops as a means of diversification for making agriculture more profitable through efficient land use, optimum utilization of natural resources (soil, water and environment) and creating skilled employment for rural masses, especially women folk. Recent efforts have been rewarding in terms of increased production and productivity and availability of a much larger volume of horticultural produce. India has emerged as the largest producer of coconut, arecanut, cashewnut, ginger, turmeric, black pepper and the second largest producer of fruits and vegetables. Among the new crops, kiwi, olive crops and oil palm have been successfully introduced for commercial cultivation in the country. Some improvement is seen in the adoption of technology for raising production.

Efforts are on to encourage private investment in hi-tech horticulture with micro-propagation, protected cultivation, drip irrigation, and integrated nutrient and pest management besides making use of latest post-harvest technology particularly in the case of perishable commodities. As a result, horticulture crop production has begun to move from rural confines to commercial ventures and has attracted young entrepreneurs, since it has proved to be intellectually satisfying and economically rewarding.

A large variety of fruits are grown in India. Of these mango, banana, citrus, pineapple, papaya, guava, sapota, jackfruit, litchi and grape and some of the tropical and sub-tropical fruits and nuts. Apple, pear, peach, plum, apricot, almond and walnut constitute the temperate fruits and nuts. Aonia, ber, pomegranate, annona, fig and phalsa are some of the and zone fruits. India produces over 46 million tonnes of fruits accounting for about 10 percent of the world production. The country ranks first in the production of mango, banana, sapota and acid lime and, in recent years recorded the highest productivity in grape.

Mango is the most important fruit covering about 39 per cent of the area accounting for 23 percent of total fruit production in the country. India's share in the world production of mango is about 54 per cent. Citrus ranks second in area and accounts for about 10 per cent of country's fruit production. Limes, lemons, sweet orange and mandarin cover bulk of the area under this group of fruits. Banana ranks third in area covering about 13 per cent of the total area. It ranks first in fruit production contributing nearly one-third of total fruit production. Apple is the fourth major fruit crop of the country with production of 1.42 million tonnes. The share of other fruits like guava and papaya is about 4 per cent while that of grapes and pineapple is about 2 per cent and litchi, about 1 per cent. The arid zones of the country are potential areas for fruits like aonia, ber, pomegranate, annona, etc. There has been a steady increase in the area and production of these fruits particularly aonia, ber and pomegranate in the country as a result of identification and development of suitable varieties and production technologies. In addition to these, date palm and fig cultivation is also finding favour in some areas.

Vegetables constitute the most important food next only to cereals and milk. Important vegetable crops grown in the country are potato, tomato, onion, brinjal, cabbage, cauliflower, okra and peas. India occupies first position in the production of cauliflower, second in onion and third in cabbage production in the world.

Traditional flowers such as jasmine, marigold, chrysanthemum, tuberose, crossandra and aster are commonly grown. Commercial cultivation of cut flowers such as rose, orchids, gladiolus, carnation, anthurium, gerbera and lilies has also become popular. The total production of flowers during 2001-02 was 0.57 million tonnes of loose flowers and 803.5 million numbers of cut flowers. Although flower cultivation has been practised in India since time immemorial, floriculture has blossomed into a viable business only in recent years. Considering the potential of this sector for generation of income and employment opportunities, promotion of involvement of women and enhancement of exports, it has been identified as an Extreme Focus Area for exports by the Government.

9.2 National Horticulture Mission

The National Horticulture Mission was launched on April 1, 2005. The Mission will ensure an end-to-end approach having backward and forward linkages covering research, production, post-harvest management, processing and marketing, under one umbrella, in an integrated manner.

To conclude, horticulture has been recognized as an important avenue for diversification in agriculture in an eco-friendly manner through efficient land use, optimum utilization of natural resources and creation of employment opportunities, particularly for unemployed youth and women. The sector was given a boost by enhancing its outlays from Rs. 1,000 crore in the Eighth Plan, to Rs. 1,454 crore in the Ninth Plan and further to Rs. 2,105 crore in the Tenth Plan. As a result, the horticulture sector has grown significantly over the years. India has maintained leadership in the production of many commodities like mango, banana, coconut, arecanut, cashew, ginger, turmeric and black pepper.

New initiatives taken in 2003-04 to boost the sector were:

- The scheme on Technology Mission for integrated development of horticulture was extended to Himachal Pradesh, Jammu and Kashmir, and Uttranchal in 2003-04.
- Additional cold storage facilities for 30.5 lakh tones were created under the cold storage scheme of the National Horticulture Board (NHB).
- The Central Government budget for 2003-04 announced the launching of schemes on Hi-Tech Horticulture & Precision Farming with an initial provision of Rs. 50 crore for 2003-04.
- A National Horticulture Mission with the objective of doubling horticulture production by 2010 was announced by the Prime Minister.

9.3 National Horticulture Board

National Horticulture Board is the agency for the

development of Horticulture in the country. NHB comes under the Ministry of Agriculture - Department of Agriculture & Cooperation. National Horticulture Board has many schemes under the Central Sector.

The schemes of the board have the following objectives:

- Develop high quality horticulture farms in identified belts and make such areas vibrant with horticultural activity which in turn will act as hubs for developing commercial horticulture.
- Develop post-harvest management infrastructure
- Strengthen Market Information System and horticulture database.
- Assist R&D programmes to develop products suited for specific varieties with improved methods and horticulture technology.
- Provide training and education to farmers and processing industry personnel for improvement agronomic practices and new technologies.
- Promote consumption of fruits/vegetables in fresh and processed form.

9.4 Technology Mission for Development of Horticulture in North Eastern Region including Sikkim

The objectives of the Mission are as follows:

1. To establish convergence and synergy among numerous ongoing governmental programme in the field of horticulture development to achieve horizontal and vertical integration of these programmes.
2. Ensure adequate, appropriate, timely and concurrent attention to all the links in the production, post harvest and consumption chain.
3. Maximise economic, ecological and social benefits from the existing investment and infrastructure created for horticulture development.
4. Promote ecologically sustainable intensification, economically desirable diversification and skilled employment.

5. Generate value addition, promote the development and dissemination of eco-technologies based on the blending of the traditional wisdom and technology with frontier knowledge such as bio-technology, information technology and space technology; and to provide the missing links in ongoing horticulture development projects.

The Technology Mission comprise of four Mini Missions viz. Mini Mission-I (MM-I), Research, Mini Mission-II (MM–II), Production and Productivity, Mini Mission–III (MM-III), Post harvest management, marketing and export and Mini Mission-IV (MM-IV), Processing. It is a Central Sector scheme.

9.5 Coconut Development Board Schemes

These schemes are Central Sector schemes to increase production and productivity of coconut. The objectives of the scheme are:

- To bring additional area under coconut in potential non-traditional areas.
- To develop new technologies for product diversification and by-product utilization.
- To strengthen mechanism for transfer of technologies.
- To elevate the income level of small and marginal farmers engaged in coconut cultivation.
- To build up sound information basis for coconut industry and market information.
- To generate ample employment opportunities in the rural sector.

The scheme provides for production and distribution of quality planting material, expansion of area under coconut, integrated farming practices for productivity improvement, technology demonstration, market promotion and human resource development.

9.6 Integrated Programmes for Development of Horticulture in Tribal/Hilly Areas

It is a Central Sector scheme. The objectives of the scheme

are:

- Production of quality planting material of improved cultivars
- New planting with seed/planking material of improved high yielding varieties
- Improving productivity through adoption of improved cultivation technology, plant protection chemicals, nutrient and water management:
- Transfer of technology through farmers participatory demonstrations, training visits of farmers, publicity through media support, extension literatures etc.
- Creation of on-farm and post harvest infrastructure such as, collection centre, packaging, transport, storage and marketing.

The project components include techno-economic feasibility study, production programmes, technology dissemination, irrigation, horticulture mechanisation, and on farm handling.

10

Fisheries

10.1 Marine Fishing Policy, 2004

Fisheries sector occupies a very important place in the socio-economic development of the country. It has been recognised as a powerful income and employment generator as it stimulates growth of a number of subsidiary industries and is a source of cheap and nutritious food besides being a foreign exchange earner. At the same time it is an instrument of livelihood for a large section of economically backward population of the country.

10.1.1 Policy Objectives: Policy objectives of the Marine Fishing Policy, 2004 are the following:

1. to augment marine fish production of the country up to the sustainable level in a responsible manner so as to boost export of sea food from the country and also to increase per capita fish protein intake of the masses,
2. to ensure socio-economic security of the artisan fishermen whose livelihood solely depends on this vocation.
3. to ensure sustainable development of marine fisheries with due concern for ecological integrity and bio-diversity.

10.1.2 Main Provisions of the Policy: These are as follows:

- **Marine Fisheries Resources:** The policy underscores the need for a departure from the open access concept in the territorial waters besides putting in place stringent management regimes. Promoting exploitation in the deep sea and oceanic waters would be another approach for reducing fishing pressure in the traditional fishing areas.
- **Harvesting of Marine Fish Resources:** The policy advocates protection, consideration and encouragement of subsistence level fishermen and technology transfer to small scale sector and infrastructure support to industrial sector. There would be exclusive areas in terms of depth and (or) distance earmarked

for non-mechanised (non-motorised) traditional craft. An area beyond this would be demarcated for mechanized and motorised craft.

- **Post-harvest Operations:** Total utilisation of harvested fish for food and non-food uses would be the central theme. Efforts would be made to fully comply with international requirements in post harvest care of catch so as to achieve highest standards in food safety. It would also be the concern of the Government to ensure that the post-harvest losses are minimized.
- **Resource Management:** Exploitation of living resources within 50 metres depth zone is showing symptoms of depletion and in certain belts in the onshore waters, it tends to cross optimum sustainable levels. The policy therefore advocates a stringent fishery management system to be in place.
- **Fishermen Welfare:** Fishing is the sole livelihood for about 10 lakh fishermen households along the coastline and this policy attaches top priority to ensuring their social security and economic well being.
- **Environmental Aspects:** The effect of environmental factors on the health of living resources needs increased attention in tune with the international awareness on the issue. Health hazards due to consumption of fish harvested from contaminated water is also becoming a matter of great concern in many parts of the world. The agencies responsible for legislation relating to environmental pollution would be urged to implement them more stringently so that the impact of pollution on fisheries can be minimized.
- **Infrastructure Development for Marine Fisheries:** Development of infrastructure for marine fisheries is of vital importance and should have an integrated approach. The facilities would inter alia include jetties, landing centres, provision for fuel, water, ice, repairs to vessels and gear. The concept of hygienic post harvest handling of fish would also be woven into the project.

- **Legislative Support:** An enabling legal framework is an essential pre-requisite for proper management and control of fisheries sector. As at present, the subject of fisheries is in the State list under article 21 of the Indian Constitution, management and control of coastal fisheries is vested with the maritime States and union territories. At the same time the Union Government carries out management and control of the fishing activities beyond territorial limits in the EEZ.

10.2 Policy for Development of Fisheries in the Union Territories of Lakshadweep and Andaman & Nicobar Islands

The waters around these two Island Groups are rich in fish resource, which are currently exploited far below the exploitable limits. Fisheries, capture, post harvest operations and marketing, is still an important means of livelihood for the inhabitants of these islands. It is, therefore considered relevant to have the policy initiatives in respect of the two UTs.

10.3 National Scheme of Welfare of Fishermen

This Centrally Sponsored Scheme envisages providing financial assistance to fishers for construction of house, community hall for recreation and common working place and installation of tube-wells for drinking water and assistance during lean period through saving cum relief component was in operation till the terminal year of the Ninth Plan. This welfare scheme has been continued during the Tenth Plan. The Plan Outlay approved for the scheme for the entire period of the Tenth Plan is Rs. 120 crore. The scheme has the following Components:

10.3.1 Development of Model Fishermen Villages: Under this component, the eligible fishermen in inland and marine sector would be provided with basic civic amenities like houses, drinking water and commonplace for recreation and work. The respective States/UT's shall provide land for development of these amenities. Cost of the development would be shared equally by the Central Government and State Governments subject to the conditions indicated below. In case of Union Territories, the entire expenditure shall be borne by the Government of India.

10.3.2 Housing: A Fishermen Village may consist of not less than 10 houses. There is no upper limit for the number of houses to be constructed in a village, which would depend on the number of eligible fishermen in that village. However, the State Governments may ensure equitable distribution of houses among all villages in proportion to the number of eligible fishermen, as far as possible. The plinth area and cost of construction of a house would be limited to 35 Sq. mts. and Rs. 40,000 respectively. The ceiling on land and cost of construction indicate the upper limit. The State Government may plan and ensure optimizing the use of available resources so that more number of houses could be built within the budgeted amount.

10.3.3 Drinking Water: A fishermen village would be provided with one tubewell for every 20 houses. Where a village consists of only 10 houses or more but less than 20 houses, one tubewell may be provided for such a village. The cost of installation of a tubewell should not exceed Rs. 30,000. However, for North-Eastern states the cost of installation of a tubewell up to Rs. 35,000 would be permissible as a special case for which the State Government should furnish adequate justification. The actual number of tubewells to be installed in a village may be rationalized on the basis of actual water requirement of the inhabitant families and the capacity of the tube wells. A fishermen village may be provided with alternative source of drinking water supply in case tubewells are not a practical proposition, provided the additional expenditure, over and above what would otherwise be admissible if tubewells were to be provided on the basis of number of houses for which the facility is intended, is met entirely by the State Government.

10.3.4 Community Halls/Workshed: As a recreation and common working place, a fishermen village with at least 75 houses will be eligible to seek assistance for construction of a community hall if found necessary. The hall will be constructed on an area not exceeding 200 sq. mts. Two toilets and a tube well will also be provided with a community hall. The total cost of the hall should not exceed Rs. 1,75,000. The State/UT's should ensure optimum utilization of the community hall by permitting its utilization as a drying yard and also as mending shed. If required, construction of walls for the community hall may be dispensed with so that it may be a structure with pillars and roofs to permit its optimum utilization as a common working place for fishermen.

10.3.5 Group Accident Insurance for Active Fishermen: Under this component, fisher folk, licensed/identified or registered with the State/UT Governments would be insured for Rs. 50,000 against death or permanent total disability and Rs. 25,000 for partial permanent disability. The insurance cover will be for a period of 12 months and a policy would be taken out by FISHCOPFED in respect of all the participating States/UT's. The annual premium payable would not exceed Rs. 15 per head – 50 per cent of which will be subsidized as grants-in-aid by the Centre and the remaining 50 per cent by the State Government. In the case of Union Territories, 100 per cent premium will be borne by the Central Government.

In case of those States/UT's, which subscribed to this component through FISHCOPFED the Central share of the assistance (100 per cent premium in case of UT's) would be released directly to FISHCOPFED and will not be routed, through States/UT's. The State Governments should, however, ensure that their share of premium is sent to FISHCOPFED well before the due date of renewal of the policy. In case of those States/UT's who do not subscribe to this component through FISHCOPFED, the release of Central share would be restricted on the basis of annual premium that would be payable had the insurance been taken through FISHCOPFED or the actual premium, whichever is less. No contribution will be collected from the fishermen. The scheme would cover fishermen in both marine and inland sectors. FISHCOPFED will be the executing agency and would operate the Scheme through any subsidiary of General Insurance Corporation of India in case of States/UT's, which opt to subscribe to the Scheme through FISHCOPFED.

Part III
Subsidies for Food Security

11. Minimum Support Prices for Agricultural Produce
12. Public Distribution System (PDS)

11

Minimum Support Prices for Agricultural Produce

For the large sections of the community which live near the margin of subsistence, a certain minimum supply of foodgrains at reasonable prices constitutes the rock-bottom of the standard of living, a fall in which would be seriously detrimental to health and efficiency. Foodgrains occupy a pivotal place in the price structure, and if this latter has to be safeguarded, as it must be, the prices of foodgrains must be held stable at levels within the reach of the poorer sections of the community.

The objectives of a sound agricultural price policy are two-fold:

- to ensure fair prices for the produce of the farmers, and
- to ensure adequate and regular supply of agricultural commodities to the consumers at reasonable prices.

Excessive fluctuations in agricultural prices generate harmful effects both for the producers and the consumers. The beneficiaries of unstable prices are the middlemen and the speculators. It is for these reasons that Government undertakes buffer stocks operations, i.e. making purchases when there is glut of produce in the market and releasing stocks during period of scarcity.

11.1 Minimum Support Prices: An Introduction

An important element of the agricultural price policy of the Government of India is the announcement every year of minimum support prices for major commodities. The co-operative societies and government agencies have helped the farmers to escape the exploitative practices of the private traders.

The Price Support Policy of the Government is directed at providing insurance to agricultural producers against any sharp fall in farm prices. The minimum guaranteed prices are fixed to set a floor below which market prices cannot fall. Till the mid 1970s, government announced two types of administered prices:

- Minimum Support Prices (MSP)
- Procurement Prices

The MSPs served as the floor prices and were fixed by the government in the nature of a long term guarantee for investment decisions of producers, with the assurance that prices of their commodities would not be allowed to fall below the level fixed by the government, even in the case of a bumper crop.

Procurement prices were the prices of kharif and rabi cereals at which the grain was to be domestically procured by public agencies (like the FCI) for release through PDS. It was announced soon after harvest began. Normally procurement price was lower than the open market price and higher than the MSP.

This policy of two official prices being announced continued with some variation up to 1973-74, in the case of paddy. In the case of wheat it was discontinued in 1969 and then revived in 1974-75 for one year only. Since there were too many demands for stepping up the MSP, in 1975-76, the present system was evolved in which only one set of prices was announced for paddy (and other kharif crops) and wheat being procured for buffer stock operations.

11.2 Methodology for Cost Calculation

The minimum support prices for major agricultural products are announced each year after taking into account the recommendations of the Commission for Agricultural Costs and Prices (CACP). The CACP, while recommending prices takes into account all important factors including cost of production, changes in input prices, input/output price parity, trends in market prices, inter-crop parity, demand and supply situation, parity between prices paid and prices received by farmers etc. Among these multiple factors that go into the formulation of support price policy, the cost of production is the most significant. Thus, for making the support price policy functionally meaningful, the minimum guaranteed prices ought to cover at least the reasonable cost of production in a normal agricultural season obtained from efficient farming.

The CACP analyses the cost of production data for various States in respect of various commodities in consultation with the states. After a meeting of the State Chief Ministers, the MPS/procurement prices are declared. With costs of production for the same crops varying between regions and also across farms within the same region and for different producers, the level of costs that could be accepted as a norm poses enormous difficulties.

In fixing the support prices, CACP relies on the cost concept which covers all items of expenses of cultivation including in that the imputed value of inputs owned by farmers such as rental value of owned land and interest on fixed capital. Some of the important cost concepts used by CACP are the C2 and C3 costs.

C2 cost includes all actual expenses in cash and kind incurred in production by actual owner plus rent paid for leased land plus imputed value of family labour plus interest on value of owned capital assets (excluding land) plus rental value of owned land (net of land revenue).

C3 Cost means Cost C2 +10 percent of cost C2 to account for managerial remuneration to the farmer.

Costs of production are calculated both on per quintal and per hectare basis. Since cost variations are large over states, CACP recommends that MSP should be considered on the basis of C2 cost. However, increases in MSP have been so substantial in case of paddy and wheat that in most of the States MSPs are way above not only the C2 cost but the C3 cost as well. For instance, weighted average of C3 costs of eight wheat growing states is presently only Rs. 532 per quintal while the weighted average of C2 cost is Rs. 483 per quintal as against which CACP recommended MSP is Rs. 620 per quintal. The producer subsidy at C2 cost is therefore Rs. 137 per quintal (MSP minus C2 cost) and Rs. 88 per quintal at C3 cost (MSP minus C3 cost).

Trends in the MSP of wheat and paddy in recent years are given in Table 11.1

Table 11.1: Minimum Support/Procurement Price of Wheat and Paddy in Recent Years (Rs./quintal)

Crop Year	Wheat		Paddy (Common)	
	MSP	Per cent change	MSP	Per cent change
1994-95	360	2.9	340	9.7
1995-96	380	5.6	360	5.9
1996-97	475	25.0	380	5.6
1997-98	510	7.4	415	9.2
1998-99	550	7.8	440	6.0
1999-00	580	5.5	490	11.4
2000-01	610	5.2	510	4.1
2001-02	620	1.6	530	3.9
2002-03	620	-	530	-
2003-04	630	1.6	550	3.8
2004-05	640	1.6	560	1.8

Source: Government of India, *Economic Survey, 2005-06*, p. 96.

Realising the importance of inter-sectoral terms of trade [1], the Government of India modified the terms of reference for the Commission for Agricultural Costs and Prices (CACP). Consequently, the CACP has been regularly taking into account the terms of trade ever since 1980 while recommending support /procurement prices for agricultural commodities.

In the meantime, Government constituted a Task Force in March 1993 (Chairman: A.S. Kahlon) to suggest methodology for constructing an index of terms of trade between agricultural and non-agricultural sectors. The Government of India now computes the terms of trade between the two sectors on the basis of the methodology recommended by the Task Force. [2]

11.3 Economic Cost of Foodgrains to FCI

The economic cost of foodgrains to FCI is of strategic importance, as it influences not only the food subsidy bill but also the country's competitiveness in international markets for foodgrains. The FCI is reimbursed the difference between the economic cost of foodgrains and the issue price. The economic cost of foodgrains to FCI has been on the rise over the years. The increase in the MSPs of rice and wheat, high State-level levies, which account for almost 50 percent of the procurement incidentals for foodgrains, and the rising trend in distribution costs have contributed to the increase in the economic costs of foodgrains over the years.

Fixing the MSP at a level equal to C2 cost (all cost in cash and kind, including the imputed cost of family labour) of the least cost State would help in containing the rising trend in economic cost of foodgrains. The major procurement States- Punjab, Haryana and Andhra Pradesh - have been imposing State taxes and levies of over 10 per cent ad valorem on the procurement of foodgrains, thereby inflating the economic cost. There is scope for rationalisation of these State levies. More decentalised procurement will help in containing the increase in the distribution and hence economic costs.

The 2004-05 (BE) projected a reduction in economic cost of wheat from Rs 952.51 per quintal in 2003-04 to Rs 924.82 per quintal and a marginal increase in the economic cost of rice from Rs 1,253.04 per quintal in 2003-04 to 1,262.51 per quintal in view of decline in distribution cost of both wheat and rice in 2004-05.

11.4 Food Subsidy Bill

Producers and consumers and within this group the vulnerable sections of the society are the major beneficiaries of food subsidy. The subsidy incurred on the supply of foodgrains through the PDS at below FCI's economic cost constitutes the consumer subsidy while the producer subsidy is the direct offshoot of the price support based procurement operations of the government. The producer subsidy together with the cost of maintaining the buffer stock accounts for the cost of buffer stock operations. The consumer subsidy together with the buffer carrying cost constitutes the food subsidy.

The food subsidy bill has increased from year to year in recent times (Table 11.2). Though pruning of the existing subsidy level is imperative and could be done by reducing operational inefficiency, the interests of the poor also have to be safeguarded. The surplus stocks of foodgrains with the government provide a vital resource for providing income support to the poor and the vulnerable. Better targeting of subsidies is now beginning to be visible. But it has been found that PDS has failed in large parts of the country, and that it needs to be restructured to be an effective tool of food security.

Table 11.2: Food Subsidy in Recent Years

(Rs. crore)

Year	Food subsidy
1996-97	6,066
1997-98	7,900
1998-99	9,100
1999-00	9,434
2000-01	12,060
2001-02	17,499
2002-03	24,176
2003-04	25,160
2004-05	25,800
2005-06	26,200

Source: Government of India, *Economic Survey, 2005-06*, p. 98.

Minimum Support Prices (MSP) lay the floor for the market price of foodgrains, especially the two dominant foodgrains: rice and wheat. With sharp increases in MSP every year despite surpluses having replaced shortages, the MSP has become the maximum selling price instead of being the floor price. This coupled with the system of open-ended procurement has made FCI the buyer of the first resort resulting in huge accumulation of surplus public stocks of foodgrains, leading to much higher commitments for government subsidy. FCI has thus become the main buyer, stockiest and seller in the domestic market. It is also the main exporter.

High statutory levies (including mandi charges, cesses and fees to commission agents) on grain purchase, not only discourage private trade but also increase FCI's cost, thus putting a pressure on the food subsidy bill. The levies imposed by the State Governments (ad valorem) differ from State to State and are highest in case of Punjab, Haryana and Andhra Pradesh.

The High Level Committee on Long Term Grain Policy recommended that government may, for open-ended procurement, in future announce a gross price, inclusive of MSP and a uniform 4 per cent allowance for State taxes as the price that its agencies would be allowed to pay. It would be better for the centre and states to agree on a ceiling on statutory levies, and announce MSPs which farmers could actually expect to receive net of all compulsory levies.

Outlining its policy on food subsidy, the Ninth Five Year Plan (1997-2002) observed, "Self-sufficiency in foodgrains for the country as a whole does not necessarily imply food and nutrition security for all. Making food available through the PDS at affordable prices has been a key element of our food security system. However, untargeted PDS has resulted in a steady rise of budgetary food subsidy. During the Ninth Plan subsidised foodgrains is proposed to be targeted only to people below the poverty line so as to ensure that budgetary subsidies reach the needy and become sustainable." [3]

National Common Minimum Programme (NCMP) of the Government pledges that all subsidies will be targeted sharply to the poor and the truly needy. In order to achieve this objective, the Ministry of Finance with the assistance of the National Institute of Public Finance and Policy (NIPFP) prepared a report on "Central Government Subsidies in India". The report examines major subsidies including food and fertilisers and recommends policies for reforms in subsidies. As regards food subsidies, the report suggests that the minimum support prices should be kept at the C2 level recommended by the CACP. To contain operational costs, reimbursement of expenses of the Food Corporation of India should be based on normative unit costs and actual quantities involved. With respect to the public distribution system, it is suggested that the system of dual prices, which encourages leakages, may be replaced by a uniform price policy along with a system of food coupons for the BPL families.

Government took special measures during 2001-02 which continued through 2002-03, such as release of foodgrains from the FCI at concessional rates for exports, offloading of the old and low quality foodgrains through tender sale and reduction in the APL issue price to bring back APL population to the PDS fold, to dispose of the excess stock of foodgrains. These measures helped in reducing the excess stock of foodgrains with the FCI. Further, the Government also adopted the policy of restraint in the announcement of the MSPs of wheat and rice (as discussed earlier in the section on minimum support price), as part of its strategy to remove market distortions, and to restore the role of private trade in the grain market, thereby easing the pressure of procurement on the FCI. Some success has been achieved in this respect, because the market prices of rice and wheat, which remained below the MSP in different parts of the country during 2001-02 and 2002-03 recovered to prevail at a level higher than the MSP during 2003-04 and, 2004-05. All these helped in tackling the problem of excess stock of foodgrains with the FCI and as already discussed earlier, the declining trend in stock levels, which started in 2003-04, continued through 2004-05.

11.5 Burgeoning Food Stocks

As a result of the partition of India in 1947, the balance between foodgrains availability and population was disturbed, leading to food shortages in new India. Therefore, the First Five Year Plan (1951-56) was mainly devoted to agricultural development. The recurring scarcities and shortages of essential food items forced the Government to adopt an elaborate system of public procurement and distribution of foodgrains.

For this purpose, the Food Corporation of India (FCI) was established in 1965, and a price support system for major agricultural crops was introduced. In spite of certain drawbacks, the system worked reasonably well till the late 1970s. Since then, production of foodgrains in the country has kept pace with the requirements of the population, owing mainly to the spread of new technology among farmers. However, the rising Minimum Support Prices (MSP) for rice and wheat induced the farmers to cultivate these two crops more than other crops. Increased production of rice and wheat led to their higher procurement by official agencies which, in turn, resulted in large accumulation of government food stocks. On the other hand, the off-take of foodgrains through the Public Distribution System (PDS) is relatively low due to (a) narrow price differential between the open market price and the price at which foodgrains are made available through the PDS, (b) altered consumption pattern of the population (towards milk, eggs and meat as against cereals) owing to improved income levels and (c) lacklustre export performance of agricultural products.

11.5.1 Macro Implications: The macro implications of burgeoning food stocks are manifold but the following two are more important. Firstly, higher procurement, along with additional storage and maintenance costs, means higher food subsidy which increases deficit on the already strained revenue account of the Central Government. Secondly, since food stocks are financed by preferential food credit, they have monetary implications as well. Higher demand for food credit can give rise to possible crowding-out effects on other sectors.

In view of the present high level of food security, there is need to focus on the distributional aspects of foodgrains rather than encouraging unsustainable levels of cereal production and procurement through the MSP.

11.5.2 Decentralised Procurement Scheme: The decentralised procurement scheme of the Government of India is in operation since 1997. Under this scheme, the designated States procure, store and also issue foodgrains as per allotments indicated by the Central Government under TPDS. The difference between the economic cost of the State Governments and the Central Issue Price is passed on to the State Governments as subsidy. The decentralised system of procurement, apart from helping to cover more farmers under the MSP of the Central Government, has the merit of economising the transport and administrative costs involved in procurement and distribution operations. Further, it helps in minimising the dependence of State Governments on the FCI for PDS requirements and reducing the complaints about quality, as consuming States themselves are the custodians of the procured foodgrains.

However, the scheme has evoked limited response from the State Governments. Out of the State Agencies' share of nearly 58 percent of total rice and 80 percent of total wheat procured by the FCI, only 33 percent rice and 13 percent wheat are contributed by the States with decentralised procurement. At present, the State Governments of West Bengal, Madhya Pradesh, Uttar Pradesh, Chhattisgarh, Uttaranchal and Tamil Nadu are implementing this scheme in a limited way. The States of Assam and Nagaland and the Union Territory of Andaman & Nicobar Islands have also evinced interest in the scheme.

The concerns of the State Governments broadly relate to financing of operations (RBI valuation norms for stocks of foodgrains) and reimbursement of expenses and release of subsidy by the Central Government (fixation of economic cost of foodgrains of State Governments and delays in the release of the subsidy). The concerns relating to the reimbursement of expenses and release of subsidy have been largely addressed through a process of consultation of the stakeholders concerned. On the request of the States, the issues relating to valuation norms have been taken up with the RBI.

Notes

1. Terms of trade between the agricultural and non-agricultural sectors is a subject of controversy among agricultural economists in

India. Terms of trade are defined as the ratio of agricultural prices to non-agricultural prices. There are two schools of thought. According to one, terms of trade have moved in favour of the agricultural sector with the result that the development of the industrial sector has slowed down. Hence, it is contended that agricultural prices should be lowered to give a boost to industries.

Contrarily, many hold the view that terms of trade have moved against the farm sector and therefore higher agricultural prices are needed to induce the farmers to produce more. The debate is inconclusive because the results of various studies are conflicting due to different methodologies and assumptions adopted by the researchers.

2. For more details on the index of terms of trade between the agricultural and non-agricultural sectors, see Reserve Bank of India, *Report on Currency and Finance*, 1998-99, pp. III-4 and 5.

3. Government of India, Planning Commission, *Ninth Five Year Plan* (1997-2002), Vol. II, p. 2.

12

Public Distribution System (PDS)

12.1 PDS: An Introduction

Food Security is one of the major components of social security. It consists of ensuring that 'food is available at all times, that all persons have means of and access to it, that it is nutritionally adequate in terms of quantity, quality and variety, and that it is acceptable within the given culture'. There are three elements in this definition, availability, access and suitability. In recent years, nutrition has been considered as part of food security, and is therefore, referred to as 'Food and Nutrition Security'.

There is enough food available in the world. Even in developing countries, the per capita food production has increased by 8 per cent on an average in the 1980s. Everybody can get 2500 calories from the available food which is 200 calorie more than the basic minimum. What is required is a well-organised public distribution system. Efforts have been made to streamline the PDS through the introduction of the Targeted Public Distribution System in June 1997. This system follows a two tier subsidised pricing structure for families Below Poverty Line (BPL) and for those Above Poverty Line. BPL population receives rice and wheat at a much lower price (hence highly subsidised) whereas APL population is supplied at a price which is much higher and closer to the economic cost. The identification of the poor under the scheme is done by the States.

A National Sample Survey has pointed out that about 5 per cent of the total population in the country sleeps without two squares meals a day.

Antyodaya Anna Yojana launched in December 2000 aims at identifying 10 million poor families and providing them with 25 kgs of foodgrains per family per month, at a price of Rs. 2 per kg.

for wheat and Rs. 3 per kg for rice, amounting to an annual allocation of foodgrains of about 30 lakh tonnes.

Similarly, the Anna Purna Scheme (2000) is for senior citizens eligible for old age pension but not receiving the pension, and whose children are not residing with them. Under this scheme 10 kg of foodgrains is provided per person, per month, free of cost. The estimated cost of this scheme is Rs. 330 crore per annum.

Public Distribution System (PDS) is the cornerstone of Government's price policy and food security system in India. It ensures availability of certain essential commodities (sugar, kerosene, rice and wheat) at affordable prices, especially for the poor. Through its agency the Food Corporation of India (FCI), the Government procures and stocks foodgrains, which are released every month for distribution through the PDS network across the country. These commodities are distributed to the public through a network of Fair Price Shops (FPS). In addition to this, the system of procurement is also used by the Government to provide minimum support prices to the farmers in order to stabilise agricultural output and income.

The FCI issues foodgrains to the State Governments at a uniform Central Issue Price (CIP) which is considerably lower than the economic cost incurred by the Central Government by way of procurement, storage, transport and distribution. The difference between the economic cost and the CIP is called the consumer subsidy. Since the FCI maintains a large buffer stock of foodgrains, it entails a substantial carrying cost. The consumer subsidy and the carrying cost together add up to the total food subsidy which is borne by the Central Government. It is an important item of the non-Plan revenue expenditure of the Government as shown in its annual budget.

12.2 Targeted Public Distribution System (TPDS)

A well-targeted and properly functioning Public Distribution System (PDS) is an important constituent of the strategy for poverty alleviation. PDS is operated under the joint responsibility of the Central and State Governments. The Central Government takes the responsibility for procurement, storage, transportation and bulk allocation of foodgrains, at subsidized prices. The responsibility of distribution to consumers including target groups through a network of 4,63,000 fair price shops rests with the State Governments.

TPDS was introduced in 1997 in order to achieve better targeting of food subsidy. Under the TPDS, a dual price mechanism for Above the Poverty Line (APL) and Below the Poverty Line (BPL) consumers prevails. The full economic cost of foodgrains is recovered from the APL consumers while foodgrains are sold at half the economic cost to BPL consumers.

The off-take from the PDS appears to be poor especially in some States like Bihar. It could be due to the fact that the economic cost has been going up, the prices at which foodgrains are supplied to people below the poverty line are also going up, and have become unaffordable to the poor in the category. It could also be due to the poor quality of the foodgrains supplied through the PDS. Besides, the quantities supplied at subsidised prices are not adequate for the sustenance of the whole family, and people have to supplement them by purchase from the open market. Thus, the implementation of the PDS does not seem to be serving the purpose of making foodgrains available to people at affordable prices. The Commission agrees with the Study Group that the food security policy calls for a review and rationalisation.

Central Government should devise a scheme, similar to the targeted PDS for foodgrains, to supply cloth free to destitutes, at subsidised prices to the people below the poverty line. The Study Group has also suggested that the Janata Cloth scheme may be revived. The Commission endorses both these recommendations of the Study Group.

12.3 Report on the High Level Committee on Long Term Grain Policy

The Department of Food and Public Distribution had constituted a High Level Committee on November 16, 2000 for formulating a long term Grain Policy for the country. The Committee submitted its final report on July 31, 2002. Some of the recommendations made by the Committee for Long Term Grain management are listed below:

1. Quality norms should be strictly adhered to while procuring foodgrains for PDS distribution.
2. Payments as statutory levies to state governments by FCI are essentially transfers from the centre to the state governments. These should be taken care of separately between the Centre and the states without involving the FCI.
3. MSP for paddy should be fixed only for a single grade.
4. APL price should be reduced to 80 percent of the economic cost and BPL price to 50 percent of the economic cost excluding statutory levies. This would also help improve the viability of the fair price shops in the distribution network.
5. Once the current high stocks are reduced, the resultant savings could be used for employment schemes, for which there was a strong felt need and which could be used to develop rural infrastructure.
6. The existing Antyodaya scheme of food support could also be expanded to become a food security system for the entire destitute population.
7. A system of universal PDS be introduced with uniform CIP, one each for rice and wheat respectively, for all consumers in all parts of the country.
8. The Central Government should announce its MSP policy before the sowing season on recommendations of the Commission for Agricultural Costs and Prices (CACP).
9. The CACP should be made an empowered statutory body.
10. In recommending MSPs which should apply only to Fair Average Quality grain, the CACP should go strictly on the basis of C2 cost of production (i.e. all costs including imputed costs of family labour, owned capital and rental on land) in more efficient regions.
11. While the Centre has to continue to take the primary responsibility for procurement, as production is dispersed

procurement should also become more dispersed and this process can definitely save costs of transportation and meet consumer needs more adequately.

12. All compulsory levy orders on rice millers under the Essential Commodities Act (ECA) should be removed with immediate effect.
13. A different problem likely to arise as a result of lower MSPs is that there will be a probability for market prices to exceed MSP and, therefore, quantities offered for sale at MSP may fall short of PDS and buffer stocks requirements. In situations where market conditions are such that MSP purchases fall short of PDS requirements. Government would need to make purchases on the basis of best terms. This may include imports, open market purchases from secondary markets or through open tender purchases or purchase from farmers at a market determined price above MSP.
14. Crop diversification is very important at the current stage of India's agricultural development, given the changing dietary patterns. There is need for special packages for diversification.
15. There should be an automatic and transparent policy of variable tariffs on both agricultural imports and exports linked to the deviation of spot international prices from their long run trends. This is required for stabilisation of prices in an open economy.
16. Barriers to private trade should be eased.
17. FCI has performed its role in its core functions reasonably well and should continue to do so keeping in mind that there has to be a work culture of total quality management.
18. It is desirable that that the FCI's role should be confined to procurement of the major cereals for the PDS.

12.4 Food Stamps and Food Credit Cards

To contain the level of food subsidy, major reforms are required in the system of marketing of food grains. Some of the steps in this direction are given below:

1. All restrictions on interstate movement of food grains should be removed once and for all.
2. The system of private trade and marketing of food grains must be strengthened.
3. The idea of having FPS across the length and breadth of the country should be looked into afresh.
4. A new system of providing food subsidy through the normal food supply shops (including the FPS) may be tried, supplemented by new/additional FPS in remote and inaccessible regions where such shops do not exist. This could be achieved through the introduction of food stamps or the food credit card system.
5. Under the system of food stamps, the State Governments could issue a subsidy entitlement card (SEC) instead of issuing ration cards. The SEC should show, among other things, the number of members in a poor family and their age and indicate their entitlement level for food stamps.
6. There could, in principle, be different levels of entitlement based on age. All adult members from a poor family, for example, could be entitled to 'a' number of food stamps per month while the entitlement for a child could be 'b' number of food stamps. There could also be a higher subsidy entitlement for old and infirm people. The SEC will indicate the total number of food stamps a family is entitled to every month.
7. Each family would collect its monthly quota of food stamps from prescribed distribution centres on showing their SEC. They could then use these food stamps at any food supply shop to buy food grains (rice and wheat) at a price (Rs x) below the market price. The retailer will then be reimbursed by the State Government.
8. There is less scope for corruption under a system of food stamps. Under the existing system, FPS owners declare on paper that they have sold a certain quantity of food to the poor at subsidized prices when, in fact, they have made huge profits by selling the food at market prices..

9. Two potential problems with the system of food stamps need to be kept in mind while designing the system. There is a distinct possibility of food stamps being counterfeited. Secondly, reimbursement of subsidy to the participating retailers can run into logistical problems. These problems are, however, minuscule compared to the problem of physically procuring, storing, transporting and delivering foodgrains to FPS across the country by the FCI and the state food corporations/agencies.
10. The food stamp system can be introduced in phases.

A food coupon system for distribution of rice and kerosene through the public distribution system (PDS) was introduced in Andhra Pradesh during 1998-1999 in order to improve the delivery system for these two commodities. Under the scheme, mere possession of the card was not enough to draw PDS rice, wheat or kerosene. The cardholder, whose photo was affixed on the card has to be physically present when obtaining the coupons. Coupons are issued once a year and coupon holders are entitled to draw rice and kerosene on a monthly basis. To help the coupon holder draw rice and kerosene in easy instalments in a month, coupons are denominated in smaller quantities like 4 kg, 8 kg etc.

12.5 Food Policy: Critical Evaluation

The policy of providing price support by raising the MSP continuously though making the terms of trade for agriculture favourable, has not only distorted domestic market prices but has also eroded our export competitiveness. While developed economies continue to protect their exports through export subsidies, Indian rice (except perhaps basmati rice) and wheat are not export competitive. An exporting country cannot have its grain prices greatly mis-aligned with free-on-board export prices. But, with MSPs of foodgrains ruling at the existing high and being totally mis-aligned with the costs of production as also free market prices, India is no longer competitive internationally.

Other consequences of the policy of high MSPs during the last five years are:

- The FCI's procurement has more than doubled.
- FCI has become the sole buyer, stockiest and seller of foodgrains.
- High MSP together with ad-valorem State taxes have eliminated private trade.
- Shortage of storage space has pushed up costs through wastage and deterioration of stocks.
- High carrying cost is a subsidy benefiting neither the consumers nor the producers.

Strong corrective steps aligning the minimum support prices with the cost of production of foodgrains are called for. Perhaps, the only solution we have at hand is to freeze the current MSP until such time it becomes equal to C2 cost or until annual procurement settles down to earlier levels of 24-30 million tonnes. Similarly, future trading, particularly in foodgrains, should be promoted first so that dependence on MSP mechanism for price stabilisation could be avoided.

The public distribution system (PDS) is recognised as a permanent feature of the strategy to control prices, reduce fluctuations and achieve an equitable distribution of essential goods. An efficient public distribution system requires a nexus between production, procurement, transportation, storage, and distribution of the selected commodities.

The working of the PDS is periodically reviewed in consultation with the State Governments and corrective measures are taken from time to time to improve the supply of various essential commodities to the consumers.

Criticising the present system of differential PDS pricing, Mid-term Appraisal of Tenth Five Year Plan (June 2005), observed, "The present system of differential PDS pricing, with very low prices for BPL consumers, is a highly inefficient way of serving the equity objective. There are heavy leakages of as much as 55 per cent according to a recent Planning Commission study. The system also distorts incentives for grain producers in non-surplus areas where FCI procurement is poor or non-existent, because it depresses grain prices below the MSP. With the Food for Work Programme in place and the expansion of Mid-Day Meals and the universalisation of Integrated Child Development Services (ICDS), there is a strong case for moving to uniform PDS pricing. In other words, the PDS, should not be viewed as a poverty reducing instrument as much as an instrument for protecting the common man (including the poor) by stabilising issue prices at a level which may imply only a limited subsidy but which insulates the consumer from sudden increases in prices due to scarcity. The procurement side of the operation should continue to aim at stabilising MSP reasonably above costs of production. Procurement support should also be extended to cover the entire country.

PDS pricing is a sensitive issue, but the proposed change is a logical consequence of the adoption of other schemes aimed at poverty alleviation. It needs to be implemented in parallel with the expansion of other social safety net schemes. The resources saved by moving towards a unified issue price should be directed to expand other poverty reducing programmes, including especially the FFW.

The urban poor are not covered by the Food for work Programme and a case can be made that they need continued subsidy benefits through the PDS. This could be attempted through a system of smart cards. A smart card may be charged with the entitlement of the person who can buy ration commodities from any trader who is linked to the smart card system. The price difference can be automatically transferred to the traders account when the holder makes a purchase." [1]

Note

1. Government of India, Planning Commission, *Mid-term Appraisal of Tenth Five Year Plan*, June 2005, pp.6-7.

Part IV
Subsidies for Industrial Development and Export Promotion

13

Industrial Development in General

13.1 Special Economic Zones

With a view to provide an internationally competitive and hassle free environment for exports, a policy was introduced on 1.4.2000 for setting up of Special Economic Zones in the country. Units may be set up in SEZ for manufacture of goods and rendering of services. All the import/export operations of the SEZ units will be on self-certification basis. The units in the Zone have to be a net foreign exchange earner but they shall not be subjected to any pre-determined value addition or minimum export performance requirements. Sales in the Domestic Tariff Area by SEZ units shall be subject to payment of full Custom Duty and import policy in force. Further Offshore banking units may be set up in the SEZs.

The policy provides for setting up of SEZ's in the public, private, joint sector or by State Governments. It was also envisaged that some of the existing Export Processing Zones would be converted into Special Economic Zones. Accordingly, the Government has converted Export Processing Zones located at Kandla and Surat (Gujarat), Cochin (Kerala), Santa Cruz (Mumbai-Maharashtra), Falta (West Bengal), Madras (Tamil Nadu), Visakhapatnam (Andhra Pradesh) and Noida (Uttar Pradesh) into a Special Economic Zones. In addition, 3 new Special Economic Zones approved for establishment at Indore (Madhya Pradesh), Manikanchan – Salt Lake (Kolkata) and Jaipur have since commended operations. In addition, approval has been given for setting up of 42 Special Economic Zones in various parts of the country in the private/joint sectors or by the State Government.

13.1.1 Facilities for Developers of Special Economic Zones: The developers of the Special Economic Zones are being provided following facilities for the development of industries in the area.

- Developer of SEZ may import/procure goods without payment of duty for the development, operation and maintenance of SEZ.
- Income tax exemption for a block of 10 year in 15 years at the option of developer as per section 80-IA of the Income Tax Act read with Appendix 14-II-N of Handbook of Procedure.
- Full freedom in allocation of developed plots to approved SEZ units on purely commercial basis.
- Full authority to provide services like water, electricity, security, restaurants, recreation centres etc. on commercial lines.
- Foreign investment permitted to develop township within the SEZ with residential areas, markets, play grounds, clubs, recreation centres etc.
- Develop Standard Design Factory (SDF) building in exiting Special Economic Zones as per guidelines.
- Income Tax exemption to Investor's in SEZ's under section 10 (23) G of Income Tax Act.
- Exemption from Service Tax
- Investment made by individuals etc. in SEZ Company also eligible for exemption u/s 88 of IT Act.
- Development promoted to transfer infrastructure facility for operations and maintenance u/s 80-I-A of IT Act
- Generation, Transmission and Distribution of Power in SEZs allowed.

13.2 National Entrepreneurship Development Board (NEDB) Scheme

The main objective of the National Entrepreneurship Development Board (NEDB) Scheme is promotion of entrepreneurship for encouraging self-employment in small scale industries and small business. The scheme covers the following activities:

- To identify and remove entry barriers for potential entrepreneurs (first generation and new entrepreneurs) including study on entrepreneurship development.
- To focus on existing entrepreneurs in micro, tiny and small sector and identify and remove constraints to survivals, growth and continuously improve performance.
- To facilitate the consolidation, growth and diversification of existing entrepreneurial venture in all possible ways.
- To support skill upgradation and renewal of learning processes among practising entrepreneurs and managers of micro, tiny, small and medium enterprises.
- To sensitise to support agencies in the area of entrepreneurship about the current requirement of growth.
- To act as catalyst to institutionalise entrepreneurship development by supporting and strengthening state level institutions for entrepreneurship development as most entrepreneurship related activities take place at the grass root level and removing various constraints to their effective functioning.
- Setting up of incubators by entrepreneurship development institutions and other organisations devoted to the promotion of entrepreneurship development.

13.3 Entrepreneurship and Business Development Centres (EBDCs)

In addition to the above activities, a new component of Entrepreneurship and Business Development Centres (EBDCs) to be established in selected Colleges/Universities/ Organisations has been included in the NEDB Scheme to motivate students to take up entrepreneurship as a career option with the objective to promote self-employment through creation of small, micro and tiny enterprises in the country which would not only provide self-employment opportunities but are also expected to create additional job opportunities in these enterprises.

13.4 National Programme for Rural Industrialisation (NPRI) for development of Clusters

A cluster is generally defined as a geographically bounded concentration of similar, related or complementary businesses with shared infrastructure, markets and services and faced with common opportunities and threats. NABARD has taken up the development of about 50 rural clusters during a period of 5 years from 1999-2000 to 2003-04. Against, this self imposed target, NABARD adopted 56 clusters for development. Considering the excellent potential in the cluster approach, it has been decided that NABARD would go in for intensive development of five selected clusters on its own and 50 additional clusters by partnering with other government agencies during 2005-06.

AGM (DD) will oversee the implementation of the programme in the identified cluster. Besides providing refinance support to the eligible units under various refinance schemes of NABARD, need based promotional support may also be considered.

The identified NGO will act as the nodal agency for implementing the project. Its close rapport with them is very important particularly in identification, planning, monitoring and assessing the development of clusters from the artisans' point of view.

The involvement Government Departments, Promotional Developmental Agencies is to be ensured right from the beginning and efforts may also be made for deriving support from higher level officers.

Banks will integrating the Cluster Action Plan into Service Area Plans and ensure focussed attention to meet the credit needs of the entrepreneurs.

13.5 Rural Entrepreneurship Development Programme (REDP)

Objective of the programme is developing entrepreneurial and activity-oriented skills among unemployed rural youth by assisting Voluntary Agencies (VAs)/Non-Governmental

Organisations (NGOs)/ Development Agencies (DAs) with good track record to conduct REDP, for those willing to set up small/ micro-enterprises.

This is one of the important NFS promotional programmes supported by NABARD for diversification of village industries with a focus on creating sustainable employment and income opportunities in a cost effective manner for the benefit of educated unemployed rural youth. NABARD has been, for last more than 13 years, supporting selected voluntary agencies/Non-Governmental Organisation (VAs/NGOs) for implementing REDPs.

NABARD provides promotional assistance to select agencies to meet the recurring expenditure in conducting REDPs. Under institutionalisation of REDP, the select institutions are provided with need-based capacity building support and long-term assurance by way of continued financial assistance, for conducting REDPs. Some of the major items that are covered under our grant assistance include the Cost of pre training survey, Publicity, Selection of candidates, Inauguration and valediction, Rent for training hall, Reading material for trainees, stationery, tool kit, Stipend in exceptional cases, Raw material, Hire charges, electricity charges, Honorarium for trainer-motivator, guest faculty, coordinator, Exposure visit of trainees, Overhead cost, Expenditure on follow up/escort services etc.

During the year 2004-05, 667 REDPs were sanctioned with a grant support of Rs. Rs.4.36 crore covering approximately 13,382 educated unemployed rural youth. As of March 2005, a total of 6248 REDPs were supported by NABARD with financial assistance of Rs 27.02 crore covering 1.70 lakh rural youth.

13.6 Rural Haat Scheme

Realising the fact that marketing has a crucial role in development of rural non-farm sector and rural haats being an integral part of a rural market system, it is felt that strengthening of these haats will have a positive impact on marketing of rural non-farm products. NABARD has, therefore, decided to support two Gram Panchayats (GP) or PACS in each DRIP district for development of infrastructural facilities in the existing/ new haats by providing grant assistance @ 80 per cent of the total project cost with an upper limit of Rs.3 lakh per haat for providing minimum infrastructural facilities in the form of raised platforms with semi-permanent roofing, sanitation arrangements, provision of drinking water, compound wall/barbed wire fencing, parking, notice board etc.

Financial support beyond Rs. 3.00 lakh will be extended by way of soft loan through Panchayati Raj Institutions (PRIs)/ Primary Agricultural Cooperative Societies (PACS) for providing some additional facilities in terms of 10-15 permanent shops with shutters for bringing in other essential services.

Soft loan extended to Gram Panchayat/PACS shall be repaid to NABARD in 5 to 7 years including an initial moratorium period of one year on half yearly basis. The rate of interest on the soft loan will be such as may be determined by NABARD from time to time.

Salient Features of the Scheme

- Project Holder – Gram Panchayat (GP)
- Project Components – Sufficient land owned by GP, Compound wall with barbed wire fencing, raised platforms covered with semi-permanent roofing, drinking water, sanitary arrangements, cycle stand, notice board.
- NABARD's Assistance – 80 per cent of project cost or Rs.3 lakh whichever is less.
- GP/Zilla Panchayat Share – At least 20 per cent of project cost.

NABARD has so far sanctioned 23 Rural Haat schemes in various DRIP districts involving grant assistance of Rs. 51.656 lakh.

14

Textile Industry

After food, clothing is the second basic necessity of human beings. Since time immemorial the human beings are using the self made cloths for wearing. These cloths have been replaced by the machine made clothes. Still there are many workers in the handloom sector who are earning their livelihood from cloth weaving and related work. Government has started many schemes for the benefit of these workers for the development of handloom sector. Besides, there are many schemes for the benefits of powerloom workers and the workers in other areas in textile industry. Some of the schemes are given below:

14.1 Technology Upgradation Fund (TUF) Scheme for Textile Industry

The scheme is operated by the Ministry of Textiles, Government of India through SIDBI and IDBI for the modernisation and technological upgradation of textile & jute industries and provides for an interest reimbursement of 5 per cent on loans availed of from eligible Primary Lending Institutions. The scheme, which was originally in operation up to 31.03.2004, had been extended up to 31.03.2007. In order to give further fillip to the scheme, Government of India, Ministry of Textiles, has decided to provide an additional incentive of 10 per cent capital subsidy over and above the 5 per cent interest subsidy under TUFs for specified textile processing machinery.

The features of the scheme of additional 10 per cent capital subsidy under TUF for specified textile processing machinery are the following:

- The additional 10 per cent capital subsidy will be admissible on the investment made in specified processing machinery during a period of one year from April 20, 2005 to April 19, 2006.

- The cut off date will be the date of disbursement of loan. Any disbursement made for the specified machinery on or after April 20, 2005 will be eligible for 10 per cent capital subsidy.
- The loan for the eligible machinery sanctioned up to the last date i.e. 19.04.2006 will be eligible for capital subsidy.
- The capital subsidy would be available to the composite units as well as to stand-alone processing units.
- The 10 per cent capital subsidy will not be available for a processing project as a whole but only on the specified processing machinery. The processing project as a whole, including the specified machinery, will continue to be eligible for 5 per cent interest incentive on the TUF compatible investment.
- The 10 per cent capital subsidy shall be available only for such projects where term loans have been sanctioned by the nodal agencies (SIDBI/IDBI) or Primary Lending Institutions (Banks etc).
- The 10 per cent capital subsidy will be worked out on the invoice price of the specified machinery. The invoice price is the basic price plus excise duty and sales tax in respect of indigenous machinery and CIF price plus actual customs duty in respect of imported machinery.
- The capital subsidy would be released by the lending agencies at the time of disbursement of term loan for the specified machinery.
- The capital subsidy can also be adjusted against promoter's contribution.
- For the purpose of releasing capital subsidy on due dates, funds in the nature of advance money would be placed by the nodal agencies (SIDBI/IDBI) with the Prime Lending Agencies. (Banks) The quantum of such advance money would be arrived at based on the subsidy forecast to be submitted by the Primary Lending Institutions (Banks) on quarterly basis to SIDBI/IDBI, based on their loan sanctions for machinery eligible for 10 per cent capital subsidy. After the first release, the subsequent releases of subsidy by

SIDBI/IDBI would depend upon the utilization of funds released earlier.

Technology levels are benchmarked in terms of specified machinery. There is no cap on funding under the scheme. The identified sectors in the textile industry, including spinning, cotton ginning & pressing, silk reeling & twisting wool scouring & combing, synthetic filament yarn texturising, crimping and twisting, manufacturing of viscose filament yarn (VFY)/viscose staple fibre (VSF), weaving/knitting including non-wovens and technical textiles, garments, made-up manufacturing, processing of fibres, yarns, fabrics, garments and made-ups and the jute sector are eligible to avail of these concessional loans for their technology upgradation requirements. Investments in common infrastructure or facilities by an industry association, trust or co-operative society and other investments specified are also eligible for funding under the scheme. Improved metal frame hand looms used by the handloom weavers have also been covered under the scheme.

14.2 Textile Workers' Rehabilitation Fund Scheme (TWRFS)

The Scheme provides interim relief to textile workers rendered unemployed due to permanent closure of any mill. Any workers would be eligible provided he/she has been engaged in a closed textile unit on the date of its closure continuously for five years or more and earning a wage equivalent of Rs. 2,500 per month or less for the mills closed between 06.06.1985 to 01.04.1993 and Rs.3,500 or less thereafter. The relief under the Scheme is available for three years on a tapering basis: to the extent of 75 per cent of the wage equivalent in the first year of the closure of the unit; 50 per cent of the wage equivalent in the second year; and 25 per cent of the wage equivalent in the third year.

14.3 Schemes for Decentralized Powerloom Sector

14.3.1 20 per cent Credit Linked Capital Subsidy Scheme for Powerloom Sector under Technology Upgradation Fund (TUF) Scheme: Weaving is a thrust area and occupies a special lace under the TUF Scheme. TUF scheme helps the small scale powerloom units by providing an additional option of availing credit linked 20 per cent capital subsidy up to a cost of Rs. 1.00 crore with the facility to obtain credit from an enlarged credit network that includes all cooperative banks and other genuine non-banking financial companies (NBFCs) recognized by the Reserve Bank of India.

14.3.2 Powerloom Service Centres (PSCs): 44 Powerloom Service Centres (PSCs) are located in major powerloom concentration areas in different States and provide a variety of technical services that include training, testing facilities, technical consultation, design development and diversification etc to powerloom units and weavers. So far 21 PSCs have been modernized and the rest are being upgraded with modern looms and related machinery and equipment. Plans are afoot to re-orient these Centres into Textile Service Centres catering to other segments of the industry as well. Most of these are under the management of autonomous bodies.

14.3.3 Support to Computer Aided Design (CAD) Centres: Similar to the PSCs, the CAD Centres also play an important role in developing new computer generated textile designs. At present there are 17 such Centres to give support to the powerloom sector all over the country. Financial assistance in the form of a grant-in-aid of Rs. 6.75 lakh per CAD Centres per annum is provided by the Ministry.

14.3.4 Group Workshed Scheme: To improve the working environment and enable powerloom workers to obtain higher productivity, this scheme, to provide subsidy for construction of worksheds, limited to 25 per cent of the unit cost of construction subject to a maximum of Rs.80 per. sq. ft has been formulated. In order to improve other infrastructure facilities the scheme envisages a link with the Textile Centre Infrastructure Development Scheme (TCIDS), which provides central assistance for improving critical infrastructure in existing or emerging textile centres.

14.3.5 Group Insurance Scheme for Powerloom Weavers: This scheme has been introduced in association with the Life Insurance Corporation of India since July 2003. This Scheme has two components:

- **Janashri Bima Yojana:** Under the scheme the powerloom workers aged between 18 to 59 years and below the poverty line (BPL) or marginally higher than the BPL are eligible for an insurance coverage of Rs. 50,000 on accidental death/ permanent disability; Rs. 25,000 on permanent partial disability; or Rs. 20,000 on natural death/partial disability. The annual premium of Rs. 200 would be shared by the Central Government, the Beneficiary, and LIC in the ratio of Rs. 60, 40 and 100 respectively.
- **Add on Scheme:** Under the scheme an additional insurance coverage of Rs. 30,000 on natural as well as accidental death is made available at annual premium of Rs. 180, which would be shared equally by Central Government and Beneficiary. On paying, a weaver can avail cumulative benefits of both the Schemes.

14.4 Health Insurance Scheme (HIS) for Handloom Weavers

The Government of India was implementing a Health Package Scheme since the year 1992-93 as a welfare measure for the benefit of handloom weavers. Now in its place, the Government of India has introduced a Health Insurance Scheme for Handloom Weavers from the Financial Year i.e. 2005-06 in collaboration with ICICI Lombard General Insurance Company Ltd.

The Health Insurance Scheme aims at financially enabling the weaver community to access the best of healthcare facilities in the country. The scheme is to cover not only the weaver but his wife and two children, cover all pre-existing diseases as well as and keeping substantial provision for OPD.

The Total premium under the scheme will be Rs.1,000 per annum, out of which Rs.800 will be contributed by Govt. of India and Rs. 200 by the Handloom weaver. The Central Govt's share of premium will be released to the ICICI Lombard directly for coverage of weavers under the scheme in instalments. Service Tax of 10.2 per cent over the annual insurance premium of Rs.1,000 will be borne by the Government of India.

In the event the claims ratio including all related costs is below 70 per cent, with the view to incentivise the scheme, the surplus shall be rolled over to the next policy period. For availing the benefits under the scheme the weaver should fulfil the following conditions:

- The weaver should be earning at least 50 per cent of his income from handloom weaving.
- All weavers, whether male or female, are eligible to be covered under the Scheme.
- The scheme will cover the weaver's family of four i.e. self, spouse and two children.
- The scheme is to cover people between age group of 1 day to 80 years.

14.5 Mahatma Gandhi Bunkar Bima Yojana (MGBBY)

The Government of India had introduced the 'Bunkar Bima Yojana' in December, 2003 which is a combination of Janshree Bima Yojana and Add-on Group Insurance Scheme. This scheme is being implemented in collaboration with the Life Insurance Corporation of India. In pursuance to the Budget Announcement made by the Hon'ble Finance Minister in his budget speech for the year 2005-06, it is proposed to implement a revised Bunkar Bima Yojana with the title "Mahatma Gandhi Bunkar Bima Yojana (MGBBY)" to cover 10 lakh weavers in the year 2005-06 and another 20 lakh weavers in 2006-07 (including 10 lakh renewal cases of 2005-06).

The basic objective of MGBBY is to provide enhanced insurance cover to the handloom weavers in the case of natural as well as accidental death and also higher sum assured. For availing of assistance under the scheme, the weaver should fulfil the following conditions:

- The weaver should be earning at least 50 per cent of his income from handloom weaving.

- All weavers, whether male or female, between the age group of 18 and 59 years are eligible to be covered under the scheme.
- Weavers being regular members of a Co-operative Society will be eligible to benefit from the scheme. While it is difficult to set a definite criterion of a regular member, ordinarily, a weaver would be considered to be a regular member if he has obtained the raw materials and supplied finished goods to the cooperatives for quantities worth his productivity of 180 days in a year. It will be up-to the Society to quantify 180 days productivity taking into each individual weaver's skill, ability and performance in past years.
- Weavers outside cooperatives can also be covered under the scheme on a certificate from the State Director in-charge of Handlooms that they are fulfilling the eligibility conditions. Weavers affiliated to State Handloom Development Corporations will also be eligible.

It will be the responsibility of the State Director in charge of Handlooms to verify the eligibility of the weavers who are proposed to be benefited in respect of whom the claims are preferred. The authority in-charge of Handlooms in the State shall finalise insurance coverage of the weavers with the Life Insurance Corporation of India. The scheme will be administered by the LIC of India. The annual premium of Rs.330 per member will be shared by GOI (Rs.150), weavers (Rs.80) and LIC's (Rs. 100) from its Social Security Fund.

Benefits:

1. In the event of death of the member, Sum Assured of Rs. 50,000 will become payable, to the nominee.
2. In the event of death by accident or partial/total permanent disability due to accident, the following benefit shall be payable:

- On death due to accident, Rs.80,000
- Permanent total disability due to accident, Rs.50,000
- Loss of 2 eyes or 2 limbs or one eye and one limb in an accident, Rs.50,000

- Loss of one eye or one limb in an accident Rs. 25,000

14.5.1 Additional Benefits: MGBBY also provides scholarship to the children of parents who are covered under it under "Shiksha Sahyog Yojana". A scholarship of Rs.300 per quarter per child is to be paid to students studying in standard IX to XII for a maximum period of four years or till they complete XII standard, whichever event occurs earlier. The scholarship will be for academic year June to May. The benefit is restricted to two children of the member covered. Both the children will be covered for scholarship. If a student fails and is detained in the same standard, he will not be eligible for scholarship for the next year in the same standard.

Once a person is admitted as a member under MGBBY, further proof of income is not necessary at the time of selection of beneficiary under the scheme. No premium is charged either to the parent of the scholarship holder or to the nodal agency. It is an additional benefit given to the children of the parents covered under MGBBY. If the premium under MGBBY is not paid on annual renewal date in such case, the child shall not be eligible for scholarship. The beneficiaries have to be selected for "Shiksha Sahayog Yojana" out of the members covered under MGBBY. The targeted beneficiary students of a State may be divided among the members covered under MGBBY in proportion to the number of lives covered within that State. The final selection shall be based on the criteria of poorest of the poor, as the number of scholarships is limited.

On introduction of MGBBY, the earlier Bunkar Bima Yojana stands discontinued and no proposals for further renewal under that scheme will be considered.

14.6 Scheme for Integrated Textiles Parks (SITP)

The scheme was launched in October 2005 with the intention of creating 25 textile parks. As on date, 7 parks have been sanctioned and 10 parks have been identified for development. An allocation has been made for 2006-07 to provide Rs.189 crore for this scheme.

14.7 Revised Textile Centres Infrastructure Development Scheme (TCIDS)

There are many areas in our country that have got a name for its textile industry. TCIDS is a part of the drive to improve infrastructure facilities at potential textile growth centres and therefore, aims at removing bottlenecks in exports so as to achieve the target of US$ 50 billion by 2010 as envisaged in the National Textile Policy, 2000. The scheme shall cover investments, which are in the nature of exigencies, or emergencies and which could not be foreseen as part of the annual plan scheme proposals. Broadly, the scheme covers investments required for quicker and strategic removal of bottlenecks and for general export facilitation. The investment must reflect its linkage to export promotion.

Traditional Textile Centres covered under the scheme are:

Tirupur, Coimbatore, Karur, Bangalore, Delhi-Noida-Gurgaon, Panipat, Ludhiana, Ahmedabad, Mumbai, Bhiwandi, Ichalkaranjee, Burhanpur, Salem-Erode, Varanasi-Mau, Meerut-Pilakhua, Surat, Solapur, Calcutta (knitting), Chennai, Cannannor, Amritsar, Baddi (Himachal Pradesh), Malegaon and Bhilwara.

Besides, the Scheme also has a provision to cover new/emerging centres including powerloom clusters as well. Balancing investment may, inter alia, relate to:

- construction of roads,
- provision of testing facilities,,
- common effluent treatment plant facilities,
- exhibition/marketing hall,
- strengthening of power supply
- improving water supply and drainage facilities, telecommunication network and IT facilities, establishment of design centres, improving warehousing facilities, facilities for movement of goods to sea ports and airports, inland container depots, air cargo complexes etc., augmentation of transport facilities especially for decongestion, facilities to improve human resources, construction of crèche buildings for apparel units

Under the Scheme funds can be given to Central/State Government Departments/Public Sector Undertakings/Other Central/State Government's agencies/recognized industrial association or entrepreneur bodies for development of infrastructure directly benefiting the textile units. The fund would not be available for individual production units.

The balancing investment should be (other than in exceptional circumstances) not in the nature of a total project by itself but an additive or adjunct to an existing or proposed facility. The Central assistance will be subject to a maximum of Rs.20 crore for a particular centre, and it would be limited to 100 per cent of the critical components of the project in respect of Common Effluent Treatment Plant, improving water supply and drainage facilities and construction of crèche buildings for Apparel Units. The other components shall be funded on 75:25 between centre and states/reputed agencies concerned.

Ministry of Textiles would cause preparation of a Master Plan identifying the critical gaps in infrastructure at textile production centres along with the blueprint for addressing them under the Scheme, which would form the basis of project desirability, through the designated nodal agencies viz. Textile Commissioner, Textiles Committee, Textile Research Associations, Textile Export Promotion Councils and Industry Associations. Nodal agencies would render assistance to the concerned State Government/ UTs in formulation of suitable projects under the Scheme. Reputed agencies like TERI, IITs, Research Institutes engaged in environment studies/projects will be involved in the preparation and implementation of projects under the Scheme. In exceptional cases, Ministry of Textiles may allow consideration of the proposals received directly from such reputed agencies.

14.8 Expiry of Agreement on Textiles and Clothing (ATC): Implications for India

The global trading regime in textiles and clothing sector has a long history. Starting with voluntary export restraints for cotton textiles in the 1950s, the Long-Term Agreement in International

Trade in Cotton Textiles (LTA) of the 1960s and early 1970s, it graduated to the Multi-Fibre Agreement (MFA) from 1974 to 1994. On January 1, 1995, MFA was replaced by the WTO Agreement on Textiles and Clothing (ATC), with a commitment to a 10-year transitional process for the ultimate removal of these quotas and fully integrating the sector into WTO rules by January 1, 2005.

India has a natural competitive advantage in terms of a strong and large multi-fibre base, abundant cheap skilled labour and presence across the entire value chain of the industry ranging from spinning, weaving, and madeups to manufacturers of garments. However, with prices expected to fall in the post-quota regime with increased international trade and competition, such an advantage may not be enough. Enhanced efficiency and productivity is a must to meet this emerging challenge of global competition. Further, while textile and cloth buyers had been sourcing products from multiple sources because of quota limitations, there is an increasing trend towards reducing the number of vendors and opting for vertically integrated companies to eliminate inefficiencies in the supply chain. Indian players need to focus on reduction in lead time through cost-cutting measures. Low labour cost benefits tend to get neutralized by high infrastructure expenses.

Most of the studies conducted to estimate the impact of ATC expiry on textile trade, share the finding that some Asian countries are most likely to benefit from the dismantling of the quotas. They predict a substantial increase in market shares for China and India. According to a recent study by CRISIL, the Indian textile and apparel industry can achieve a potential size of US$ 85 billion by 2010, with a domestic market size of US$ 45 billion and nearly 60 per cent of exports comprising of garments. The potential translates to creation of 12 million job opportunities, 5 million directly in the textile industry, and 7 million in allied sectors.

The Indian companies have been expanding capacities in anticipation of the opportunities emerging from the phase-out of the quota system. Under the Technology Up-gradation Fund

Schemes (TUFS), applications with a project cost of Rs. 18,467 crore have been sanctioned for a loan amount of Rs. 8,505 crore. Indian textile industry needs to make for more investments in the coming years to capitalise on the post-quota regime opportunities. Assuming a capital-to-turnover ratio of one, there is a need to invest Rs. 1,40,000 crore in the next six years to achieve the vision of reaching the textile and clothing exports target of US$ 40 billion by 2010 and to meet the growing domestic demand.

Close attention needs to be paid to the composition, volume and value of products as well as competitive strengths vis-à-vis countries like China, Sri Lanka, Bangladesh and Pakistan. Textiles contribute around 19 per cent of India's total annual export earnings. Despite India's comparative advantage, a number of constraints continue to restrict the growth of Indian textile markets abroad. These include:

- more than 60 per cent of the fabric production in the decentralised power loom sector, which is unable to compete with the cheaper and flawless fabric from state of the art plants of China or Taiwan;
- infrastructure constraints; and
- emergence of Preferential Trade Arrangements (PTA) as an important factor in the global textile trade.

Ensuring a technology-induced self-sustained and multi-fibre base to enlarge its share in global exports of textiles and clothing remains as the major challenges before the Indian textile industry.

Areas where national policy measures will be necessary include

- reduction of disincentives for the factory mode of production
- introduction of a more flexible labour policy,
- removal of policy bias against synthetic fibres,
- modernization and technological upgradation of the sector and
- easing of other trade and investment constraints.

14.8.1 Measures Taken by the Government: With the phasing out of quota regime on January 1, 2005 and the full integration of the textiles sector in the WTO, Indian textiles industry is at the crossroads. To make preparations for the new opportunity, Government, in recent years, took various measures which, *inter alia*, included the following:

- revamping textile legislation, regulation and inspection system,
- introduction of an optional CENVAT regime in cotton textile,
- rationalization of duty on man-made fibres,
- removing the small-scale reservation of the woven garment sector,
- enhancing the investment ceiling for small-scale units in the knitwear sector,
- setting up of the Technology Upgradation Fund Scheme (TUFS),
- new schemes of Apparel Parks for Exports,
- Textile Centres Infrastructure Development Scheme,
- introduction of a Technology Mission on Cotton to improve the productivity and quality of cotton.
- FDI is freely allowed in the sector.
- Basic customs duty on designated textile machinery and spare parts have been reduced,
- Additional Excise Duty on Textiles & Textile Articles (AT&T) and Additional Excise Duty (Goods of Special Importance) Act have been abolished.

15

Food Processing Industry

15.1 India's Food Processing Industry: An Introduction

The shelf life of foodgrains is over 3 years or even more as against fruits and vegetables whose shelf life ranges between 1 week and 3 months. Currently hardly 1 per cent of over 140 million tonnes of fruits and vegetables produces in the country goes through the processing route. Hence strategies for diversified agriculture should involve a separate road map for value addition in fruits and vegetables sector. Creation of essential infrastructure for preservation, cold storage, refrigerated transportation, rapid transit, grading, processing, packaging and quality control would be the key areas for such a strategy.

Though India is one of the major food producers in the world, it accounts for less than 1.5 per cent of international food trade. A strong and dynamic food processing industry is important for diversification and commercialization of agriculture. It ensures value addition to the agricultural products, generates employment, enhances income of farmers and creates surplus for export of agro foods. A number of policy initiatives have been taken to promote this sector. Foreign direct investment of around US $1 billion has already been approved in India's food processing industry since 1991. Many Indian firms are seeking foreign partners for joint ventures to avail of their technological advantage.

India is the second largest producer of fruits and vegetables. Processing of fruits and vegetables is an important segment in the development efforts of the Government of India. Presently, the fruits and vegetable sector is highly decentralized, with a large number of processing units operating in the small scale and cottage industry sector. The installed capacity of fruits and vegetables processing industry has been steadily increasing. The efforts of the government to give a boost to the food products exports have found results in recent years. Response from the foreign as well local investors in this sector has been very encouraging.

15.1.1 Food Parks: The Ministry of Food Processing is setting up food parks in different parts of the country. The idea behind setting up of food parks is to enable small and medium entrepreneurs find access to capital-intensive facilities, such as cold storage, warehouse, quality control labs, effluent treatment plants etc. Development of such facilities is expected to make the food processing units in the food parks cost competitive besides improving their market accessibility. So far 30 food parks have been sanctioned in different parts of the country. The Ministry is also in the process of introducing a new Plan Scheme for development of infrastructure like cold storage etc. for the benefit of food processing units in addition to the scheme of food parks already in existence.

15.1.2 Quality Management: The Ministry is also operating schemes on the Promotion of Total Quality Management including ISO 9000, ISO 14000, Hazard Analysis and Critical Control Points (HACCP), Good Manufacturing Practices, Good Hygienic Practices etc. with the following objectives:

- To motivate the food processing industries for adoption of food safety and quality assurance mechanism.
- To prepare them to face the global competition in the international trades in the post WTO era.
- To enable adherence to a stringent quality in hygiene norms.
- To enhance product acceptance by overseas buyers.
- To keep Indian Food Industry technologically abreast of international best practices.

In addition, Ministry of Food Processing is also working towards the promotion of bar coding on food packages, as the bar coding is on its way to become almost a compulsory requirement in the global market.

To encourage the food processing in the country, Ministry of Food Processing Industries has following schemes under its control.

15.2 Scheme for Technology Upgradation

The assistance is provided for Modernization of Processing units of

- Milk Products
- Meat and Poultry
- Fishery Products
- Cereal, pulses, Oil seeds
- Oleoresins, Spices, Coconut, Mushroom, Hops etc

15.3 Scheme for Human Resource Development

This scheme has the following components:

- Setting up of Food Processing & Training Centre (FPTC)
- Creation of Infrastructure facilities for running Degree/Diploma Courses and Training Programmes for Food Processing
- Training Programmes sponsored by Ministry of Food Processing Industries
- Entrepreneurship Development Programme

15.4 Scheme for Quality Assurance, Codex Standards and Research & Development

This scheme has the following components:

- Total Quality Management (TQM)
- Promotion of Quality Assurance and Safety Concept
- Bar Coding
- Strengthening of Codex Cell
- Setting up of Quality Control Laboratory
- R & D in Processed Food Sector

15.5 Scheme for Backward and Forward Integration and other Promotional Activities

This scheme has the following components:

- Backward Linkages
- Forward Integration

- Generic Advertisement
- Promotional activities such as participation in Exhibition, Fairs, Supporting Seminars, Workshops, Conferences etc. and Studies and Surveys
- Strengthening of Industry Associations
- Food Fortification

15.6 Scheme for Infrastructure Development

This scheme has the following components:

- Development of Food Park,
- Packaging Centre,
- Modernised Abattoirs,
- Integrated Cold Storage, facilities,

Recognizing the enormous benefits that the food processing industry can bring to agriculture and job creation, and to consumers, food processing is being treated as a priority sector for bank credit. NABARD will create a separate window with a corpus of Rs. 1,000 crore for refinancing loans to the sector, especially for agro-processing infrastructure and market development. Government will also set up the National Institute of Food Technology Entrepreneurship and Management. The Paddy Processing Research Centre at Thanjavur will be developed into a national-level institute.

16

Small and Village Industries

In view of the importance of small-scale industries, Government continues to lay emphasis on their growth and various measures have been taken to enable them to stand in competition with large and medium scale industries. Small industries are helped by the Government in the following manner:

16.1 Credit Linked Capital Subsidy Scheme (CLCSS) for Technology Upgradation of SSI

The Scheme was launched by the Government of India during 2000-01 with the aim to facilitate technology upgradation by SSI units in the specified products/sub-sectors by providing 12 per cent capital subsidy for induction of proven technologies. The scheme covers 30 sub sectors/products. NABARD, as nodal agency is implementing the scheme through good working RRBs and Cooperative banks (since December 4, 2002) and Commercial banks (since January 17, 2005). The scheme is applicable to the units financed by scheduled Commercial banks, RRBs, Cooperative banks, NSIC, SFCs and NEDFI. The Scheme will be in operation for a period of 5 years from October 01, 2000 to September 30, 2005, or till the time sanction of capital subsidy by the Nodal agencies reaches Rs.600 crore. The eligible borrowers under the scheme are sole proprietorships, partnerships, cooperative societies, private and public limited companies in SSI sector. Preference shall be given to women entrepreneurs. The scheme is to benefit the entrepreneurs in the Tiny Industries and SSI sector.

With a view to expedite identification and approval of eligible PLIs to implement the scheme as well as sanction and release of admissible subsidy to the eligible units through the identified PLIs, the Regional Offices of NABARD located in all the States have been delegated powers.

Revised guidelines under the scheme are as under.

- The Scheme will be in operation till 31.03.2007 or till the time sanction of the capital subsidy by the nodal agencies reaches Rupees Six Hundred crore, whichever is earlier
- Maximum Ceiling of loan under the scheme is Rs.1 crore.
- The rate of subsidy is 15 per cent.
- The admissible subsidy will be calculated on the amount of purchase price of plant and machinery acquired by the unit for implementation of the project. Irrespective of the size of investment in Plant & Machinery, the ceiling of loan for all the units is Rs. 1 crore.

16.2 Excise Duty Concessions

In line with Government's policy of encouraging small-scale industries, a wide range of concessions and exemptions from excise duty is available to small producers to enable them to stand in competition with large-scale manufacturers. Also, relatively simple and concessional procedures are followed for the assessment and collection of excises from the small-scale sector. As a part of the Comprehensive Policy Package on SSI and Tiny Sector announced by the Prime Minister on August 30, 2000, the excise exemption limit for SSI was raised from Rs. 50 lakh to Rs. 1 crore with effect from September 1, 2000.

Though preferential treatment to small units and labour-intensive methods of production is desirable, the misuse of these concessions has created doubts as regards the ultimate beneficiaries of such facilities. Concerned about the misuse of excise concessions, the Finance Minister in his 2001-2002 budget speech announced the withdrawal of exemption on the following items: cotton yarn, ball or roller bearings, arms and ammunition for private use.

16.3 Priority in the Disbursement of Loans by the Financial Institutions

The composite loan scheme of SIDBI and commercial banks is designed to ease operational difficulties of the small borrowers by providing term loans and working capital through a single window. As a part of the Comprehensive Package on SSI announced by the Prime Minister on August 30, 2000, the limit for composite loan was raised from Rs. 10 lakh to 25 lakh.

16.4 Other Concessions

These include

- import of raw material and machinery and the supply of these materials through small industries corporations and other agencies,
- direct assistance like consultancy, training through a wide network of promotional bodies such as Small Industries Service Institutes (SISI),
- price and purchase preference to products manufactured in small scale sector in Government purchase programme.

Khadi and Village Industries Commission (KVIC) is providing various kinds of Assistance for generating employment in rural areas. Some of the schemes of KVIC are given below:

16.5 Rural Employment Generation Programme: Margin Money Scheme (MMS) for Village Industries

The scheme is in operation since July 1997. The objectives of the programme are to accelerate the growth of employment in rural areas and to check the migration of the labour force from rural areas to urban areas.

16.5.1 Margin Money: Margin money (own stake) to be contributed by the borrower 10 per cent, Margin money to be contributed by SC/ST members and other weaker section borrower - 5 per cent

16.5.2 Margin Money from KVIC

- For projects up to Rs. 10 lakh 25 per cent of the project outlay will be provided by KVIC as Margin Money by way of subsidy.
- Projects above Rs. 10 lakh and up to Rs. 25 lakh 25 per cent up to Rs. 10 Lakh plus 10 per cent for the remaining cost.

- SC/ST/OBC/Women/Physically handicapped/Ex-Service men and minority community beneficiary/institutions and beneficiaries hailing from hill, border and tribal areas and North-Eastern Region, Sikkim, Andaman and Nikobar Islands and Lakshdweep - 30 per cent up to Rs. 10 lakh

Choice of selection of he borrowers is left to the banks. Credit decision fully rests with the banks subject to technical viability and financial feasibility of the project. NABARD refinance is available for this scheme to the banks. During the year 2004-05, the number of projects financed was 23,453 as against the 24,747 number of projects financed in the previous year. Further in Employment Generation through the Scheme, the Andhra Pradesh stood at No. 1 followed by Uttar Pradesh, Rajasthan, Madhya Pradesh, West Bengal and Haryana.

16.6 Janashree Bima Yojna

This scheme from LIC is for the Khadi workers aged between 18 to 59 years living below or marginally above poverty line. The claim is payable only on death. The claim payable on death due to natural causes is Rs. 20,000. Death due to accident or permanent disability i.e. loss of both eyes or both the limbs claim payable is Rs. 50,000. On partial disability or loss of one eye or limb the claim payable is Rs. 25,000.

16.7 Shiksha Sahayog Yojana

This is a scholarship scheme launched on 31.12.2001 for the benefit of children of members of Janashree Bima Yojana. Students studying in 9th to 12th standards (including ITI), whose parents are covered under Janashree Bima Yojana are eligible A maximum of 2 children per family are eligible under the scheme. If a student fails and is detained in the same standard, he will not be eligible for scholarship for the next year in the same standard.

Financial Assistance: Scholarship of Rs. 300 per quarter per child will be paid for a maximum period of four years. The benefit is restricted to two children per member (family) only. No premium is charged for the scholarship. Premium of Rs. 100 per member per annum (half of the premium) is borne by the Government of India from Social Security Fund.

16.8 Product Development Design Intervention & Packaging (PRODIP)

The scheme provides for the financial assistance for development of the product, its design and packaging. Proper 'design' is required not only for products (output) but also has to be an integral part of inputs that is in production processes, tools etc. In as much as the pillar of the KVI sector is the artisan, KVI lays great emphasis on this area, that is in improving hand tools and small machines, reducing drudgery and improving the quality of work environment and the productivity of artisans. The role of visual design and brand-identity for sales outlets is also important. There is need for common logos, shop and layout design, proper labelling and packaging of KVI products.

In the last few years, KVIC had/has initiated a number of design related projects, more of a pilot nature. They include:

- 'Khubsoorat' Khadi -an effort to sell designer khadi products
- Developing packaging for 'Sarvodaya' brand KVI products through National Institute of Packaging, Mumbai.
- Involving nationally reputed star textile designers in designing khadi wear for display and sale in selected Delhi outlets.
- Associating with National Institute of Design, Ahmedabad (NID) under UNDP project for design intervention in khadi production, processes and garments in nine institutions of Maharashtra and Gujarat.

In order to embark with full vigour in the field of design, and to take up design projects in a big way 'organisational preparedness' within KVIC is a preliminary requirement. For this purpose, the following initiatives have/are being taken: KVIC will operate this scheme on 'Project Approach' basis.

16.9 District Rural Industries Project (DRIP)

With the objective of creating significant number of sustainable employment opportunities in rural areas through enhanced credit flow to RNFS with complementary financial and non-financial promotional support, NABARD on a pilot basis had launched this integrated area-based credit intensification programme in collaboration with Government, Banks and other development agencies with focus on district during 1993-94 in 5 districts with a view to evolving a role model for rural industrialization. The project is extended to 75 more districts, under various phases. During 2005-06, the project is being extended to 26 additional districts under Phase VII. This is a participatory programme of State Govt., Banks, NGOs and Developmental agencies for credit intensification towards development of RNFS.

NABARD is providing the following assistance under DRIP scheme

- Conduct of Detailed Potential Survey of the district to map the RNFS potentials.
- Extending 100 per cent refinance to banks for their lending under ARF (NFS).
- Extension of financial assistance in the form of grants to select agencies for promotional programmes.
- Direct association/involvement of AGM (DD) and RO in various forums/promotional interventions - Organisation of special programmes/meets.
- Use of consultants/consultancy agencies for specific activities/studies.
- An extensive and intensive strategy for training/skill upgradation/sensitisation of PLIs, NGOs and Govt. functionaries.
- Guiding and reviewing the progress of DRIP through Project Coordination and Guidance Committees set up at District/State level.
- Disseminating the lessons learnt under DRIP to all the Project Partners.
- Sponsoring Monitoring and Evaluation studies.

DRIP has amply demonstrated that with clearly defined objectives, identified potentials, coordinated operational strategy, orientation/sensitisation/training, participatory approach and close monitoring, intensification of credit for setting up of NFS units and employment generation are feasible even without subsidy. Demand-led production could be accelerated within proper entrepreneurial environment, institutional linkage and synergy of efforts. Many of DRIP tools/strategies/experiments have potential for successful replication.

16.10 Scheme of Fund for Regeneration of Traditional Industries (SFURTI)

The objectives of the Scheme are:

- to develop clusters of traditional industries in various parts of the country over a period of five years commencing 2005-06;
- to make traditional industries more competitive with more market-driven,
- productive, profitable and sustained employment for traditional industry artisans and rural entrepreneurs;
- to strengthen the local governance systems of industry clusters, with the active participation of the local stakeholders, so that they are enabled to undertake development initiatives by themselves; and
- to build up innovated and traditional skills, improved technologies, advanced processes, market intelligence and new models of public-private partnerships, so as to gradually replicate similar models of cluster-based regenerated traditional industries.

The target sectors and potential beneficiaries will include:

- Artisans, workers, machinery makers, raw material providers, entrepreneurs, institutional and private business development service (BDS) providers engaged in traditional industries and working in selected clusters of khadi, coir and village industries, including leather and pottery.
- Artisan guilds, cooperatives, consortiums, networks of enterprises, self-help groups (SHGs), enterprise associations, etc.

- Implementing agencies, field functionaries of Government institutions/organisations and policy makers, directly engaged in traditional industries.

16.11 Skill Upgradation & Design Development for Handloom Weavers (SUDHA)

Objective of the programme is to assist weaver members of Primary Weavers Co-operative Societies (PWCS) or VAs/NGOs and other promotional agencies involved in the development of handloom weavers through skill up gradation, design development/product mix, quality improvement, marketing etc.

Handloom weavers, who have been practicing the age-old techniques of weaving, continuing with same old patterns, colour combinations and designs not having much market demand in the upcountry market are the target group under the scheme.

16.11.1 Implementing Agencies:

- Apex Handloom Coop. Marketing Federations
- Apex/Regional Weavers Coop Societies,
- Registered Coop Societies, VAs/NGOs working in the field of development of Handloom Sector.

16.11.2 Eligible Purposes:

- Market Survey(by concerned agencies)
- Design development to improve the marketability of handloom, both in domestic and international markets.
- Skill up gradation/improvement for adoption of improved looms, usage of standard inputs, better dyeing and printing, processing and weaving practices etc.
- Hiring of consultants or appointment of experts for a shorter period.
- Quality control
- Special marketing efforts like preparation of broachers, pamphlets, branding and other marketing oriented measures,
- Exposure visits
- Orientation/ Sensitisation Workshops.

17

Export Promotion

Exports have come to be regarded as an engine of economic growth in the wake of liberalization and structural reforms in the economy.

Exports have acquired added significance in the wake of liberalisation wave sweeping across the world. The trend towards market economy in almost all the countries of the world has increased the role of exports in developmental efforts. Exports have become an important indicator of a country's economic performance.

Although non-traditional items (gems and jewellery, readymade garments, engineering goods and chemicals) have entered into India's exports in a big way yet traditional items of exports, viz. marine products, tea, coffee, spices and coir occupy a dominant place in our export basket. These items have been the backbone of India's export efforts for long.

A series of measures have been initiated with the object of stepping up exports. The measures in question include organisational changes, increased facilities, and incentives and diversification of trade.

- Export Promotion Councils, for cotton textiles, silk and rayon, engineering goods, chemicals, tobacco, spices, cashew, leather, plastics, sports goods and mica;
- establishment of the Export Risks Insurance Corporation;
- assignment to Commodity Boards for tea, coffee and coir of the duties of Export Promotion Councils;
- increased facilities for publicity, fairs, exhibitions etc;
- removal of export controls and quota restrictions;
- abolition of most export duties;
- refund of excise duties;
- special import licences for raw materials for exports;

- priorities for transport facilities;
- development of trading relations with USSR and countries in Eastern Europe.

17.1 Central Assistance to States for Developing Export Infrastructure and other Allied Activities

The objective of the scheme is to involve the states in the export effort by providing assistance to the State Governments for creating appropriate infrastructure for the development and growth of exports.

The scheme shall provide an outlay for development of export infrastructure which will be distributed to the States according to pre-defined criteria. The existing EPIP, EPZ and CIB schemes shall be merged with the new scheme. The scheme for Export Development Fund (EDF) for the North East and Sikkim (implemented since 2000-2001) shall also stand merged with the new scheme. After the merger of the schemes in respect of EPIP,EPZ, CIB and EDF for NER and Sikkim with the new scheme, the ongoing projects under the schemes shall be funded by the States from the resources provided under the new scheme.
The activities aimed at development of infrastructure for exports can be funded from the scheme provided such activities have an overwhelming export content and their linkage with exports is fully established. The specific purposes for which the funds allocated under the Scheme can be sanctioned and utilised are as follows:

- Creation of new Export Promotion Industrial Parks/Zones (including Special Economic Zones (SEZs)/Agri-Business Zones) and augmenting facilities in the existing ones.
- Setting up of electronic and other related infrastructure in export conclave.
- Equity participation in infrastructure projects including the setting up of SEZs.
- Meeting requirements of capital outlay of EPIPs/EPZs/SEZs

- Development of complementary infrastructure such as roads connecting the production centres with the ports, setting up of Inland Container Depots and Container Freight Stations,
- Stabilising power supply through additional transformers and islanding of export production centres etc.
- Development of minor ports and jetties of a particular specification to serve export purpose.
- Assistance for setting up common effluent treatment.
- Projects of national and regional importance.
- Activities permitted as per EDF in relation to North East and Sikkim.

17.1.1 Allocation of Funds: The outlay of the scheme will have two components. 80 per cent of the funds (State component) shall be earmarked for allocation to the States on the basis of the approved criteria to be utilised for the approved purposes. The balance 20 per cent (central component), and amounts equivalent to un-utilised portion of the funds allocated to the States in the past year(s), if any, shall be retained at the central level for meeting the requirements of inter state projects, capital outlays of EPZs, activities relating to promotion of exports from the NER as per the existing guidelines of EDF and any other activity considered important by the Central Government from the regional or the national perspective.

17.2 Marketing Development Assistance (MDA) of the Ministry of Commerce

This has been one of the important measures being undertaken by the Government of India through the Department of Commerce and Industry to stimulate and diversify the country's export trade. Besides providing assistance to the exporters in undertaking export market development programmes like participation in Buyer Seller Meet/Trade Fair and Exhibitions/Trade Delegations etc. through its own external Market Development Assistance Scheme, Coir Board has also been facilitating the exporters to avail of the assistance available for various export market development programmes under the

MDA Scheme of the Ministry of Commerce and Industry. The Ministry has issued revised guidelines which will come into force with effect from April 1, 2004. The revised guidelines are given below:

Following are the Agencies through which MDA Scheme is implemented:

- Export Promotion Councils
- Approved Organizations consisting of Commodity Boards, Development Authorities and FIEO.
- Other approved trade bodies like Export Inspection Council, FICCI, Associated Chamber of Commerce and Industry, CII etc.

Following are the Activities covered under the Assistance Scheme.

- Buyer Seller Meet
- Trade Fairs and Exhibitions
- Trade Delegations

Eligibility Criteria:

- Exporting Companies with an FOB of exports up to Rs.5 crore in the preceding year will only be eligible for MDA assistance.
- The beneficiary exporter should have completed twelve months membership continuously with the concerned EPC/Commodity Board/Approved Trade Bodies.
- MDA will be granted for export market development programmes (as identified above) only to those exporters who participate in those programmes led by EPCs/Commodity Boards etc. (Note that the requirement of beneficiary firm participating along-with the EPC/Commodity Board for being eligible for MDA was not there in as per the existing guidelines for availing MDA.

17.3 Export Promotion: Market Access Initiative (MAI)

It is an Export Promotion Scheme to promote India's exports on a sustained basis, during the tenth five year Plan. The scheme is formulated on focus product- focus country approach to evolve specific strategy for specific market and specific product through market studies/survey. Main aim of the scheme is to identify the priorities of research relevant to the Department of Commerce and to sponsor research studies consistent with the priorities;, WTO Studies for evolving WTO compatible strategy; to support EPCs/Trade Promotion Organisations in undertaking market studies/survey for evolving proper strategies and to support marketing projects abroad based on focus product - focus country approach. Under marketing projects, the following activities will be funded:

a. Opening of Showrooms
b. Opening of Warehouses
c. (c)Display in international departmental stores
d. Publicity Campaign and Brand Promotion
e. Participation in Trade Fairs, etc., abroad
f. Research and Product Development
g. Reverse visits of the prominent buyers etc. from the project focus countries.

17.4 Export Development Fund for the North Eastern Region

Following the announcements made by the Prime Minister in respect of measures for the development of exports from the North-Eastern region in Shillong on January 21-22, 2000, an Export Development Fund (EDF) has been set up with the objective of using the resources for the development of exports from the region. The features of the Scheme and the guidelines for consideration of proposals in respect of the Scheme are given below:

Fund:

- The Fund shall be set up with an initial corpus of Rs. 5 Crore.
- Further contribution to EDF may be provided by the Ministry of Commerce & Industry from any other budgetary and non-budgetary sources as identified by the Government.

- It will be managed by the Agricultural & Processed Food Products Export Development Authority (APEDA) under the instructions of the Department of Commerce.

Objective: The objective of the Fund is to assist specific activities for promotion of exports from the North-Eastern region of the country including Sikkim. All activities, which have a linkage with the exports from the region and are designed to help exports, shall be eligible for assistance from the Fund.

Scope: Following activities will be eligible for assistance from the Fund:

- Setting up of pioneering/pilot projects aimed at exports
- Provision of equipment and machinery for the pioneering/pilot projects aimed at exports
- Creation of Common facilities for facilitating exports
- Facility for testing and standardisation as well as quality improvement of export products
- Funding related to the exchange of trade delegations
- Any other activity as notified by the Department of Commerce having a bearing on export promotion in the North-East

Eligible Agencies: Under the scheme, funds may be given to:

- Central/State Governments
- Public Sector undertakings of Central/State Governments
- Other agencies of Central/State Governments
- Export Promotion Councils/Commodity Boards
- Apex Trade bodies recognised under the EXIM policy of Government of India and other apex bodies recognised for this purpose by the Empowered Committee.
- Individual Production/Service Units dedicated to exports.

17.5 Foreign Trade Policy (FTP) 2004-09

In a radical move, the Government of India announced, on August 31, 2004, a new Foreign Trade Policy for the period 2004-09, replacing the hitherto nomenclature of EXIM Policy by Foreign Trade Policy (FTP). A vigorous export-led growth strategy of doubling India's share in global merchandise trade in the next five years, with a focus on the sectors having prospects for export expansion and potential for employment, generation, constitute the main plank of the Policy. These measures are expected to enhance international competitiveness and aid in further increasing the acceptability of Indian exports.

17.5.1 Objectives and Strategy: The new Foreign Trade Policy (FTP) takes an integrated view of the overall development of India's foreign trade and essentially provides a roadmap for the development of this sector. It is built around two major objectives of doubling India's share of global merchandise trade by 2009 and using trade policy as an effective instrument of economic growth with a thrust on employment generation. Key strategies to achieve these objectives, inter alia, include: unshackling of controls and creating an atmosphere of trust and transparency; simplifying procedures and bringing down transaction costs; neutralizing incidence of all levies on inputs used in export products; facilitating development of India as a global hub for manufacturing, trading and services; identifying and nurturing special focus areas to generate additional employment opportunities, particularly in semi-urban and rural areas; facilitating technological and infrastructural upgradation of the Indian economy, especially through import of capital goods and equipment; avoiding inverted duty structure and ensuring that domestic sectors are not disadvantaged in trade agreements; upgrading the infrastructure network related to the entire foreign trade chain to international standards; revitalizing the Board of Trade by redefining its role and inducting into it experts on trade policy; and activating Indian Embassies as key players in the export strategy.

17.5.2 Special Focus Initiatives: The FTP 2004 has identified certain thrust sectors having prospects for export expansion and potential for employment generation. These thrust sectors include agriculture, handlooms and handicrafts, gems & jewellery and leather and footwear sectors. Sector specific policy initiative for the thrust sectors include, for agriculture sector, introduction of a new scheme called *Vishesh Krishi Upaj Yojana* (Special Agricultural Produce Scheme) to boost exports of fruits, vegetables, flowers, minor forest produce and their value added products. Under the scheme, exports of these products qualify for duty free credit entitlement (5 per cent *of f.o.b* value of exports) for importing inputs and other goods. Other components for agriculture sector include duty free import of capital goods under Export Promotion Capital Goods (EPCG) scheme, permitting the installation of capital goods imported under EPCG for agriculture anywhere in the Agri-Export Zone (AEZ), utilizing funds from the Assistance to States for Infrastructure Development of Exports (ASIDE) scheme for development of AEZs, liberalization of import of seeds, bulbs, tubers and planting material, and liberalization of the export of plant portions, derivatives and extracts to promote export of medicinal plants and herbal products.

The special focus initiative for handlooms and handicraft sectors include extension of facilities like enhancing (to 5 per cent of *f.o.b* value of exports) duty free import of trimmings and embellishments for handlooms and handicrafts, exemption of samples from countervailing duty (CVD), authorizing Handicraft Export Promotion Council to import trimmings, embellishments and samples for small manufacturers, and establishment of a new Handicraft Special Economic Zone. Major policy announcements under gems and jewellery sector encompass: permission for duty free import of consumables for metals other than gold and platinum up to 2 per cent of *f.o.b* value of exports; duty free re-import entitlement for rejected jewellery allowed up to 2 per cent of *f.o.b* value of exports; increase in duty free import of commercial samples of jewellery to Rs.1 lakh, and permission to import of gold of 18 carat and above under the replenishment scheme. Specific policy initiatives in leather and footwear sector are mainly in the form of reduction in the incidence of customs duties on the inputs and plants and machinery. The major policy announcements for this sector include: increase in the limit for duty free entitlements of import trimmings, embellishments and footwear components for leather industry to 3 per cent of *f.o.b* value of exports and that for duty free import of specified items for leather sector to 5 per cent of *f.o.b* value of exports; import of machinery and equipment for Effluent Treatment Plants for leather industry exempted from customs duty; and re-export of unsuitable imported materials (such as raw hides and skin and wet blue leathers) has been permitted. The threshold limit of designated '*Towns of Export Excellence*' has also been reduced from Rs.1,000 crore to Rs.250 crore in the above thrust sectors.

17.5.3 New Export Promotion Schemes: A new scheme to accelerate growth of exports called *Target Plus* has been introduced. Under the scheme, exporters achieving a quantum growth in exports are entitled to duty free credit based on incremental exports substantially higher than the general actual export target fixed. Rewards are granted based on a tiered approach. For incremental growth of over 20 per cent, 25 per cent and 100 per cent, the duty free credits are 5 per cent, 10 per cent and 15 per cent of *f.o.b* value of incremental exports.

Another new scheme called *Vishesh Krishi Upaj Yojana* has been introduced to boost exports of fruits, vegetables, flowers, minor forest produce and their value added products. Exports of these products qualify for duty free credit entitlement equivalent to 5 per cent of *f.o.b* value of exports. The entitlement is freely transferable and can be used for import of a variety of inputs and goods. To accelerate growth in export of services so as to create a powerful and unique *Served from India* brand instantly recognized and respected the world over, the earlier duty free export credit (DFEC) scheme for services has been revamped and re-cast into the *Served from India* scheme. Individual service providers who earn foreign exchange of at least Rs.5 lakh, and other service providers who earn foreign exchange of at least Rs.10 lakh are eligible for a duty-credit entitlement of 10 per cent of total foreign exchange earned by them. In the case of stand-alone restaurants, the entitlement is 20 per cent, whereas in the case of hotels, it is 5 per cent. Hotels and restaurants can use their duty credit entitlement for import of food items and alcoholic beverages.

To make India into a global trading-hub, a new scheme to establish Free Trade and Warehousing Zones (FTWZs) has been introduced to create trade-related infrastructure to facilitate the import and export of goods and services with freedom to carry out trade transactions in convertible currencies. Besides permitting FDI up to 100 per cent in the development and establishment of these zones, each zone would have minimum outlay of Rs. 100 crore and five lakh sq. mts. built up area. Units in the FTWZs qualify for all other benefits as applicable for SEZ units.

17.5.4 Simplification, Rationalization and Modifications of Ongoing Schemes: EPCG scheme has been further improved upon by providing additional flexibility for fulfillment of export obligation, facilitating and providing incentives for technological upgradation, permitting transfer of capital goods to group companies and managed hotels, doing away with the requirement of certificate from Central Excise (in the case of movable capital goods in the service sector) and improving the viability of specified projects by calculating their export obligation based on concessional duty permitted to them. Import of second hand capital goods without any restriction on age has been permitted and the minimum depreciated value for plant and machinery to be re-located into India has been reduced from Rs. 50 crore to Rs. 25 crore. The new policy has allowed transfer of the import entitlement under Duty Free Replenishment Certificate (DFRC) scheme in respect of fuel to the marketing agencies authorized by the Ministry of Petroleum and Natural Gas to facilitate sourcing of such imports by individual exporters.

The Duty Entitlement Passbook (DEPB) scheme will continue until replaced by a new scheme to be drawn up in consultation with exporters. Additional benefits have been provided to Export Oriented Units (EOU), including exemption from service tax in proportion to their exported goods and services, permission to retain 100 per cent of export earnings in Export Earners Foreign Currency (EEFC) accounts, extension of income tax benefits on plant and machinery to DTA units which convert to EOU/Electronic Hardware Technology Park (EHTP)/Software

Technology Park (STP)/Bio-technology Park (BTP) units, allowing import of capital goods on self-certification basis and permission to dispose of (for EOU in textile and garment manufacture) leftover materials and fabrics up to 2 per cent of *c.i.f* value or quantity of import on payment of duty on transaction value only. Minimum investment criterion has also been waived for brass hardware and hand-made jewellery EOUs (this facility already exists for handicrafts, agriculture, floriculture, aquaculture, animal husbandry, IT and services). The FTP proposes setting up of BTPs by granting all facilities of 100 per cent EOUs. The FTP 2004 has introduced a new rationalized scheme of categorization of status holders as Star Export Houses, with benchmark for export performance (during the current and previous three years) varying from Rs. 15 crore (for One Star Export House) to Rs. 5,000 crore (for Five Star Export House). The new scheme is likely to bestow status on a large number of hitherto unrecognized small exporters. Such Star Export Houses will be eligible for a number of privileges including fast-track clearance procedures, exemption from furnishing of bank guarantee, eligibility for consideration under Target Plus Scheme, etc.

17.5.5 Simplification of Rules and Procedures and Institutional Measures: Policy measures announced to further rationalize/simplify the rules and procedures include exemption for exporters with minimum turnover of Rs. 5 crore and good track record from furnishing bank guarantee in any of the schemes, service tax exemption for exports of all goods and services, increase in validity of all licences/entitlements issued under various schemes uniformly to 24 months, reduction in number of returns and forms to be filed, delegation of more power to zonal and regional offices, and time-bound introduction of electronic data interface (EDI). Institutional measures proposed in the FTP 2004 include revamping and revitalizing the Board of Trade, setting up of an exclusive Services Export Promotion Council to map opportunities for key services in key markets and setting up of Common Facility Centres for use of professional home-based service providers in state and district level towns. Pragati Maidan in Delhi is proposed to be transformed into a world class complex, with state-of-the-art, environmentally controlled, visitor friendly exhibition areas and marts. The FTP 2004 also proposes provision to deserving exporters, on the recommendation of the Export Promotion Councils, of financial assistance for meeting the costs of legal expenses connected with trade related matters.

Part V
Subsidies for Employment and Labour Welfare

18

Urban Employment Schemes

Economic security is one of the main components of human security. It constitutes the crux of social security in the conventional sense. Economic security requires employment and an assured source of a basic income adequate for meeting one's basic needs.

A primary objective of state policy should be to generate greater productive work opportunities in the growth process itself, by concentrating on sectors, sub-sectors and technologies which are more labour-oriented, in regions characterised by higher rates of unemployment and under-employment. Recognising the high incidence of under-employment and increasing casualisation of labour, there is a need to enhance employment opportunities for the poor, particularly for those who are in seasonal occupation.

As in other developing countries, unemployment is a serious problem of the Indian economy. The poverty of the masses in India is closely related to the problem of unemployment.

Unemployment is a situation when willing workers fail to get jobs at the prevailing wage rates. In other words, unemployment means involuntary idleness, i.e. the time for which individuals are available for and willing to, but are not able to find work. From social point of view, unemployment means wastage of the precious labour resources of the country. For an individual, unemployment is a painful and demoralising experience. Employment to be gainful and sustainable has to be productive in character.

Unemployment is a multi-dimensional phenomenon in India. It is not restricted to one sector or group of population. Instead, it is a widespread disease touching almost every segment of the society.

To deal with the unemployment problem, Government of India has launched, from time to time, various employment schemes.

18.1 Nehru Rozgar Yojana (NRY)

Introduction: Nehru Rozgar Yojana (NRY) is a centrally sponsored programme. It provides for setting up of self-employment ventures and wage employment through the creation of assets in Urban Local Bodies (ULB). NRY consists of three schemes:

1. Scheme for setting up of Urban Micro Enterprises (SUME) in all urban settlements and providing training and infrastructure (T&I) support.
2. Scheme for Urban Wage Employment (SUWE) for-creation of socially and economically useful public assets in ULB areas with population up to one lakh.
3. Scheme of Employment through Housing and Shelter Upgradation (SHASU) in low-income neighbourhoods mainly for urban poor and economically weaker sections and training and infrastructure support for promotion of construction skills.

The Government of India in October 1989 launched the scheme. The Programme was recast in March 1990. The programme subsumed with Swarn Jayanti Shahari Rozgar Yojana on its start on 1.12.1997.

Target Group: Under NRY, urban poor having an annual income of less than Rs. 11,850 at 1991-92 prices are eligible for assistance in the shape of employment, loan and subsidy. The beneficiaries were to be identified by the ULB by conducting household surveys. While the largest target group of the Yojana is the urban poor, women and those belonging to SC/ST constitute special target groups. Thirty per cent of the beneficiaries under the schemes of SUME and SHASU were to be women.

This scheme covers urban settlements with population between 1 lakh and 20 lakh.

Subsidy under SUME was 25 per cent with a ceiling of

Rs. 4,000 for beneficiaries belonging to the general category and Rs. 5,000 for women and those belonging to SC/ST. The expenditure on subsidy was shared between the Centre and the State Governments equally and from April 1, 1992 in the ratio of 60 to 40. Besides the subsidy, 75 per cent of the unit cost of each self-employment venture was to be provided as loans by scheduled banks at subsidised rates of interest.

Under SUWE (Scheme for Urban Wage Employment), the entire expenditure was to be a grant to be shared between the Centre and the State Governments/Urban Local Bodies on 80:20 basis and on 60:40 basis from April 1, 1992. Subsidy under SHASU was 25 per cent of the unit cost with a ceiling of Rs. 1,000 and 75 per cent of the cost with the ceiling of Rs. 3,000 was to be provided by Housing and Urban Development Corporation (HUDCO) as an interest bearing loan. The expenditure on subsidy was shared between the Centre and State Governments in the ratio: 80:20 and from April 1, 1992 on 60:40 basis. Subsequently, it was decided that funds would be provided by the Centre to HUDCO which in turn would provide funds on project to project basis to State level agencies like Slum Clearance Boards, Housing Boards etc.

The Central share of funds under NRY schemes was to be allocated to the different States/Union Territories on the basis of their urban population and incidence of urban poverty.

Organisational Set up: At the National level, the Ministry of Urban Development was responsible for planning and monitoring of the Yojana. At the State level, the Secretary, Local Self-Government or the Secretary, Urban Development as the nodal officer was responsible for coordination and monitoring of the Programme. At the district level District Nehru Rozgar Yojana Committee was responsible for formulating the different schemes for smaller municipalities in the district and for coordination and implementation of the programme.

Training and infrastructural support (T&I): The outlay on training and infrastructural support component of SUME consisted of three elements of expenditure viz.

- training to urban poor beneficiaries - seventy per cent;
- support to training institutions - fifteen per cent and
- infrastructural support for setting up micro enterprises - fifteen per cent.

It was intended that spare capacity available in ITIs, Polytechnics and other suitable institutions run by Government, private or voluntary organisations be utilised for three months courses for batches of 25 persons. The average training expenditure per trainee was Rs. 1,200 for full course (per month for trainer: Rs. 1,000, stipend for trainee: Rs. 250, materials: Rs. 100 and per course: Rs. 750 on account of miscellaneous office expenses).

Scheme for Urban Wage Employment (SUWE): The below poverty line households living in the urban areas having a population of up to one lakh were to be covered by SUWE. Eligible beneficiaries were required to be identified by the ULBs to provide wage employment by utilising their labour for construction of socially and economically useful public assets in their jurisdiction through groups of beneficiaries organised into associations/guilds/cooperatives etc. The selection of projects and approval of estimates was to be done by ULBs in consultation with District NRY Committee.

The scheme envisaged taking up of municipal works for construction of socially and economically useful public assets like low cost water supply, pour flush community latrines, drainage related earthworks and community facilities etc. For urban settlements below 20000 population, the ratio of material and labour was 50:50 and for population between 20000 and 1 lakh, 60:40.

Scheme of Housing and Shelter Upgradation (SHASU): The scheme was to enable households belonging to economically weaker sections to construct simple dwelling units or to upgrade them with improvement of roof, walls, flooring, additional rooms etc. and the scheme was to be considered for declared slums areas, inner cities and areas predominantly inhabited by low income groups at a per capita cost of Rs. 4,000. ULBs were to formulate the projects in consultation with the State nodal agency and HUDCO was to finally approve them. The scheme was to be implemented in urban settlements with a population between one lakh and 20 lakh.

The ULBs were to identify the potential beneficiaries taking assistance from neighbourhood committees, urban basic services units, where existing, and NGOs.

Training and Infrastructure Support (T&I): The scheme envisaged training and infrastructural support (T&I) for promotion of construction skills among beneficiaries consisting of three elements viz.

- Training of urban poor beneficiaries: seventy per cent
- Support to training institutions: fifteen per cent and
- Creating training and infrastructure with fifteen per cent of funds released through HUDCO.

The average expenditure per trainee (for a batch of 25 trainees) was Rs. 1,500 for a full course of 3 months (average expenditure per month per trainer: Rs. 1,000, material per trainee: Rs. 150, stipend per trainee: Rs. 300 and miscellaneous office expenses per course: Rs. 1,000).

The interest earned on NRY funds was to be utilised on infrastructural support to beneficiaries and support to training institutions on certain specified objects but the Ministry had no information about the details of interest earned by each State and its proper utilisation by them.

Monitoring and Evaluation: The general features and operational guidelines for NRY issued by the Ministry did not envisage submission of periodical monthly progress reports by the States. The Ministry had, however, held three meetings between March 1990 to April 1993 with the representatives of the State Governments. However, as per the Management Information System (MIS) introduced by the Ministry in April 1992, monthly and bi-monthly reports were to be sent to the State headquarters by the district headquarters. In turn the State Governments were required to send their reports to the Ministry by 14th of every month. No evaluation of the NRY programme had been conducted so far.

A test-check of monitoring arrangements in the 24 States selected for audit revealed that state level monitoring Committees/cells had been set up in only 10 States, (Arunachal Pradesh, Jammu & Kashmir, Kerala, Gujarat, Goa, Punjab, Meghalaya, Mizoram, Orissa and Tripura).

With reference to results of the audit, in selected implementing agencies conducted by the State Accountants General in the Ministry, it was stated that these facts had not come to its notice. In Orissa, in 2 ULBs test-checked, no survey was conducted to identify the beneficiaries. In Assam, records in support of survey of the beneficiaries, housing conditions, slum pockets, water, electricity, drainage and sewerage etc. were not shown to audit.

18.2 Self- Employment Programme for Urban Poor (SEPUP)

Introduction: The Government of India, Ministry of Finance has formulated this scheme in consultation with the Reserve Bank of India for providing self-employment to the urban poor living in metropolitan, urban and semi-urban centres.

The objective of the programme is to enable identified eligible families living below subsistence level in Metropolitan areas, cities and towns with population exceeding 10000 (according to 1981 census) to undertake self employment ventures with the help of subsidy and bank credit.

All public sector banks shoulder the responsibility of implementing the scheme through their branches located in the scheme areas.

This scheme was launched on August 15, 1986.

Area of Operation: The scheme will cover all metropolitan, urban and semi-urban centres with population exceeding 10000 according to 1981 census. The population criteria were relaxed by the Reserve Bank of India subsequently and the scheme was extended to other centres with less than 10000 population provided that the area is not covered by IRDP.

Target: From each urban area one beneficiary for each 300 population (as per 1981 census) is to be assisted under the programme. From the year 1990-91, physical target under the programme was changed to one beneficiary for every 600 population of the centre as per 1981 census. The share of the SC/ST will be 30 per cent both number-wise and amount-wise

The urban poor families whose total income of the family members included in the ration card should not exceed Rs. 600 per month. 30 per cent of the loan amount and number of accounts should go to SC/ST beneficiaries.

Eligibility Criteria: The persons eligible under the scheme are:

- Permanent resident of the areas for at least 3 years (banks to obtain the declaration in the specified format.
- His/her name should appear in the ration card.
- Total family income as per ration card should not be more than Rs. 600 per month. Income of the children below the age of 14 years is to be excluded while arriving at the total income of the family for the purpose of the eligibility under SEPUP.
- Applicant should not have borrowed from any other bank/financial institution for similar purpose, and
- Applicant should have aptitude and the previous experience in the activity applied for.

Procedure for Implementation: The scheme is to be implemented through selected branches of public sector banks only. The selection is to be done by a committee of bankers to be constituted in each city/town by the public sector bank having the lead responsibility for the district. The bank will also act as a convenor of the committee, which will have one or two more banks having maximum number of branches in the centre as members. The committee in turn will divide the city in to convenient zones and form a separate local committee of bankers for the zone. The convenor will inform the public about the scheme, creation of zones, the bank offices which will receive applications from the concerned zones, constitution of zonal committees etc. The zonal convenor bank will receive the applications from the area and will place them in the committee for scrutiny. The meetings should be called as early as possible to clear the applications. The committee will forward the applications to the concerned branch. The loan should be sanctioned within 14 days from the date of application received from convenor. The financing bank branch should communicate the sanction to the borrower and the zonal committee.

Loan Amount, Subsidy and Margin: Loan amount under the scheme is up to Rs. 5,000, 25 per cent subsidy is available under the scheme. The subsidy is kept as fixed deposit. Interest on subsidy is to be created to the loan account. Subsidy is to be provided by the Reserve Bank of India. No margin to be obtained from the borrowers. Where the project cost exceeds Rs. 5000, banks, under usual terms and conditions subject to the proposals being found viable, could provide the assistance.

Hypothecation of the goods purchased is to be treated as security for the loan.

The rate of interest under the scheme will be 10 per cent per annum.

Purpose of Loan: The Reserve Bank of India has suggested the following activities for the purpose of loan. Agarbatti making, beedi rolling, black smithy, book binding, card board box making, carpentry, chair caning, clay moulding, cycle thela, mobile shop, rickshaw pulling, weaving, shoe repairing, pottery, vegetable vendors, launderers and press, plumbers, pan beedi shop, scooter repair shop, furniture and painting shop, tea shop, stove repair shop, ready made garments, paper bag vending, magazine/newspaper stall, fruit/juice vendors, tyre retreading, newspaper boys, milk vendors, fish vendors etc.

Coordinating Agency: Identification of the beneficiaries to be done by the bankers committee set up by the Lead Bank. The programme is to be implemented through selected branches of public sector banks only.

Loan Pass Books: Each borrower is to be issued the loan pass book with full details like name of the person, address. Purpose of loan, rate of interest, period of loan, monthly instalments of loan, subsidy amount etc.

Repayment Programme: Loan is repayable in 33 monthly instalments with an initial holiday of 3 months (total loan period 36 months). Repayment schedule should be fixed for net amount of loan after excluding subsidy. Subsidy to be kept in fixed deposit is adjusted on repayment of 75 per cent of the loan amount.

Monitoring: The progress of the scheme will be monitored and supervised by the bankers committee at each centre/zone with cooperation of all and on the basis of data. The head offices of banks should also monitor the implementation of the scheme by their branches wherever they have been given the responsibility. The head office of each bank will submit district-wise data in respect of loans sanctioned and disbursed by its branches under the scheme on a fortnightly basis.

Evaluation: A quick study on implementation of SEPUP in selected districts revealed the following deficiencies:

1. The Local Bankers Committee in some centres did not perform their role relating to the scrutiny and sponsoring of applications effectively.
2. Adequate publicity was not given at some centres.
3. Flow of instructions from the controlling offices of the banks to the designated branches was slow which resulted in non-adherence of the time schedule at several stages.
4. Branches were not keen to observe the time schedule prescribed.
5. Repayment instalments were fixed for total loan amount including subsidy and the number was less than the prescribed number i.e. 33.
6. Banks obtained affidavit for income in all cases instead of doubtful cases only.
7. Banks insisted for third party guarantee in some centres.
8. Fixed deposit receipts were not created in the names of beneficiaries in some banks.
9. In some branches application forms were not distributed to the intending applicants who had collected at the branches as per the advertisements.

The scheme has been merged with the Scheme for Urban Micro Enterprises (SUME) on its commencement on 15th August 1989.

18.3 Swarna Jayanti Shahari Rozgar Yojana (SJSRY)

In December 1997, the Urban Self-Employment Programme (USEP) and the Urban Wage Employment Programme (UWEP), which are the two special components of the SJSRY, substituted for various programmes operated earlier for urban poverty alleviation. The SJSRY is funded on a 75:25 basis between the Centre and the States. In 2003-04, the central allocation of Rs. 94.50 crore plus Rs. 10.50 crore for North-Eastern Region including Sikkim was fully utilized. Even 2004-05 saw the release of the entire budgetary allocation of Rs. 122 crore. In 2005-06, out of an allocation of Rs. 160 crore, Rs. 84.52 crore had been utilized until November 30, 2005.

19

Rural Employment Schemes

19.1 Swarnjayanti Gram Swarozgar Yojana [SGSY]

The programme was started with effect from 01.04.1999 after review and restructuring of the following programs:

1. Integrated Rural Development Programme (IRDP) and allied programmes namely
   - Training of Rural Youth for Self Employment (TRYSEM),
   - Development of Women and Children in Rural Areas (DWCRA),
   - Supply of Improved Toolkits in Rural Areas (SITRA) and
   - Ganga Kalyan Yojana (GKY), besides
2. Million Wells Scheme (MWS).

Loan-cum-subsidy for the Group Activity: The SGSY will primarily follow the group approach. The group is entitled to Subsidy of 50 per cent of the project cost subject to per capita subsidy of Rs.10,000 or Rs. 1.25 lakh, whichever is less. The cost of the group formation and development should be met from the funds provided under the SGSY. Considering the experiences of the NGOs involved in the development of SHGs in the country , it is estimated that an amount of Rs. 10,000 per group would be the investment required over 3-4 years. Rs. 10,000 per group as mentioned above for formation and development of Self Help Group, is the maximum ceiling, however, the actual amount may be decided by the District Level SGSY Committee based on the local prevailing situations.

Payment of the amount to the NGOs/CBOs/Community Coordinators/Animators will be made in four instalments in the manner given below:

- 20 per cent of the funds at the beginning when the formation of Self Help Group is commenced by the NGO/CBOs/Community Coordinator/Animator. This money could be utilised during the formation stage. During this period the group should open an account in the service area Bank Branch and they should be imparted Basic Orientation training on the concept of Self Help Group, Group dynamics, maintenance of records and books of accounts, conducting group meetings and financial transactions.

- 30 per cent after the group qualifies for Revolving Fund or get linked to the Bank by way of availing Credit and continue to work satisfactorily.
- 40 per cent after the group take up an economic activity and
- 10 per cent after the start of economic activity by the group and adherence to repayment schedule of the loan sanctioned by the Bank.

Subsidy: Subsidy under SGSY will be uniform at 30 per cent of the project cost, subject to a maximum of Rs. 7,500. In respect of SC/STs, however, these will be 50 per cent and Rs. 10,000 respectively. For groups of Swarozgaris (SHGs), the subsidy would be at 50 per cent of the project cost subject to per capita subsidy of Rs. 10,000 or Rs.1.25 lakh, whichever is less. There will be no monetary limit on subsidy for irrigation projects.

Back-end Subsidy: Subsidy will be back-ended. Banks would disburse the full project cost including subsidy to the Swarozgaris as loan. The benefits of subsidy will also be available to Swarozgaris who prefer to avail themselves of required working capital in the form of cash credit. The operation of subsidy amount by the bank will be as follows:

Identification of training institutions: Data on the available training Infrastructure should be collected so as to make an optimal use of the existing Infrastructure facilities at the District as well as the block levels. The facilities may include institutions such as it is, Polytechnics, Krishi Vigyan Kendras, Khadi and Village Industries Boards, State Institutes of Rural Development, Extension Training Centres, reputed voluntary organizations and any departmental facilities available in that area. The DRDA will be entitled to meet the expenses, incurred by the training institution for conduct of the training programme, from out of the

SGSY- Training fund, but such expenses should not exceed Rs.15 per trainee per day.

SGSY Training Fund: Up to 10 per cent of SGSY funds will be set aside as training fund and will be utilized to provide both orientation and training programmes to the Swarozgaris, as indicated above. A separate Head of Account should be opened for this purpose.

The DRDA will be entitled to meet the expenses, incurred by the training institution for both Basic Orientation and Skill Development Training from out of the SGSY Fund. The Basic Orientation Training may include topics on concept of Self Help, group dynamics, conflict resolution, conduct of group meetings, maintenance of records, awareness about social and family welfare programmes etc. The training for skill development may include skill upgradation through exposure to latest tools and technology, value addition and diversification of products, entrepreneur development, marketing skills, packaging, labelling etc.

The DRDA will be entitled to meet the expenses for training from out of the SGSY Fund. The Institutional training cost may be fixed at Rs. 15 per day per trainee only for imparting training, if no boarding and lodging facility is provided to the participants, and at Rs. 35 per day per trainee in case the Institution provides boarding and lodging also with training. If the Institution does not provide boarding and lodging then the participants may be paid Rs. 25 per trainee day to meet the cost of boarding and lodging. Swarozgaris may be allowed one time to and fro travelling cost from their place of residence to the Training Institute.

Further, DRDAs may incur an expenditure of Rs. 200 per trainee per month for payment of honorarium to master craftsman engaged for imparting skill development training to Swarozgaris identified and selected for economic activity and Rs. 100 per month per trainee, as allowance for raw materials required for the training. However, the total expenditure on Basic Orientation and skill development training will not exceed Rs. 5,000 per trainee. The State Government will decide duration of Skill development training. It will depend upon the activities and in order to ensure uniformity of the duration of training for all the Districts.

19.2 Sampoorna Grameen Rozgar Yojana (SGRY)

There are following two major Programmes for Wage-Employment Generation in the rural areas by the Ministry of Rural Development:

1. Employment Assurance Scheme (EAS) dedicated to wage-employment itself and
2. Jawahar Gram Samridhi Yojana (JGSY).for Infrastructure creation at the village level

   The new programme was launched on September 25, 2001.

- The Sampoorna Grameen Rozgar Yojana (SGRY) a Centrally Sponsored Scheme (CSS) is being implemented with the total outlay of Rs. 10,000 crore.
- Under the Scheme, 50 lakh tones of foodgrains amounting to about Rs. 5,000 crore (at economic cost) is being provided every year, free of cost, to the State Governments and Union Territory Administrations.
- Rs. 5,000 crore has been kept to meet the cash component of wages and material cost.
- The cost of the cash component of the Programme is shared by the Centre and State in the ratio of 75:25.
- The payment of food grains is to be made by the Ministry of Rural Development to the Food Corporation of India (FCI) directly.
- About 100 crore mandays of employment are envisaged to be generated every year in the rural areas through the SGRY.
- Every worker seeking employment under the SGRY will be provided minimum 5 kgs. of foodgrains (in kind) per manday as part of wages.

The balance of wages will be paid in cash so that they are assured of the notified minimum wages.

19.3 Prime Ministers Gram Sadak Rozgar Yojana (PMGSRY)

The scheme was on December 25, 2000. The scheme is a 100 per cent Centrally Sponsored Scheme. 50 per cent of the Cess on High Speed Diesel (HSD) is earmarked for this Programme. Once the Core Network is prepared, it is possible to estimate the length of roads for New Connectivity as well as Upgradation for every District. States may, each year, distribute the State's Allocation among the Districts giving 80 per cent on the basis of road length required for providing connectivity to Unconnected Habitations and 20 per cent on the basis of road length requiring Upgradation under the PMGSY.

In making the District-wise allocation, the number of Habitations taken up under the PMGSY or any other Programme would be excluded from the total number of Unconnected Habitations (even if the road works are still under execution). The figures of connected as well as Unconnected Habitations in any District would keep on changing every year till such time as all Unconnected Habitations (of the stipulated population size) have been covered in the District. The Pradhan Mantri Gram Sadak Yojana does not provide for any staff costs.

19.4 The National Rural Employment Guarantee Scheme (NREGS)

The scheme was launched on February 2, 2006. This scheme is the primary instrument to combat rural unemployment and hunger poverty. National Rural Employment Guarantee Act 2005 was passed on September 5, 2005. The Act provides for the enhancement of livelihood security of the households in rural areas of the country by providing at least one hundred days of guaranteed wage employment in every financial year to every household whose adult members volunteer to do skilled/unskilled manual work. The Act extends to the whole of India except the State of Jammu and Kashmir.

Financial Outlay: In the current year, under a clutch of schemes including the Food for Work programme, a sum of Rs. 11,700 crore is expected to be spent on rural employment. For

2006-07, the total allocation for rural employment will be Rs. 14,300 crore. Of this, Rs. 11,300 crore (including NER component) will be under the NREG Act and Rs. 3,000 crore (including NER component) will be under SGRY. Since there is a legal guarantee of employment under the NREG Act, more funds will be provided according to need. Provided further that the wage rate specified from time to time under any such notification shall not be at a rate less than sixty rupees per day. Until such time as a wage rate is fixed by the Central Government in respect of Act. If the Programme Officer is not in a position to disburse the unemployment disbursement allowance in time or at all for any reason beyond his control, he shall report the matter to of the District Programme Coordinator and announce such reasons in a notice to be displayed on his notice board and the notice board of the Gram Panchayat and such other certain conspicuous places as he may deem necessary. Every case of non-payment or delayed payment of unemployment allowance shall be reported in the annual report submitted by the District Programme Coordinator to the State Government along with the reasons for such non-payment or delayed payment. The State Government shall take all measures to make the payment of unemployment allowance to the concerned household as expeditiously as possible.

Disentitlement: An applicant who do not receive unemployment allowance in certain circumstances.

a. does not accept the employment provided to his household under a Scheme; or
b. does not report for work within fifteen days of being notified by the Programme Officer or the implementing agency to report for the work; or
c. continuously remains absent from work, without obtaining a permission from the concerned implementing agency for a period of more than one week or remains absent for a total period of more than one week in any month, shall not be eligible to claim the unemployment allowance payable under this Act for a period of three months but shall be eligible to seek employment under the Scheme at any time.

The Programme Officer shall prepare a plan for the Block under his jurisdiction by consolidating the project proposals prepared by the Gram Panchayats and the proposals received from intermediate panchayats.

- The Gram Panchayat shall be responsible for identification of the of the Gram projects in the Gram Panchayat area to be taken up under a Scheme as per the Panchayats. recommendations of the Gram Sabha and the Ward Sabhas and for executing and supervising such works.
- A Gram Panchayat may take up any project under a Scheme within the area of the Gram Panchayat as may be sanctioned by the Programme Officer.
- Every Gram Panchayat shall, after considering the recommendations of the Gram Sabha and the Ward Sabhas, prepare a development plan and maintain a shelf of possible works to be taken up under the Scheme as and when demand for work arises.

Minimum Features of a Rural Employment Guarantee Scheme:

1. The focus of the Scheme shall be on the following works in their order of priority-

- water conservation and water harvesting;
- drought proofing (including afforestation and tree plantation);
- irrigation canals including micro and minor irrigation works;
- provision of irrigation facility to land owned by households belonging to the Scheduled Castes and Scheduled Tribes or to land of beneficiaries of land reforms or that of the beneficiaries under the Indira Awas Yojana of the Govt. of India;
- renovation of traditional water bodies including desilting of tanks;
- land development;
- flood control and protection works including drainage in water logged areas;
- rural connectivity to provide all-weather access; and

- any other work which may be notified by the Central Government in consultation with the State Government.

2. Creation of durable assets and strengthening the livelihood resource base of the rural poor shall be an important objective of the Scheme.
3. The works taken up under the scheme shall be in rural areas.
4. The State Council shall prepare a list of preferred works for different areas based on their ability to create durable assets.
5. The Scheme shall be subject to appropriate arrangements as may be laid down by the State Government under the rules issued by it for proper maintenance of the public assets created under the Scheme.
6. Under no circumstances shall the labourers be paid less than the wage rate.
7. When wages are directly linked with the quantity of work, the wages shall be paid according to the schedule of rates fixed by the State Government for different types of work every year, in consultation with the State Council.
8. The schedule of rates of wages for unskilled labourers shall be so fixed that a person working for seven hours would normally earn a wage equal to the wage rate}
9. The cost of material component of projects including the wages of the skilled and semi-skilled workers taken up under the Scheme shall not exceed forty per cent of the total project costs.
10. It shall be open to the Programme Officer and Gram Panchayat to direct any person who applied for employment under the Scheme to do work of any type permissible under it.
11. The Scheme shall not permit engaging any contractor for implementation of the projects under it.
12. As far as practicable, a task funded under the Scheme shall be performed by using manual labour and not machines.
13. Every Scheme shall contain adequate provisions for ensuring transparency and accountability at all level of implementation.
14. Provisions for regular inspection and supervision of works taken up under the Scheme shall be made to ensure proper

quality of work as well as to ensure that the total wages paid for the completion of the work is commensurate with the quality and quantity of work done.

Conditions for Guaranteed Rural Employment and Minimum Entitlements of Labourers:

1. The adult members of every household. who
- reside in any rural areas; and
- are willing to do unskilled manual work, may submit their names, age and the address of the household to the Gram Panchayat at the village level (hereafter in this Schedule referred to as the Gram Panchayat) in the jurisdiction of which they reside for registration of their household for issuance of a job card.
2. It shall be the duty of the Gram Panchayat to register the household, after making such enquiry as it deems fit and issue a job card containing such details of adult members of the household affixing their photographs, as may be specified by the State Government in the Scheme.
3. The registration made under paragraph 2 shall be for such period as may be laid in the Scheme, but in any case not less than five years, and may be renewed from time to time.
4. Every adult member of a registered household whose name appears in the job card shall be entitled to apply for unskilled manual work under the Scheme.
5. All registered persons belonging to a household shall be entitled to employment in accordance with the Scheme made under the provisions of this Act, for as many days as each applicant may request, subject to a maximum of one hundred days per household in a given financial year.
6. The Programme Officer shall ensure that every applicant referred to in paragraph shall be provided unskilled manual work in accordance with the provisions of the Scheme within fifteen days of receipt of an application or from the date he seeks work in case of advance application, whichever is later: Provided that priority shall be given to women in such a way

that at least one-third of the beneficiaries shall be women who have registered and requested for work under this Act.

7. Applications for work must be for at least fourteen days of continuous work.
8. There shall be no limit on the number of days of employment for which a person may apply, or on the number of days of employment actually provided to him subject to the aggregate entitlement of the household.
9. Applications for work may be submitted in writing either to the Gram Panchayat or to the Programme Officer, as may be specified in the Scheme.
10. The Gram Panchayat and Programme Officer, as the case may be, shall be bound to accept valid applications and to issue a dated receipt to the applicant. Group applications may also be submitted.
11. Applicants who are provided with work shall be so intimated in writing, by mailing a letter sent to him at the address given in the job card and by a public notice displayed at the office of the Panchayats at the district, intermediate or village level.
12. As far as possible, employment shall be provided within a radius of five kilometers of the village where the applicant resides at the time of applying.
13. new work under the Scheme shall be commenced only if-

- at least fifty labourers become available for such work; and
- the labourers cannot be absorbed in the ongoing works: Provided that this condition shall not be applicable for new works, as determined by the State Government in hilly areas and in respect of afforestation.

14. In cases the employment is provided outside such radius, it must be provided within the Block, and the labourers shall be paid ten per cent of the wage rate as extra wages to meet additional transportation and living expenses.
15. A period of unemployment shall ordinarily be at least fourteen days continuously with not more than six days in a week.

16. In all cases where unemployment allowance is paid, or due to be paid, the Programme Officer shall inform the District Programme Coordinator in writing the reasons why it was not possible for him to provide employment or cause to provide employment to the applicants.
17. The District Programme Coordinator shall, in his Annual Report to the State Council, explain as to why employment could not be provided in cases where payment of unemployment allowance is involved.
18. Provision shall be made in the Scheme for advance applications, that is, applications which may be submitted in advance of the date from which employment is sought.
19. Provision shall be made in the Scheme for submission of multiple applications by the same person provided that the corresponding periods for which employment is sought do not overlap.
20. The Gram Panchayat shall prepare and maintain or cause to be prepared and maintained such registers, vouchers and other documents in such form and in such manner as may be specified in the Scheme containing particulars of job cards and passbooks issued, name, age and address of the head of the household and the adult members of the household registered with the Gram Panchayat.
21. The Gram Panchayat shall send such list or lists of the names and addresses of households and their adult members registered with it and supply such other information to the concerned Programme Officer at such periods and in such form as may be specified in the Scheme.
22. A list of persons who are provided with the work shall be displayed on the notice board of the Gram Panchayat and at the office of the Programme Officer and at such other p laces as the Programme Officer may deem necessary and the list shall be open for inspection by the State Government and any person interested.
23. If the Gram panchayat is satisfied at any time that a person has registered with it by furnishing false information, it may

direct the Programme Officer to direct his name to be struck off from the register and direct the applicant to return the job card: Provided that no such action under this paragraph shall be directed unless the applicant has been given an opportunity of being heard in the presence of two independent persons.

24. If any personal injury is caused to any person employed under the Scheme by accident arising out of and in the course of his employment, he shall be entitled to, free of charge, such medical treatment as is admissible under the Scheme.
25. Where hospitalisation of the injured worker is necessary, the State Government shall arrange for such hospitalisation including accommodation, treatment, medicines and payment of daily allowance not less than half of the wage rate required to be paid had the injured been engaged in the work.
26. If a person employed under a Scheme dies or becomes permanently disabled by accident arising out of and in the course of employment, he shall be paid by the implementing agency an ex-gratia payment at the rate of twenty-five thousand rupees or such amount as may be notified by the Central Government, and the amount shall be paid to the legal heirs of the deceased or the disabled, as the case may be.
27. The facilities of safe drinking water, shade for children and periods of rest, first-aid box with adequate material for emergency treatment for minor injuries and other health hazards connected with the work being performed shall be provided at the work site.
28. In case the number of children below the age of six years accompanying the women working at any site is five or more, provisions shall be made to depute one of such women worker to look after such children.
29. The person deputed under paragraph 28 shall be paid wage rate.
30. In case the payment of wages is not made within the period specified under the Scheme, the labourers shall be entitled to receive payment of compensation as per the provisions of the Payment of Wages Act, 1936 (4 of 1936).

31. The wage s under a Scheme may be paid either wholly in cash or in cash and kin provided that at least one-fourth of the wages shall be paid in cash only.

Performance: There is good response in the country towards this scheme. Till March 2006, the Gram Panchayats have received 2.15 crore applications for the people from 181 districts out of the 200 districts selected under the scheme. Job Cards have been issued to 79.69 lakh applicants.

19.5 Pilot Intensive Rural Employment Project (PIREP)

Unemployment is a major problem not only in rural areas but also in urban areas. Unemployment is a main reason for the poverty of the people. This programme started as a pilot project to find answer to the rural unemployment problem in India. The projects were started as research and action projects.

The programme commenced in November 1972 during the Fourth Five-Year Plan.

Under the Programme 15 Pilot Projects were started and these projects were expected to be completed in October 1975. A survey was to be conducted of all the persons in need of the work in a block. Workers to be registered under the project and employment offered to them.

Objectives: The project aimed at providing employment to one third of the unemployed persons each year thus covering all unemployed persons in three years in selected blocks in the country situated in different economic and ecological conditions.

Minor irrigation, soil conservation, afforestation, common orchards, pisciculture, road construction, rural godowns school building construction, other agricultural schemes etc. were the works undertaken under the project.

Evaluation: A committee was set up under the Chairmanship of Prof. Dantwala to supervise and guide the economists who were entrusted with the evaluation work of the Pilot Intensive Rural Employment Programme (PIREP). The evaluation of the programme revealed the following:

1. All the persons registered did not turn up for the work.

2. The number of workers registered for the project was not as per the data given in the survey.
3. The demand for the work was not consistent and works has to be adjusted as per the availability of labour.
4. Planning of the projects and integration with other departments was not proper hence the results were not as expected.
5. The kind component was not sufficient to give the people sufficient durable income generating assets.

19.6 Crash Scheme for Rural Employment

The chronic unemployment is a very small part of Indian unemployment scene as only a few persons remain unemployed throughout the year. Most of the unemployed gets some or the other work, may be only for few days in a month. The rural unemployment estimated in 1971 was 14.21 million persons-years. This position was very alarming. To provide employment in rural areas, works like road construction, land reclamation, protection from floods, drainage, minor irrigation, soil conservation, afforestation etc. were undertaken under this programme. The scheme covered the areas not covered by other employment schemes for marginal farmers, small farmers and agricultural labourers.

Objectives: The objective of the programme was to alleviate unemployment and under-employment in rural areas. The aim of the programme was to provide employment to 1000 persons on an average continuously over a working season of 10 months in a year and that each project should be labour intensive and should result in a work of durable nature. More employment opportunities were available in rural areas through these programmes.

It was also expected that this programme would provide regular employment to the people who go in for development of animal husbandry, fisheries, dairy etc. for semi-skilled, skilled and unskilled labourers.

This scheme was implemented during the last 3 years of

Fourth Five-Year Plan and started in the year 1971-72. The scheme period expired in March 1974.

The outlay of the scheme was Rs. 50 crore per year. The programme was for three years with an allocation of Rs. 150 crore.

The Crash Scheme was not treated as successful as it could not make significant impact in removing unemployment. The reason given for the failure was that the rural youths could not be placed at the place of labour demand at the minimum prescribed wages.

19.7 Training of Rural Youth for Self Employment (TRYSEM)

This programme started on August 15, 1979 as a centrally sponsored scheme. The main object of this programme is to provide training in necessary skill and technology to the rural youth between the age of 18 to 35 years in agriculture, allied activities, industries, services and business. In each blocks 40 youths were to be given training each year, thus covering 2 lakh youths in the country each year. After the training these youths are provided financial assistance under IRDP. This is a sub programme of IRDP. During the sixth plan 10.15 lakh and during the seventh plan 9.99 lakh youths were trained under the scheme. Out of the 9.99 lakh youths trained in seventh plan, 4.65 lakh started their own business and 1.31 lakh youths got the service.

Main thrust of the scheme is to equip rural youths with the necessary skills and technology to undertake self-employment.

The programme commenced in the year 1979. With the extension of IRDP in all blocks of the country, TRYSEM is being implemented as a part of IRDP.

The selection of the beneficiaries is based on the income criteria. In the beginning of the implementation of the scheme a family having an income of Rs. 3,500 or less per year is considered for selection. The priority in selection is given to the poorest families. Only one beneficiary is taken from one family. Preference is given to the persons having entrepreneurial aptitude.

Priority is given to scheduled caste, scheduled tribes, ex-service men and persons attended 9 months National Adult Education Programme. Women candidates should be one third of the trainees.

Technical training to the selected candidates is to be provided through technical institutes and master trainers, master craft men, skilled artisans, industrial and servicing units, commercial and business establishments etc.

Financial Assistance: Financial assistance to be given is of two types:

A. Recurring: Following types of recurring expenditure is incurred under the scheme (June 2, 1981). The amount has changed time to time under various heads.

- **Stipend to trainees:** Stipend to trainees is available for undergoing training through institutions or master craftsmen. In case the training is conducted in the village of the trainee, the rate of the stipend shall be up to Rs. 50 both in case of institutions as well as master-craftsmen. In case the training is held outside the trainee's village and the institution/master craftsman does not provide the accommodation to him free of cost, the rate of stipend shall be up to Rs. 125 per month. In such cases the rate of daily stipend for courses of duration of less than a month shall be up to Rs. 5 per trainee.
- **Training expenses:** Training institution also receives the expenses incurred on the training.
- **Raw material:** Institution/master craftsmen are given the money for raw material used for the training.
- **Tool kits:** The trainees are provided with free tool kit required for the trade.
- **Payment to master trainers:** A reward is given to master trainers for each candidate for successful completion of the training.

B. Non-Recurring: There is a provision for strengthening existing training infrastructure in the form of construction of dormitories, classrooms and workshops and purchase of equipments and aids.

Positive Points:

1. Of the total beneficiaries covered in the sample, around 96 per cent were in the prescribed age-group of 18-35 years and only 2 per cent were below 18 years and 1 per cent above 35 years.
2. The participation of Scheduled Castes (SCs) and Schedules Tribes (STs) under the programme was found to be 39.51 per cent for SCs and 12.89 per cent for STs respectively. This was more than the minimum norm of 50 per cent prescribed for SC/ST communities under the guidelines.
3. Majority of the beneficiaries (57.14 per cent) were exposed to training for a period of 12-26 weeks as prescribed in the guidelines and nearly 33 per cent for more than 26 weeks.
4. Roughly 91.93 per cent of the beneficiaries acquired vocational/technical knowledge as a result of TRYSEM training.
5. As to the competence of Master Craftsmen who imparted TRYSEM training, high percentage of beneficiaries, i.e. 88.82 per cent found them competent.
6. Majority of the beneficiaries, (58.33 per cent) expressed confidence in taking up self-employment after the TRYSEM training.
7. As to the type of enterprises taken up by the beneficiaries after training, it was found that majority of the trainees, i.e. 62 per cent took up self-employment in the secondary sector, 33 per cent in the tertiary sector and the remaining 5 per cent in the primary sector.
8. Roughly, 73.88 per cent of the beneficiaries could derive average monthly turnover up to Rs. 1,000 as a result to self-employment taken up by them after the training.
9. As a result of self-employment activities, a very high percentage, i.e. 91 per cent of the beneficiaries had an average net income up to Rs.500 per month.
10. A large number of beneficiaries, i.e. 92.19 per cent had their self-employment activities very near, i.e. up to 2 kms. from their place of residence. This was primarily due to the fact that roughly 89.25 per cent of them had no conveyance

facilities of their own.

11. Majority of the Master Craftsman, i.e. 57.29 per cent were selected on the basis of their long experience in the craft/trade of their specialisation.

Areas of Concern:

1. Of the total number of beneficiaries who got training under TRYSEM, roughly 47.19 per cent were unemployed after training.
2. At the all-India level, 63.25 per cent considered the monthly stipend paid to them as inadequate.
3. In comparison to the beneficiaries who underwent TRYSEM training, the number of beneficiaries who were provided with tool-kits during the training was very inadequate.
4. Of the major lacunae observed in the training programme by the trainees, a large percentage, i.e. 68.18 per cent of the trainees felt that the duration of training was inadequate.
5. Majority of the beneficiaries, i.e. 66.52 per cent expressed lack of funds' as the major reason for not taking up self-employment independently after the training.
6. Majority of the beneficiaries, i.e. 46.85 per cent felt 'lack of funds' as the major bottleneck for taking up self-employment activities.
7. A major proportion of TRYSEM trainees i.e. 53.57 per cent did not apply for loan under IRDP. Of the total beneficiaries who applied for loan unit IRDP (i.e. 46.43 per cent), only about 50 per cent were given assistance under IRDP.
8. A large number of beneficiaries, i.e. 62.91 per cent felt no improvement in their socio-economic conditions as a result of TRYSEM training.
9. As regards socio-economic conditions of the beneficiaries, the survey revealed that 70.64 per cent of the beneficiaries were living in 'Kuccha Houses'; 61.58 per cent without drinking water; and 54.31 per cent without electricity.

19.8 National Rural Employment Programme (NREP)

Introduction: The genesis of this programme goes to the

Food for Work Programme. People in villages with no or very less productive assets need wage employment to sustain their family. The employment in agriculture is also seasonal. Besides this with the more number of small and marginal farmers in the villages, their family members do most of the work in the farm, hence the wage employment is also limited. This programme caters to the needs of this segment of rural areas.

Objectives: The objectives of the programmes are as follows:

- Generation of opportunity for wage employment.
- Creation of durable community assets. and
- Improvement of the nutritional status of the rural poor.

National Rural Employment Programme was launched in October 1980 by restructuring Food for Work Programme.

NREP operates all over the country. Backward regions and areas having larger incidences of unemployment are given priority.

The target was to provide 300 to 400 million mandays of employment every year. As part of the wages, workers employed under the programme are given the foodgrains. It was decided to provide food grain at subsidised rates, lower than the normal distribution price to these workers.

Financing Pattern: The programme is Centrally sponsored and centre and state will share the costs on 50:50 basis. The central Government will provide its share in the form of foodgrains to the extent of surplus foodgrains available and rest in the form of cash.

Works Undertaken: Each DRDA has to prepare a portfolio of projects to be taken up under the programme. DRDA is required to ensure proper linkages with other rural development programmes at the planning stage. The work is executed through Panchayati Raj institutions. The work undertaken under the programme was to strengthen the basic infrastructure of the rural areas.

Some of the work undertaken under the programmes was:

- Community irrigation wells
- Minor irrigation projects

- Rural roads
- Panchayat Ghars
- Balwadi Bhavans
- Village Ponds
- Drinking Water wells etc.

Evaluation: The programme has achieved its basic objectives. It has also provided additional benefits like ensuring payment of minimum wages and improving the availability of foodgrains and checking the migration of rural people to cities. However the following points have called for attention for improvement.

- There was no coordination with the needs of the identified beneficiaries of the Integrated Rural Development Programme.
- The programme was basically to provide for use of local material for house construction. But it was observed that there is a tendency of using more construction material from outside the village. This has resulted in less employment generation in the local areas.
- This programme was conceived as an additional wage generation programme. But in implementation it was observed that the implementation agencies are taking it as general development programme.
- Many a times the amount received from various departments like Irrigation, Public Works Department etc. were shown as a matching grant from the States. This has resulted in reduction in the employment generation during the VI Five-Year Plan.

To improve the effectiveness of NREP it was combined with Rural Landless Employment Guarantee Programme in 1989 and renamed as Jawahar Rozgar Yojana.

19.9 Rural Landless Employment Guarantee Programme (RLEGP)

Objectives: The objectives of the programme are as follows:

- To improve and expand employment opportunities for the rural landless with a view to providing employment for at least one member of every landless labour household for up to 100 days in a year and

- To create durable assets for strengthening the rural infrastructure which will lead to rapid growth of the rural economy.

Area of Operation: Area of operation of the programme is whole of the country. Ranging from a village to the State individual projects can cover any area. Backward areas having predominant population of unemployed landless labourer and the areas with low wage pockets are to be given priority.

Financial Assistance: The programme is funded entirely by the Central Government. The programme envisages that the expenditure on wage component should not be more than 50 per cent of the cost of a project. The Government, at par with the minimum agricultural wages, fixes the wages paid under NREP. The work is undertaken directly by the Government and contractors are eliminated. For distribution of foodgrains also the work is undertaken directly and not through contractors. Panchayati Raj institutions are involved in planning and execution of the programme.

This programme was launched in August 1983. The programme is more or less on the lines of Employment Guarantee Scheme of Maharashtra.

Programme Implementation: The implementation of the programme is the responsibility of the State Governments. To ensure adherence to minimum technical standards in formulating projects, besides providing a coordinated approach for the whole country, the projects proposed by the States Governments are considered for approval by a committee comprising representatives of the Central and State Governments. The projects taken up should be relevant to the (i) Minimum Needs Programme, (ii) Development of infrastructure or (iii) Improvement of the productivity of the areas. The workers employed in RLEGP are given foodgrains at the rate of Rs. 1 per kg per manday as a part of their wage as is done in NREP. Since the cost of the foodgrains is subsidized, rate charged is lower than those prevailing under the public distribution system.

Target and Achievement: The programme was to achieve the 3,600 lakh mandays of employment with the provision of resources of Rs. 600 crore during the last 2 years of VI Five-Year Plan i.e. 1983-85. The programme could achieve 72 per cent of the target by providing 2,600 lakh mandays of employment.

The Programme was renamed as Jawahar Rozgar Yojana in 1989.

19.10 Employment Assurance Scheme (EAS)

This is an employment oriented development programme. Central and States share the expense of this programme in the ratio of 80:20. The Central assistance under the scheme is given directly to the District Board/District Rural Development Agency. The programme incharge is the District Magistrate or the Deputy Commissioner. The part of the wages may be paid in the form of foodgrains.

The Employment Assurance Scheme (EAS) was introduced on October 2, 1993.

The primary objective of the Employment Assurance Scheme is to provide gainful employment during lean agricultural season in manual work to all able bodied adults in rural areas who are in need and desirous of work, but cannot find it. The secondary objective is the creation of economic infrastructure and community assets for sustained employment and development.

Area of Operation: In the beginning the scheme was introduced in the rural areas of 1778 blocks of 261 districts in which the Revamped Public Distribution System (RPDS) was in operation. The blocks selected were in the drought prone areas, desert areas, tribal areas and hill areas. During 1994-95, EAS was extended to 409 blocks under DPAP/DDP and Modified Area Development Approach (MADA) blocks having larger concentration of tribal population. In March, 1995 the scheme was further extended to 256 blocks (233 flood prone blocks in the States of Uttar Pradesh, Bihar and Assam, and 23 blocks of Jammu and Kashmir in view of the special conditions prevailing there).

The Intensified Jawahar Rozgar Yojana (IJRY) was merged with Employment Assurance Scheme from January 1, 1996. Consequently, 722 non-EAS blocks in 120 IJRY districts were also covered under EAS. On universalization, the remaining blocks were covered under the scheme in two phases i.e. 1123 blocks in 1996-97 and 1121 blocks in 1997-98. At present, the scheme is being implemented in all the 5448 rural blocks of the country.

Salient Features of the Scheme:

1. The scheme is operative in all the rural blocks of the country.
2. It is a demand driven scheme with no fixed earmarking of annual funds for any district or block.
3. The Central assistance under the scheme is directly released block-wise to DRDA/ZPs based on the demand for wage employment and expenditure.
4. All adult rural poor normally residing in the villages are covered.
5. A maximum of 2 adults per family are provided the assurance of up to 100 days of employment.
6. New works will not be opened under this scheme if employment potential is available through plan and non-plan works already in progress and utilising the same could fulfil the assurance.
7. Works should be labour intensive which result in the creation of durable productive assets.
8. As an individual beneficiary oriented scheme, on the lands of BPL families, horticulture development is a permitted activity.
9. Implementing agencies are Block Development Officers, District Officers of various line Departments and PRIs at all three levels.
10. The desirous workers have to get themselves registered with village level workers or Gram Panchayats and are issued a family card.
11. When about 10 workers demand work, new projects can be

started by the block level officer for providing employment.

12. The State Level Coordination committee for the Rural Development programmes is responsible for the overall supervision, guidance and monitoring of EAS.

Block-wise Entitlement of Funds under EAS: As per the present classification of blocks into 'A', 'B' and 'C' categories, the central share of each instalment to the blocks is Rs. 40 lakh, Rs. 30 lakh and Rs. 20 lakh respectively. The State share is Rs.10 lakh, Rs. 7.50 lakh and Rs. 5 lakh respectively.

The shelf of projects for new works to be taken up in each of the categories should not exceed 150 per cent of the funds expected by a block in two instalments. The classification of the blocks into 'A', 'B' and 'C' categories was made earlier on the basis of the criteria of backwardness and size of the population. These were mostly blocks in hilly, tribal, drought prone and desert areas. These criteria were followed up to the merger of IJRY with EAS. As per this criteria blocks with population above 196287 were put in 'A' category; blocks with population between 196287 and 65585 were put in 'B' category and blocks with population below 65585 were put in 'C' category. Consequent upon universalization of EAS all the remaining blocks have been put in 'C' category for the purpose of determining the entitlement of funds by each.

Some Recently Introduced Changes in EAS:

1. Panchayati Raj Institutions of all three levels have been included as Implementing Agencies.
2. The shelf of Projects would be prepared based on suggestions of Gram Sabhas and Panchayats as well as from other sources like line departments, people's representatives etc. as per felt needs of the people.
3. Registration of wage-seekers would be done in Gram Panchayats and work-site etc.
4. The implementing agencies have been permitted to utilize one person from among the beneficiaries group as facilitator in maintenance of muster roll, payment of wages, monitoring of quality of works etc. Such person will be eligible to receive

wages applicable to unskilled labourers.

5. The States have been requested to evolve and publish "Rural Standard Schedule of Rates" as has already been done by some States to eliminate the role of contractors in EAS works.
6. To make the implementation of the programme more transparent instructions have been issued to all the states to exhibit prominently the details of funds received, works sanctioned, estimated cost, quantity of material used, workers engaged and wage rates etc. in the Panchayat Office/work site. The accounts for the Gram Panchayats are also open for scrutiny by the Gram Sabha.
7. To avoid multiplicity of Committees a decision has been taken to merge District and Block level EAS Committees with the existing Vigilance and Monitoring Committees.

19.11 Rural Employment Generation Programme of Khadi and Village Industries Commission (KVIC): Margin Money Scheme (MMS) for Village Industries

Introduction: The Rural Employment Generation Programme was started as per the recommendations of the High Powered Committee on Khadi and Village Industries headed by the then Prime Minister in May 1994. The committee among other things recommended the accelerated growth of rural employment generation programmes. Accordingly the scheme was formulated by the KVIC and discussed in the Conference of Industry Ministers in August 1996 and decided to implement the Scheme throughout the country.

The Khadi and Village and Industries Commission was set up in 1957 by an Act of Parliament. The Commission is entrusted with the responsibility of organising, promoting and implementing programmes for the development of the various industries like processing and preservation of fruits, bamboo and cane works, oil Ghani, khadi cloths, palm gur, match boxes, leather tanning, hand made paper, non-edible oil and soap etc. It helps in providing self-employment to many persons in their own area besides increase in production of the concerned raw material.

The Commission arranges for the training of the rural artisans and also procures machinery, equipments, raw materials for distribution among the artisans and arrange for marketing of the goods produced by the artisans.

The objectives of the programme are to accelerate the growth of employment in rural areas and to check the migration of the labour force from rural areas to urban areas.

The scheme is in operation since July 1997.

Eligibility Criteria: Margin Money Assistance is provided where total project cost is as follows:

1. For institutions/cooperative societies, Trusts registered with KVIC/KVIB - up to Rs. 25 lakh
2. For the individuals (artisans and entrepreneurs) - up to Rs. 10 lakh.

Projects more than the above ceiling limit are not eligible for margin money. The scheme is not applicable to partnership firms and private limited companies. The registration for the institutions, cooperative societies, Trusts with KVIC/KVIB is not a pre-condition under the scheme.

The scheme is applicable to all viable village industry projects (except Khadi and polyvastra) which produce any goods or renders any services with or without use of power and in which fixed capital investment per head of artisan or worker does not exceed Rs. 50,000.

Area of Operation: Scheme is in operation in all rural areas. Rural areas mean areas comprised in any village and includes area comprised in any town, the population of which does not exceed 20000 or such other figure as the Central Government may specify from time to time.

Financial Assistance: Bank will sanction 90 per cent (95 per cent in case of SC/ST/WS) of the project cost as loan. KVIC will place a lump sum deposit of margin money at the head office of the bank. This will be available for adjustment by banks to the borrowers loan account after a period of two years from the date of disbursement of loan. Banks are required to furnish the quarterly progress report of adjustment of margin money directly to KVIC. The margin money should be kept in term deposit with a lock-in period of two years in the name of beneficiary. This is later to be adjusted against outstanding loan component. The interest on bank loan has to be charged on the entire bank loan.

Margin Money: Margin money (own stake) to be contributed by the borrower is 10 per cent Margin money to be contributed by SC/ST members and other weaker section borrower - 5 per cent.

Margin Money from KVIC:

- For projects up to Rs. 10 lakh 25 per cent of the project outlay will be provided by KVIC as Margin Money by way of subsidy.
- Projects above Rs. 10 lakh and up to Rs. 25 lakh- 25 per cent up to Rs. 10 lakh plus 10 per cent for the remaining cost.
- SC/ST/OBC/Women/Physically handicapped/Ex-Service men and minority community institutions and beneficiaries hailing from hill, border and tribal areas and North-Eastern Region, Sikkim, Andaman and Nikobar Islands and Lakshdweep - 30 per cent up to Rs. 10 lakh.

Choice of selection of the borrowers is left to the banks. Credit decision fully rests with the banks subject to technical viability and financial feasibility of the project. NABARD refinance is available for this scheme to the banks.

Modalities of the scheme financed through banks

1. KVIC will place a lumpsum deposit of Margin Money in advance with the designated nodal branches of PSBs in Savings Bank Account in the name of KVIC, at State/Regional Offices of KVIC. KVIC also places lumpsum Margin Money with State KVIBs.
2. Banks will ensure that each project fulfils the criteria of "Village Industries", "Per Capita Fixed Investment", "Own Contribution" and is located in "Rural Area".
3. Banks will appraise project feasibility technically as well as economically and take their own credit decision on the basis of viability of each project.
4. Banks must ensure investment of "own contribution" of the entrepreneur, individual, institution, Co-operative Society,

SHGs etc. @ 10 per cent of the total cost of the project for General category and 5 per cent in the case of the Weaker Section beneficiary/ institutions.

5. Once the Margin Money is released in favour of the loanee, it should be kept in Term Deposit for 2 years at branch level in the name of the beneficiary/institution. No interest be paid by the Bank on Term Deposit and no interest be charged for corresponding loan portion.
6. Since "Margin Money" is to be provided in the form of back-ended Subsidy (Grant), it will be credited to the borrower's loan account after 2 years from the date of first disbursement to the borrower/institution. (In case, the Bank's advance goes "bad" before the 2 year period is over, Margin Money will be adjusted by the banks to liquidate loan liability of the borrower either in part or full.)
7. In case any recovery is effected subsequently by the Bank from any source whatsoever, such recovery will be utilised by the Bank for liquidating their outstanding dues first. Any surplus will be remitted to KVIC.
8. Margin Money will be one time assistance from KVIC. For any enhancement of Credit Limit, the KVIC's Margin Money assistance will not be available.
9. More than one project by a single family under REGP is not to be permitted.

Feedback and Reporting System: The Banks will submit the Margin Money claim to the Commission every quarter certifying that the criteria laid down for availing the benefits of Rural Employment Generation Programme (REGP) have been complied with by the Banks, meticulously. The Bank will submit a State-wise Quarterly Progress Report to the Commission regarding the number of units financed under the Scheme, total limit/ credit sanctioned, funds released and Margin Money placed at their disposal, utilised.

Marketing Linkages: There are over 7050 sales outlets run by voluntary organisations/institutions/Societies/Trusts assisted by KVIC/ KVIBs. These sales outlets are part of the marketing support system for Khadi and V.I. products of institutions/ entrepreneurs assisted by KVIC/KVIBs/Banks. This Directorate has also released the funds to State/Regional Offices of KVIC to conduct the Exhibitions, Workshops and Awareness Camp etc. in support of marketing linkages. Special care has been taken for A&N Island, J&K and Goa.

Registration: Registration with KVIC/KVIBs under the scheme is mandatory. Beneficiary will have to register either with KVIC or KVIB. For registration with KVIC they will have to apply on the prescribed form and duly recommended by the concerned Financing Bank. The application should be accompanied by registration fees @ 1 per cent of the project cost by demand draft drawn in favour of Chief Executive Officer of the Commission payable at State Bank of India, Vile Parel (West) Branch, Mumbai-56. Registration is valid for three financial years. For further renewal of the registration fee @ 0.5 per cent of the project cost is to be paid to the KVIC.

REGP Training: The beneficiary should undergo EDP training at KVIC accredited training centres before release of second instalment of loan by the bank.

Negative List under Margin Money (REGP) Scheme:

- Any Industry/Business connected with Meat (Slaughtered) i.e. processing, canning and/or servicing items made of it as food, production/manufacturing or sale of intoxicant items like Beedi/Pan/Cigar/Cigarette etc., any Hotel or Dhaba or Sales outlet serving liquor, preparation/producing tobacco as raw materials, Tapping of Toddy for sale.
- Any Industry/Business connected with cultivation of crops/plantation like Tea, Coffee, Rubber etc. sericulture (cocoon rearing), activities related to Horticulture, Floriculture, Animal Husbandry like Pisciculture, Piggery, Poultry etc.
- Khadi & Polyvastra and any project producing yarn and cloth.
- Manufacturing of Polythene Carry bags of less than 20 microns thickness and manufacture of carry bags or containers made of recycled plastics for storing, carrying,

dispensing or Packaging of food stuff and any other item which causes environmental problems.

- Industries such as processing of Pashmina Wool and such other products like hand spinning and hand weaving, taking advantage of Khadi Programme under the purview of Certification Rules and availing sales rebate.

Industries under the Purview of KVIC: Village industries under the preview of KVIC are classified in seven major groups as follows:

Group I: Mineral-based Industries

1. Cottage Pottery
2. Lime stone, lime shell and other lime products
3. Stone cutting, crushing, carving and engraving for temples and buildings
4. Utility articles made out of stone
5. Slate and slate pencil making
6. Manufacture of plaster of Paris
7. Utensils washing powder
8. Fuel requiting
9. Jewellery making out of gold, silver, stone shell or synthetic materials
10. Manufacture of Gulal and Rangoli
11. Bangles manufacturing
12. Manufacture of paints, pigments, varnishes and distempers
13. Manufacture of glass toys
14. Glass decoration, cutting, designing and polishing
15. Gem Cutting

Group II: Forest-based Industries

16. Handmade paper
17. Manufacture of *Katha*
18. Manufacture of Gums and resins
19. Manufacture of shellac
20. Cottage match industry, manufacture of fire works and agarbattis
21. Bamboo and cane work
22. Manufacture of paper cups, plates, bags and other paper

containers

23. Manufacture of exercise book binding, envelop making, register making including all other stationary items made out of paper
24. *Khus tattis* and broom making
25. Collection, processing and packing of forest products
26. Photo framing
27. Manufacture of jute products (under fiber industry).

Group III: Agro-based and Food Industries

28. Processing, packing and marketing of cereals, pulses, spices, condiments, masala etc.
29. Noodle making
30. Power *atta chakki*
31. Dalia making
32. Mini rice shelling unit
33. Palm Gur making and other palm products industry
34. Manufacture of cane *gur* and *khandsari*
35. Indian sweets making
36. *Raswanti*- Sugarcane juice catering unit
37. Bee keeping
38. Fruits and vegetable processing, preservation and canning including pickles
39. Oil Ghani
40. Menthol Oil
41. Fibre, other than coir
42. Collection of forest plants and fruits for medicinal purpose
43. Processing of maize and ragi
44. Pith work, manufacturer of pith mats and garlands etc.
45. Cashew processing
46. Leaf cup making
47. Milk Products making unit
48. Cattle feed, poultry feed making

Group IV: Polymer and Chemical-based Industries

49. Flaying, curing and tanning of hides and skins and ancillary industries connected with the same and cottage leather industry

50. Cottage soap industry
51. Manufacturer of rubber goods (dipped latex products)
52. Products out of rexene PVC etc.
53. Horn and bone including ivory products
54. Candle, camphor and sealing wax making
55. manufacturer of packing items of plastic
56. Manufacture of *bindi*
57. Manufacture of *menhdi*
58. Manufacturer of essential oils
59. Manufacturer of shampoos
60. Manufacturer of hair oils
61. Detergents and washing powder making (non-toxic).

Group V: Engineering and Non-Conventional Energy

62. Carpentry
63. Blacksmithy
64. Manufacture of household aluminium utensils
65. Manufacture and use of methane (Gobar) gas from cow dung and other waste products (such as flesh of dead animals, night soil etc.)
66. Vermiculture and waste disposal
67. Manufacture of paper pins and clips, safety pins, stove pins.
68. Manufacture of decorative bulbs, bottles, glass etc.
69. Umbrella assembling
70. Solar and wind energy implements
71. Manufacture of hand made utensils out of copper
72. Manufacture of hand made utensils out of bell metal
73. Other articles made out of brass, copper and bell metal
74. Production of radios
75. Production of cassette player whether or not fitted with radio
76. Production of cassette recorder whether or not fitted with radio
77. Production of voltage stabilizer
78. Manufacture of electronic clocks and alarm time pieces
79. Carved wood and artistic furniture making
80. Tin smithy

81. Motor winding
82. Wire net making
83. Iron grill making
84. Manufacture of rural transport vehicles such as hand carts, bullock carts small boats, assembly of bicycles, cycle rickshaw, motorized carts etc.
85. Manufacture of musical instruments.

Group VI: Textile Industry (excluding Khadi)

86. Polyvastra which means any cloth woven on handloom in India from yarn handspun in India from a mixture of man made fiber yarn hand spun in India with either with cotton, silk or woollen yarn hand spun in India or with any two or all of such yarn
87. Manufacture of *Lokvastra* cloth
88. Hosiery
89. Tailoring and preparation of readymade garments
90. Batick works
91. Toys and doll making
92. Thread Balls and woollen balling, *Lachhi* making
93. Embroidery
94. Manufacture of surgical bandages
95. Stove wicks
96. Embroidery of fabrics

Group VII: Service Industry

97. Laundry
98. Barber
99. Plumbing
100. Servicing of electronic wiring and electronic domestic appliances and equipments
101. Repairs of diesel engines, pump sets etc.
102. Tire vulcanizing unit
103. Agriculture servicing for sprayers, insecticide, pump sets etc.
104. Hiring of sound system like loud speaker, amplifier, mike etc.
105. Battery charging
106. Art board painting
107. Cycle repair shops

108. Masonary
109. Band troupe
110. Motorized local boat (fiber glass)
111. Motor cycle to ply as taxi (for Goa only)
112. Musical instruments (for Goa only)
113. Dhabas (not serving liquor)
114. Tea stall
115. Iodized salt.

20

Employment Schemes for Ex-Servicemen

20.1 Self Employment Programme For Ex-Servicemen (SEMPEX)

About 60000 of our armed forces personnel retire every year in the prime of their youth. To provide self-employment to such personnel, this scheme has been promoted by the Director General (Resettlement). Assistant Director, Ex-Servicemen in the Zila Sainik Board coordinates the scheme and sponsor the applications. Ex-Servicemen, war widows of ex-servicemen and disabled service personnel registered with Zila Sainik Boards or Kshetriya Sainik Boards are eligible to apply for the assistance. Majority of service personnel at the time of retirement is at an age where they have numerous unfinished domestic responsibilities, which necessitate their taking up of a second occupation. A total of 18,01,145 Ex-Servicemen (ESM) and 3,72,179 widows have been registered as on June 30, 2003. The Government of India bears 50 per cent of the expenditure incurred on the organisations of RSBs while the remaining expenditure is borne by the respective State Governments. It is not possible to provide government jobs to all ex-servicemen after their retirement from the Armed Forces, Government has formulated several schemes for encouraging and giving financial support by way of loans to ex-Servicemen entrepreneurs intending to set up small and medium industries. Important self Employment Schemes for ex-servicemen are SEMFEX-I, SEMFEX-II and SEMFEX-III. The activities covered under the scheme include tiny, Small Scale Industries and Small Scale Service and Khadi and Village Industries.

20.1.1 SEMFEX-I Scheme: For eligibility under the scheme the age should be up to 60 years, should not have any outstanding loans, should be unemployed. A certificate to this effect that ex-service man has not taken any benefit from DGR/RSB/ZSB previously. The eligible ex-servicemen interested in the scheme should apply to the respective RSB/ZSB. Ceiling for loan is Rs.15 lakh. Rate of Interest on Soft seed assistance - 6 per cent and on Term Loan is as per directive by RBI from time to time.

20.1.2 SEMFEX–II-Scheme: SEMFEX II aims at providing credit to ex-servicemen, widows of ex-servicemen and disabled service personnel for undertaking farm, non farm and service sector activities in rural areas. The Soft Loan Assistance for Margin Money Scheme forms part of SEMFEX II. Based on the request from financing banks, it has been decided to dispense with the condition of availability of refinance from NABARD towards the term-loan component by banks under SEMFEX II involving margin money loan up to Rs. 5 lakh. As such, banks are now eligible to avail cent percent interest free refinance from NABARD under Soft Loan Assistance for Margin Money Scheme up to Rs 5 lakh without availing refinance for the term loan component of projects undertaken by borrowers under SEMFEX II. The scope of the Scheme has been enlarged to the borrowers of SRWTO scheme under SEMFEX-II also, on a very selective basis, subject to the condition that the margin money assistance shall not exceed 10 per cent of the cost of the vehicles. With due regard to the services rendered by Ex-servicemen in defending motherland, Banks may consider, at their discretion, reducing/waiving of service charges to be levied under the scheme.

There is no age limit under the scheme. The ex-servicemen should have Registration with ZSB/RSB. He should not have any outstanding loans. Partnership with non ex-servicemen is allowed subject to limitation of 25 per cent. Project should be located in rural area and in case of towns population should not exceed 10,000. A certificate to the effect that the ex-servicemen has not taken any benefit from DGR/RSB/ZSB previously duly notarised. Registration with Zila Sainik Board/Rajya Sainik Board is required for the scheme.

20.1.3 SEMFEX-III Scheme: Ex-servicemen, widows and disabled ex-servicemen are eligible to take up Khadi Village are eligible under the programme.
Industries Commission programmes. There is no age restriction except that the applicant should not be below 21 years of age. The scheme is operative in villages having population of not more than 10,000.

Financial Assistance

- 50 per cent grant and 50 per cent loan of the total estimate of the cost of construction of buildings, worksheds, godowns etc. @ Rs.180 per sq. feet is provided.
- Financial assistance for the supply of approved implements, equipment tools and
- machinery is sanctioned on the basis of 65 per cent grant and35 per cent loan.
- Financial grant is sanctioned by KVIC for meeting the salary and other incidental expenses of one technical man for a duration of five years. In the first year the grant of Rs.10,000 and then at reduced scale for next four years is provided by KVIC.
- The KVIC sanctions assistance for exhibitions, conferences, seminars and symposia etc. The expenditure on these is sanctioned as 100 per cent grant.

20.2 Scheme for Preparing Ex-Servicemen for Self-Employment (PEXSEM)

Generally ex-servicemen prefers to settle down in their own villages or rural areas than in urban areas or in any other avocation or employment away from their homes. The basic objective of PEXSEM is to impart training to retiring or retired defence personnel and ex-servicemen settled in rural areas, which may help them in getting employment as well as self-employment close to their homes in rural areas. And also to give them such technical and financial assistance to the extent possible in order to help them start a small self-employment venture. A stipend of Rs. 250 per month will be given to the beneficiaries to meet the boarding and lodging expenses travelling expenses of Rs. 100 is also provided. A training fee of Rs. 50 per month and Rs. 200 for raw material and literature is also available. In consultation with the District Industries Centre and Bank the project is prepared. Bank is required to provide need based financial assistance to the beneficiary. Banks may sanction loans up to Rs. 50,000 to the ex-servicemen trained under the PEXSEM scheme. This loan limit was raised from July 19, 1994. Earlier maximum permissible advance under PEXSEM was Rs. 25,000.

Subsidy: A subsidy to the extent of 33 per cent of the project cost with a maximum of Rs. 3,000 is available from the department. Subsidy amount has been raised to Rs. 5000 or 33 per cent whichever is less from July 19, 1994. Subsidy will be released to the bank by Zila Sainik Board at the time of disbursal of final instalment of loan to ex-servicemen. An interest subsidy is also available on the bank loan from the Kshetriya Sainik Board.

21

Other Employment Schemes

21.1 National Food for Work Programme (NFFWP)

The NFFWP was launched as a CSS in November 2004 in the 150 most backward districts to generate additional supplementary wage employment with food security. States receive food grains under NFFWP free of cost. The focus of the programme is on works relating to water conservation, drought proofing (including afforestation/tree plantation), land development, flood-control/ protection (including drainage in waterlogged areas), and rural connectivity in terms of all-weather roads. In 2004-05, allocation of Rs. 2,020 crore and 20 lakh tonnes of foodgrains generated 7.85 crore persondays of employment. In 2005-06, of the allocation of Rs. 4,500 crore and 15 lakh tonnes of food grains (Revised), Rs. 2,219 crore and 11.58 lakh metric tonnes of foodgrains had been released up to January 27, 2006. About 17.03 lakh persondays were generated up to December 2005.

21.2 Prime Minister's Rozgar Yojana for Educated Unemployed Youth (PMRY)

This programme was launched in selected places on October 2, 1993 and was extended to all areas since 1.4.1994 and SEEUY was merged with this programme. The objective was to provide employment to more than a million persons by setting up 7 lakh micro enterprises by the Educated Unemployed Youth. The loan may be considered in the form of composite loan (Term loan and working capital) not exceeding Rs. 1 lakh to each applicant. 5 per cent margin is to be contributed by the borrower. The loan amount for other than business sector was increased to Rs. 2 lakh from 01.04.1999.

Subsidy: A subsidy of 15 per cent of the loan disbursed subject to a maximum of Rs. 7,500 to each beneficiary will be provided by the Government. Subsidy is paid by the Reserve

Bank of India. Subsidy is to be kept in Fixed Deposit by the Bank. No interest is to be paid on the subsidy amount retained by the banks. Also the banks would charge no interest on the portion of loan representing subsidy. The date of the FDR will be the date of last installment of loan released by the branch as the subsidy amount is remitted in advance to the Head Office of the Bank. If PMRY loan is closed prematurely, the borrower will not be eligible for the subsidy. Similarly subsidy will not be available in case of mis-utilisation of loan, abandonment of the project by the borrower, ineligibility of the borrower due to his not complying with the criteria laid down under the scheme.

21.3 Food for Work Programme

Introduction: The problem in rural areas is of seasonal employment, unemployment and under employment. Agricultural activities in the villages can not provide regular sufficient work to the entire landless labourer. These people are to be provided work in nearby areas in agriculture and allied activities sector so as to avoid migration to other places. To provide supplementary employment opportunities this programme was started. The wages were paid in the form of foodgrains, hence the nomenclature Food for Work or Food for Employment programme was given. The foodgrains was released to the states as per their requirement.

This programme was launched in 1977.

Objectives: The objectives of the programme were as follows:

- To provide opportunities of work for the poor persons living in the rural areas especially during the periods when there is no work in agriculture.
- To utilise the stocks of foodgrains available with Central Government as a resource for meeting the additional expenditure required for the purpose.
- To create durable infrastructure assets for the villages in the form of roads, tanks etc. and maintenance of public works in the state and in local bodies.

Implementation: The following works were allowed in the

programme:

- soil conservation,
- bunding,
- flood protection,
- afforestation
- provision of drainage
- Irrigation,
- Construction of irrigation channels to the fields,
- Construction of school buildings,
- Construction of community centres etc.

This programme stamped success in rural areas by creating a large number of durable assets for the local communities. The programme was later on renamed as National Rural Employment Programme from October 1980. As a part of Employment Assurance Scheme, a new Food for Work Programme was started in January 2000-01 in eight drought affected States. The detail is given below.

New Food for Work Programme (FFWP): This is another Food for Work Programme. Earlier programme was started in 1977. As part of the Employment Assurance Scheme (EAS), this Programme was started in January, 2000-01 in following eight drought-affected States.

1. Chhattisgarh,
2. Gujarat,
3. Himachal Pradesh,
4. Madhya Pradesh,
5. Maharashtra,
6. Orissa,
7. Rajasthan and
8. Uttaranchal.

The Food for Work Programmes (FFWP) was later expanded to form a part of any wage employment scheme of the Central or State Governments being implemented in the notified districts during periods of natural calamities, such as drought, flood, cyclone or earthquake. Now the programme is in operation in the States of Andhra Pradesh, Bihar, Chhattisgarh, Gujarat, Himachal

Pradesh, Karnataka, Kerala, Madhya Pradesh, Maharashtra, Orissa and Rajasthan. For the States/Areas, which are formally notified natural calamities affected, the programme will continue up to of March 31, 2002.

Implementation: The Food for Work Programme is a general scheme, which can form a part of any wage employment scheme of the Central or State Government being implemented in the notified district of the State during the period of Natural Calamities. The cash component of the wage and material is met from the Scheme under which it is being implemented. The cost of transportation of foodgrains from FCI godowns to the worksites/PDS and its distribution is the responsibility of the State Government. Government of India makes available appropriate quantity of foodgrains to each of the affected States. Foodgrains are supplied to the States as additionality and free of cost. The cost is borne by the Government of India with a view of enabling the State Governments to provide adequate wage employment opportunities to the needy rural poor. The eligibility criteria for employment are relaxed so as to include both BPL and APL families.

The States may make payment of wages partly in kind (up to 5 kg. of foodgrains per manday) and partly in cash. The State Governments are free to calculate the cost of foodgrains paid in wages, at either BPL rates, or APL rates, or any rate between these two rates. The workers are paid the balance wages in cash, so that they are assured of the notified Minimum wages. Free foodgrains are treated as additionality to the on going schemes. For foodgrains released, Ministry of Rural Development directly makes payment to the FCI on submission of bills against the lifting of foodgrains by the States. Supply of foodgrains is made to the workmen preferably at the work site. The official supervising the work (decided by the State Government) under the Food for Work Programme, will be responsible for the distribution of food grains at the work site or through PDS. The payment of wages, cash as well as foodgrains must be made weekly. The works for the Food for Work Programme should be executed in accordance with the Guidelines of that Scheme under which they are taken up. In other words, there will be no relaxation in the product output.

Since the Food for Work Programme is meant for providing wage employment in the natural calamity affected States, preference shall be given to labour-intensive works like below. As far as possible, the works to be taken up should result into durable assets.

1. The work should be such which would help in drought-proofing such as moisture conservation works,
2. watershed development works,
3. water harvesting,
4. digging up, de-silting of village ponds/tanks and water courses and
5. construction of rural links roads (Kutcha Road) etc.

21.4 Jawahar Rozgar Yojana (JRY)

Introduction: This programme was launched on April 28, 1989 and National Rural Employment Programme and Rural Landless Employment Guarantee Programme have been merged with this programme. The programme is sponsored by the Central Government. The share of Central and State Government assistance was 80:20. Now the share of states has been restricted to 10 per cent. Road construction, irrigation and other infrastructure development is being undertaken under this scheme so as to avoid additional funds for such work.

Aims and Objectives: The programme aims at providing wage employment to at least one member of each rural poor family for 50 to 100 days in a year near to his residence.

1. Primary Objective: Primary objective of the scheme is the generation of additional gainful employment for the unemployed and the under employed in the rural areas.
2. Secondary Objectives.

- Creation of productive community assets for direct and continuing benefits to the priority groups and for strengthening rural economic and social infrastructure which lead to rapid growth of rural economy and steady rise in the income levels of the rural poor.

- Improvement in the overall quality of life in rural areas.

Target Group and Special Safeguards for Certain Sections: The JRY is targeted to benefit people living below the poverty line in rural areas. Preference, however, is given to the Scheduled Castes, the Scheduled Tribes and freed bonded labourers. At least 30 per cent of employment is to be provided to women under the Yojana. 22.5 per cent of funds have to be spent on individual beneficiary schemes for the direct benefit of SCs/STs.

Allocation Procedure: JRY is a Centrally Sponsored Scheme. The expenditure under the programme is shared between the Centre and the States in the ratio of 80:20. Central assistance is provided to the States on the basis of proportion of rural poor in a State/UT to the total rural poor in the country. From the States to the districts, the allocation is made on the index of backwardness formulated on the basis of equal weightage to the proportion of rural Scheduled Caste/Scheduled Tribes population in a district to total rural SC/ST population in the State and the inverse of per capital production of agricultural workers in that district.

Implementing Agencies: The Panchayati Raj Institutions implement JRY in a decentralised fashion. The major share of funds is utilized at the village level by the Gram Panchayats. At the district level the responsibility of co-ordination, guidance and monitoring is vested with the DRDA/Zila Parishad (ZP). Funds under JRY are distributed among DRDAs/ZPs, Intermediate Panchayats/Village Panchayats in a district in the ratio of 15:15:70. The resources allocated to DRDA/ZP, intermediate panchayats and gram panchayats are to be spent within the geographical boundaries of each unit. These funds cannot be diverted under any circumstances except where two or more intermediate level Panchayats/Gram Panchayats decide to pool the resources together to take up a work for their common benefit.

Monitoring of JRY: The performance of JRY is monitored

regularly by the Centre and the State Governments. To facilitate proper monitoring, emphasis is laid on building a strong data base and periodical feedback through monthly and annual progress reports. The physical and financial achievement under the programme is monitored at the Central level through monthly and annual progress reports received from the States. The Department of Rural Employment and Poverty Alleviation has evolved a system to ensure that the guidelines are followed strictly. The utilisation certificates, audit reports and other parameters such as matching grants from the States, minimum expenditure etc. are examined before the release of second instalment. Periodical reviews are carried out by the Central Government in the meeting of Secretaries of the State Governments. Senior officials of the Ministry also see operation of various Rural Development programmes during their visits to the States under the Area Officers Scheme. The scheme is supervised by officials of DRDA/ZP at the district level. The State Level Coordination Committee (SLCC) for the rural development programmes monitors the programmes at the State Level. State Government officials also inspect the programmes. For better monitoring and to check diversion, embezzlement and misappropriation of rural development funds including JRY, Government of India has issued instructions to all the State Governments for constitution of Vigilance and Monitoring Committees at State/District and Block level. In many States these committees have been constituted and have started functioning.

Concurrent Evaluation of JRY: The Ministry of Rural Areas and Employment undertook the concurrent evaluation of JRY. The evaluation was done from June 1993 to May 1994 covering 470 districts, 933 blocks and 4700 Village Panchayats. Findings revealed that 82.16 per cent of available funds were spent on community development projects. The construction of rural link roads received the highest priority and average wages paid per mandays of the unskilled workers were more or less on the lines of minimum wages prescribed under the Act. The wage and non-wage component of the expenditure was 52.84:47.16. By and large, payment of wages to workers was made either on a daily basis or weekly basis; muster rolls were maintained; of the total assets created, 76.11 per cent were found to be in good/satisfactory condition; the share of SCs/STs in generation of employment was satisfactory; roughly, 11 mandays of employment were created during the reference period; family members of the workers also received employment during the last 30 days preceding the date of survey and 76.96 per cent of the assets were created by village panchayat. The evaluation, however, has highlighted some inadequacies. More than 50 per cent of elected panchayat heads were not imparted training for implementation of JRY works. The share of women in employment generation was less than the prescribed 30 per cent. 49.97 per cent of the works could not be completed on account of shortage of funds. Some discrepancies were observed between payment of wages to male and female workers. The use of locally available material in various works undertaken by Panchayats was not appreciable.

Changes were brought about in the guidelines to sharpen its focus on the genuinely needy and deserving persons in tune with the social and moral commitments towards socially deprived sections of the society. In light of the outcome of the reviews of the Yojana and experience gained through time in implementing the Yojana, the following changes were introduced:

- Preference in employment under the Yojana to the parents of child labourers withdrawn from hazardous/non-hazardous occupation;
- Foodgrains to be given as a part of wages under JRY at the rate of 1 kg. per person-day at the same price fixed for the people below the poverty line under Targeted PDS. Distribution of foodgrains, however, is optional on the part of the State Governments;
- Earmarking of three per cent of the funds to create barrier free infrastructures like a pucca path or a street connecting the house of the beneficiaries or a sloped entrance in the house of the beneficiaries or in public places like Panchayat Ghar,

schools, hospitals, park etc. in favour physically handicapped persons living below poverty line in rural areas;

- Keeping of funds under JRY in separate saving bank accounts of ZP/DRDA.

JRY is implemented by the village panchayats with active participation of people. The programme, therefore, empowers the village panchayats and the people. The programme also contributes significantly in creating social and community assets and economic infrastructures at the village level. Steps are being taken to restructure and entrust the implementation of JRY entirely to the Village Panchayats. So that the panchayats have reasonable autonomy in implementation of the programme and have freedom from bureaucratic control in approval and technical scrutiny of the works and at the same time become effective in development of the basic infrastructures at the village level.

21.5 Scheme for Providing Self-Employment to Educated Unemployed Youth (SEEUY)

Introduction: This Scheme was formulated by the Government of India, Ministry of Industry, in consultation with Reserve Bank of India. This programme was started to provide financial assistance to 2.5 lakh educated unemployed youths per year in the country.

Objective of the scheme was to encourage educated unemployed youth including women to take up self employment ventures in industry and services sector.

The programme is sponsored by the Central Government.

The programme commenced on August 15, 1983.

The project operates in all the areas in the country except cities with a population of more than 10 lakh as per the 1981 census. The educated unemployed youth is the target group under the scheme.

Eligibility Criteria:

- The total family income should not be more than Rs. 10,000 per year,
- Minimum educational qualification should be X or ITI pass,

- Age should be between 18 to 35 years, and
- He/she should not be employed,
- Joint loans can also be considered under the Scheme.

Nodal Agency: District Industries Centres are assigned operational responsibility of the scheme at District level. DIC will function as a nodal agency in consultation for formulation of self-employment plan in consultation with the lead bank of the concerned area. DIC will also be responsible for implementation, monitoring and overall guidance of the State Governments. DIC will formulate location specific plans of action that would be based on realistic demand assessment for various services and projects and the number of entrepreneurs, which each particular line of production and services would be able to absorb. The concerned Small Industries Service Institute will assist the DIC in carrying out surveys, assessment of potentials and preparation of projects.

Implementation: Appropriate publicity will be given to the scheme by the DIC. Implementation of the scheme by DIC would involve identification of beneficiary, selection of specific vocations, identification of the support system required by the beneficiaries, escort services and close liaison with the banks and other local agencies concerned with industry, trade and service sector.

Identification of the Beneficiaries: Identification of the beneficiaries is to be done through the Task Force and the General Manager of the District Industries Centre is the Chairman of the task force. Task force consists of the Representatives of DIC, Lead Bank and SISI. Task force has to play a crucial role in implementation of the scheme. The entrepreneurs will apply to DIC on plain paper.

The Task force is responsible for the following:

- Motivating and selecting the beneficiaries under the scheme.
- Identifying and preparing the schemes.
- Determine the avocation and schemes for each entrepreneur.
- Recommending loans for each entrepreneur.
- Getting speedy clearances from various authorities.

Loan Amount: Loan amount for various types of ventures is as follows:

- Industrial ventures Rs. 35,000 (from 1986-87). Earlier it was Rs. 25,000 only.
- For Service ventures Rs. 25,000
- For Business ventures Rs.15000

It was decided that there is no bar on providing loan for financing any viable activity including dairy poultry etc. under the scheme as a part of business venture. It should be ensured that there is no overlap between this scheme and IRDP. It should be seen that forward and backward linkages are available for such ventures.

Where a unit require additional assistance to expand its activities, assistance for such purpose should be provided outside the scheme under normal terms and conditions.

Subsidy: 25 per cent subsidy is available under the scheme. Subsidy is to be claimed from Reserve Bank of India and is to be kept as term deposit in the bank and interest to be credited to the loan account. Subsidy is to be adjusted against last instalment due.

Margin: No margin is to be obtained from the borrower up to a loan of Rs. 25,000. The subsidy received is to be treated as margin. Above loan of Rs. 25,000 usual margin as per bank rules is to be obtained.

Security: No security or guarantee was to be obtained for the loans up to Rs. 25,000. Assets created out of loan to be hypothecated. For loans above Rs. 25,000 bank may take margin and security as per bank's usual norms.

Rate of Interest: The rate of Interest on composite loan would be as 10 per cent in backward areas and 12 per cent in other areas. Loans exceeding Rs. 25,000 for industrial ventures will attract interest as applicable as per under RBI interest rate directives, for term loans to SSI units i.e. 12.5 per cent in backward areas and 13.5 per cent in other areas.

Training: Many of the educated unemployed may have some basic knowledge about financial management, accounting, inventory management etc. and training courses will not be generally necessary except in industries sector. However for those who require some basic training and advice about selection and use of equipment, the State Governments would utilise the services of Industrial Training Institutes, polytechnics etc. to provide training to them, DIC and SISI will coordinate all training courses, wherever necessary.

Other Inputs: For trade and services sites may have to be preferentially organised from State/Municipal authorities. Those opting for industrial venture should be given preference.

Repayment: The loans are repayable in 3 to 7 years depending upon the nature and the profitability of the venture with an initial holiday of 6 to 18 months.

Recovery: The recovery of the loan will be responsibility of the banks concerned. Local Bank managers would be allowed sufficient flexibility in dealing with cases of default. In the case of bonafide default, rescheduling would be preferred.

Monitoring: District Industries Centre would monitor the scheme. The bank branches will send monthly progress report to DIC. The monthly progress report will be sent to District Advisory Committee of DICs of which District Magistrate is the Chairman. The committee will sort out problems of implementation/coordination and monitoring. Head Offices of the Banks will review the progress of the scheme on quarterly basis. Banks will verify the assets created out of the loan amount within one month of the disbursal to ensure proper end use of funds.

Evaluation: The evaluation studies have shown that

- The Task force forwarded applications without any scrutiny.
- Beneficiaries belonging to affluent sections have been selected.
- Ineligible beneficiaries have been financed in certain cases.
- Loans have been given for the purpose of extension of existing business.
- Same activity has been financed in the same area without verifying the scope of the activity in that area.
- Some of the borrowers have not purchased the assets after getting the loan.

- Representatives of the banks are not regular in attending the meetings.
- In many cases the bank was represented by a junior officer, who is not fully convergent with the appraisal technique of the proposals.
- Income generation was not sufficient due to improper location of the unit, lack of product demand, lack of infrastructure, lack of experience in the activity and the competition from the existing business in the area.
- Borrowers not traceable.
- Borrowers not completing formalities.
- Assets sold after the purchase.
- Funds utilised for other purpose.

Part VI
Subsidies for Energy and Transport Development

22

Electric Power

In India, power is in the Concurrent List of the Constitution and hence reforms in this sector have to be undertaken by the Central as well as State Governments.

22.1 Salient Features of India's Power Sector

Supply of electricity commenced in India in the 1880s with the commissioning of a small 130 KW hydroelectric plant at Darjeeling, now in West Bengal. A thermal power plant based on coal was set up in Calcutta in 1897. For the next 50 years, that is, up to Independence, the supply of electricity was confined mainly in and around urban centres, chiefly for lighting purposes. Almost all the initial ventures were due to the enterprise of private entrepreneurs.

Legal provisions to support and regulate electricity were put in place through the Indian Electricity Act (1910). Shortly after Independence, a second Act – Electricity (Supply) Act, 1948 – was formulated, paving the way for establishing Electricity Boards in the States of the Union. The State Electricity Boards (SEBs) have played the pivotal role in the rapid expansion of the country's electricity network.

The production of power was reserved for the public sector in the Industrial Policy Resolution of 1956. Since then, almost all new investment (barring those by existing Licensees) in power generation, transmission and distribution has been made in the public sector.

According to *Economic Survey, 2002-03*, electricity generation in the country which was only 5.1 billion units (KWh) in 1951 which had increased to about 515 billion units by 2001-02. Despite this achievement, the power sector has been plagued by serious shortage of supply vis-à-vis demand.

Coal, oil, gas and hydroelectric potential constitute the conventional sources for electricity generation in the country. Of these coal-based thermal power plants and in some regions, hydro-power have been the mainstay of electricity generation. Oil, natural gas and nuclear power account for a smaller proportion.

Approximately 64 percent of the coal output is consumed in power generation. The total coal reserves are assessed at 186 billion tonnes. The country also has some 5 billion tonnes of lignite deposits suitable for power generation. Electricity extracted from these fuels can therefore, meet the growing needs for over next 100 years and beyond.

While the country has large oil/gas bearing sedimentary basins, proven reserves are placed at 728 million tonnes of crude oil and 686 billion cubic metres of gas. The entry of the private sector into oil exploration is expected to establish additional reserves. Also, oil companies in the Arab countries have shown keenness to make large quantities of natural gas available through pipeline. For the present, however, power generation based on gas will be limited because of demand for hydrocarbon resources from other sectors like transportation, petrochemicals, fertilisers, etc. on the one hand and availability of cheaper coal sources on the other.

As regards hydel generation, it is assessed that exploitable potential at 60 percent load factor is 84,000 MW which could yield 442 billion units of 'firm' generation annually, and a further 150 billion units of 'infirm' seasonal electricity. Currently, hydro-electric schemes in operation account for just 14.5 per cent of the potential and those under execution for a further 7.2 per cent. Some 78 per cent of the country's hydel potential thus remains to be exploited.

The country also possesses renewable energy sources in abundance. Potential generation capacity, according to official estimates, is 126,000 MW, of which, wind-based generation – which has begun to be exploited in the southern and western regions – is estimated at 20,000 MW, small hydro potential at 10,000 MW and bio-mass energy at 17,000 MW. The largest source (79,000 MW), however, is of ocean, thermal, tidal and wave power, technologies for which are yet to be established through pilot schemes. Subject to cost-effective technologies being developed, solar energy is also available in abundance for tapping.

Although coal, oil, gas and hydro-electric potential constitute the conventional sources of electricity generation, coal-based thermal power plants and hydro-power have been the mainstay. It is assessed that 78 percent of the country's hydel potential remains as yet unexploited. Besides, wind and solar energy are also available for tapping. There is little doubt that coal-based generation will continue to be the bedrock of India's power sector for the foreseeable future. But with logistical and environment related issues coming to the fore, an integrated medium and long term fuel policy for power needs to be hammered out urgently.

Domestic and agricultural segments, power for both of which is subsidised, have shown maximum growth in the consumption in the last three decades. This has contributed to the worsening of the SEBs' financial situation. Domestic consumption is certain to remain a high-growth area whereas growth in agricultural consumption is expected to taper. Long-term projections indicate a fairly stable division of demand with the domestic and agricultural components together accounting for about 47 per cent of the total with commercial, industrial and others making up the rest. Thus, unless major power tariff reforms are carried out, the financial problems of the SEBs will continue.

Additions to installed capacity during the Eighth Plan period were originally planned at 30,538 MW, but due to the shortfall experienced in the first three years, actual likely capacity addition is now estimated at only 18,023 MW inclusive of 1,348 MW in the private sector. The main reasons for this shortfall are deficiencies in project management, problems related to external-aided projects, law and order problems and resource constraints. Due to this serious slippage in planned capacity addition, the shortage in peaking and energy at the end of the Eighth Plan are projected to be as much as 29 per cent and 15 per cent respectively. Clearly, there is an urgent need to accelerate investment in power in both the public and private sector immediately. The costs of any further delay in the clearing of power projects will inflict incalculable costs in the economy.

Transmission and distribution (T&D) losses are alarmingly high in India. As against deemed normal T&D losses of 8 to 10 per cent, in India they were in excess of 20 per cent up to 1993-94. So far as financial performance is concerned, only two of the 18 SEBs of the country are expected to reach the target of ensuring a minimum return of 3 per cent of the value of fixed assets in use as specified by the Electricity (Supply) Act, 1948. At the root of the chronic inability of SEBs to raise needed investments is the uneconomic subsidised pricing of electricity for domestic and agricultural segments. According to provisional figures, average tariff per unit (kwh) sold was 133 paise in 1994-95 as against cost per unit of 160 paise.

22.2 Power Subsidies at the Level of States

Electric power is one of the main sectors for subsidization not only in India but in the whole world. It is said that the politics of power is played with the power subsidies. Almost all the States in India are providing different kind of subsidies to various categories of consumers. This results in huge operational losses to the State Exchequer and other categories of customers are paying excess charges than the actual cost of production and distribution. Most of the State Electricity Boards are in red and various steps are being thought to bring them in black. Free electricity to farmers for irrigation is the major area of power subsidy and various State Governments are handling this in different manners. It is not possible to calculate the actual hidden cost of electricity by an individual as it includes the cost not recovered or less recovered from subsidised category.

Tamil Nadu has already committed itself to power sector reforms. Government has signed a Memorandum of Understanding with the Union Power Ministry hence it has to make the Electricity Board viable and even profitable by 2003.

The board has to ensure 100 per cent metering of all supplies, contain transmission and distribution losses and cut down on the subsidies. Government has to decide on various aspects of subsidy and reimbursement of the cost of electricity to the Board for free supply to a section of consumers.

Karnataka and Andhra Pradesh have also tried to cut electricity subsidies and increase the tariffs. As it is the rule that one sector of the economy is used to subsidize another sector, there should be no net subsidies to the power sector. The 1996 balance sheet of the Karnataka Electricity Board showed that there were no net subsidies. But there were cross- subsidies where some categories of consumers like industrial, commercial and AEH were subsidising other consumers, particularly agricultural consumers. The decisions regarding subsidies always have to take into account the necessity of helping some sections of society which is poor.

In the area of power reforms, the Karnataka State had enacted the Karnataka Electricity Reform Act (1999), and had introduced a power policy based on future privatisation of distribution. For the purpose the Karnataka Electricity Regulatory Commission (KERC) was established the in the year 2000, which immediately awarded Karnataka's first power tariff increase since 1998.

Free power scheme was started in Punjab in 1997 and the scheme was cited as the reason for the financial problems of the State. It also resulted in over exploitation of groundwater and further lowering of water table at a faster pace. State, assured the farmers to provide free electricity from August 15, 2005, and has gone back from its words after a meeting which decided that the power will not be free but bonus may be provided to some farmers who fulfils certain conditions. Again it declared free power to all the farmers in the State from September 1, 2005.

The Calcutta Electric Supply Corporation's (CESC) had fixed the average tariff for the lowest bracket of consumers at 160 paise a unit; for the middle class and the affluent class at 225 paise and 490 paise respectively; and for industrial consumers at around 460 paise.

Delhi Government has to provide Rs. 160 to Rs. 180 crore to private electricity supply company as subsidy due to taking back the electricity tariff hike, In other way the taxpayer's money is being used to subsidize their own electricity bills. The purpose for privatizing the power was that this will reduce the expenditure on total operating costs, staff; transmission, theft etc. and the electricity cost will reduce. Greater efficiency in private sector is thought to phase out subsidies.

Haryana Government is also providing subsidies to various categories of consumers. Power companies get subsidy from the government on supplying power to the agricultural sector.

The World Bank has also expressed anxiety at the enormous subsidies being given by the State government in power sector and asked it to take up fiscal reforms to bring this under control through implementation of the purchaser-provider model. The report says that the open-ended power subsidy obligation was the biggest threat to the budget. Though the government has extensive liabilities in the power sector, it has little control over them. No government agency should be allowed to escape budget discipline, which is what the power sector does now. Otherwise, the State's fiscal position will remain fragile. The bank also called for rationalisation of the classification systems. It wanted India to improve audit methodology and reporting practices of states.

22.3 Effects of Power Subsidies

1. Social costs (externalities) are paid through taxes instead of energy prices, distorting the true cost of energy.
2. Subsidies favor mature, conventional energy sources (such as fossil fuels, fission nuclear & hydro) over emerging sources like solar and wind.
3. Subsidies encourage use of polluting and environmentally risky energy sources (such as fossil fuels and nuclear energy).
4. Skewed subsidies steer even larger amounts of private investment into capital-intensive but uneconomic projects, forcing up interest rates.

5. Uneconomic energy investments make everyone pay bloated energy bills for decades to come, making industry less competitive abroad.

It has been suggested to reduce the subsidy to make permanent solution for many alternate energy resources like solar energy, bio gas, tidal wave energy, wind energy etc For all these though the initially the cost is high, the long time cost is minimal.

22.4 Poor Performance of State Electricity Boards (SEBs)

In fact, financial difficulties of the SEBs lie at the heart of the problems of the power sector. The financial position of all the State Electricity utilities has deteriorated quite rapidly in the past decade. Barring Himachal Pradesh State Electricity Board (HPSEB) and Maharashtra State Electricity Board (MSEB), all other SEBs have recorded losses (excluding subsidy booked in the accounts) between 1992-93 and 2001-02 ranging from Rs. 4 crore to Rs. 3,682 crore. A highly disturbing feature is that losses have been rapidly increasing over the decade of the 1990s.

According to the Planning Commission during the year 2001-02, the commercial loss (excluding subsidy) was of the order of Rs. 24,063 crore. Such huge losses have adversely affected operations, and the ability of the electricity utilities to reliably supply electricity to the consumers. Owing to inadequate revenues, all state utilities have defaulted in payments to central PSUs including NTPC, Power Grid Corporation, NHPC, Coal India Limited, Railways and have accumulated substantial arrears.

The main reason of the financial crises of SEBs is losses in transmission and distribution (T&D losses). T&D losses correspond to electricity produced but not paid for. T&D losses of SEBs rose from 24.8 per cent in 1997-98 to 26.5 percent in 1998-99 and further to 30.9 per cent in 1999-2000. T&D losses are caused by a variety of problems, including energy sold at low voltage, sparsely distributed loads over large rural areas, inadequate investments in the distribution system, improper billing and theft. Indiscriminate grid extension despite low load densities (as measured by demand in MW divided by the length of the T&D system) has resulted in inefficiencies.

In the ultimate analysis, the basic problem being faced by the sector is the gap between user charges and the cost of supply. Despite reform efforts, the gap between the cost of supply and average tariff has actually worsened over recent years from a level of 23 paise in 1992-93 to about 110 paise in 2001-02. Revenues dropped from 82.2 percent of costs in 1992-93 to 68.6 per cent in 2001-02 (Table 22.1). This suggests that as of yet, reforms in the functioning of SEBs have not yielded the desired results, and motivates a prime focus upon the functioning of SEBs in power reforms.

Table 22.1: Recovery of Cost through Tariff

Year	Average cost/unit (paise)	Average tariff/unit (paise)	Percent recovery of cost
1992-93	128.2	105.4	82.2
1993-94	149.1	116.7	78.3
1994-95	163.4	129.0	78.3
1995-96	179.6	139.0	77.4
1996-97	215.6	165.3	76.7
1997-98	239.7	180.3	75.2
1998-99	263.1	186.8	71.0
1999-00	305.1	207.0	67.8
2000-01	327.3	226.3	69.1
2001-02	349.9	239.9	68.6

Source: Ministry of Power

To examine the issue of outstanding dues of SEBs, an Expert Group was constituted under the Chairmanship of Shri Montek Singh Ahluwalia, the then Member (Energy), Planning Commission to recommend a one-time settlement of dues payable by State Electricity Boards (SEBs) to Central Public sector Undertakings (CPSUs) and dues from the CPSUs to the State Power Utilities. The recommendations of the Expert Group have been accepted by the Government of India. The scheme would facilitate the settlement of outstanding dues of Rs. 41,852 crore of the SEBs payable to CPSU's as on September 30, 2001 after writing off Rs. 9,610 crore.

22.5 Accelerated Power Development Reforms Program (APDRP)

In addition to the Electricity Act, the central government created the Accelerated Power Development Reforms Program (APDRP). The budgetary allocation for 2003-04 for APDRP was Rs. 3,500 crore. This offers fiscal support to State governments which undertake a reforms program which would bring down the aggregate technical and commercial (AT&C) losses from the conventional levels of around 50 per cent to a target of 15 per cent. APDRP, and other similar incentive-linked programs, are part of a new strategy of linking fiscal transfers from the centre to the States, to institutional reform programs at the State level. So far, investment projects amounting to Rs. 15,642 crore have been sanctioned under APDRP covering 466 towns in the country. An amount of Rs. 882.5 crore has been released under the incentive component to the states of Gujarat, Haryana, Maharashtra, Andhra Pradesh and Rajasthan in the first two year.

23

Petroleum Products

23.1 Petroleum Subsidies

Prior to April 2002, prices of motor spirit, high speed diesel, kerosene for public distribution system (PDS) and domestic liquified petroleum gas (LPG) were decided by the Government and administered through the Oil Coordination Committee (OCC), and there was an elaborate system of cross-subsidisation of PDS kerosene and domestic LPG through higher prices of motor spirit. The subsidies on kerosene alone reached Rs. 8,151 crore in 1999-2000 and started to decline thereafter. Similarly, subsidy on LPG increased up to 2000-01 and started to decline thereafter. The net result from cross-subsidization of products by petroleum companies, predominantly public sector companies both in the upstream and downstream sectors, constituted the so-called oil-pool surplus or deficit. These balances were carried on the books of the state-owned oil companies, and occasionally settled by Government intervention. Thus, subsidisation in the oil sector was in the nature of a quasi-fiscal operation.

By a gazette notification in November 1997, Government set a timetable for a phased transition from an administered price regime to a market-determined system with continued subsidization of PDS kerosene and LPG, but on a gradually reducing scale. Subsidies on kerosene and LPG for household use were to be phased down over time to smaller price subsidies of 33.3 per cent and 15 per cent, respectively, by end-March 2002. As part of the energy sector reforms, the prices of many petroleum products, for example, naphtha, furnace oil, low-sulphur heavy stock (LSHS), light diesel oil (LDO) and bitumen, have been liberalized since April, 1998. One important achievement was the linking of high speed diesel prices to international prices and an elimination of subsidy since September

1997 for some time. However, LPG and kerosene, consumed mainly by the domestic sector, continue to be heavily subsidized.

The phased reduction in subsidies has fallen behind schedule. In March 2002, Government decided that the subsidy on domestic LPG and PDS kerosene would be provided on a specified flat-rate basis from the Consolidated Fund from April 1, 2002. In this situation, Government reimburses the firms for the cost of the subsidy, which is carried as a line item in the budget and called the petroleum subsidy.

23.2 Rising Petroleum Prices and Subsidy Burden

The unprecedented and steep rise in the international prices of crude and petroleum products has led to an increase in the explicit subsidy bill in the Central Government's budget from Rs. 5,225 crore in 2002-03 to Rs. 6,573 crore in 2003-04. Moreover, there were reports of under-recoveries by public sector oil marketing companies leading to demand for greater subsidies.

Retail selling prices of motor spirit and high speed diesel for the consumers are calculated by taking into account:

1. Basic price at refinery level on import parity basis,
2. Freight up to depots,
3. Marketing cost and margin,
4. State-specific irrecoverable levies,
5. Excise duty,
6. Delivery charges from depot to retail pump outlet,
7. Sales tax and other local levies, and
8. Dealers' commission.

The basic selling prices of motor spirit and high speed diesel are uniform at all refinery locations throughout the country. As per the existing arrangement between the oil marketing companies and refineries, the element at (1) is revised on a fortnightly basis in line with movements in international prices. The marketing costs and margins, dealers' commission, and delivery charges within free delivery zones are also uniform. The prices at various locations vary depending upon the distance from the refinery, rate of sales tax and other local levies.

Although the oil marketing companies were granted freedom to fix retail selling prices of motor spirit and high speed diesel on a fortnightly basis, in practice, this arrangement has not appeared to have worked in quite a transparent manner. For example, there was no revision of motor spirit and high speed diesel prices between January 1, 2004 and June 16, 2004, while the prices of crude and petroleum products in international markets increased rapidly.

In order to mitigate the hardship of oil companies, Government worked out a new methodology with effect from August 1, 2004 allowing the oil marketing companies limited freedom to revise the prices of motor spirit and high speed diesel within a price band. Oil companies are permitted to adjust prices on their own within a band of 10 per cent of the mean of rolling average import-parity price including cost of freight of the previous 12 months and last quarter. When prices move beyond this band, the oil marketing companies have to approach the government to modulate the excise duty rates.

23.3 Policy Options

LPG subsidy benefits largely the higher expenditure groups in the urban areas, and may be regressive. With regard to kerosene, on a per capita basis, the urban areas receive a larger subsidy. The limited availability of subsidized kerosene in rural areas biases its use in favour of lighting rather than cooking. Moreover, the kerosene subsidy in rural areas is regressive as higher expenditure groups receive more subsidized kerosene than lower expenditure groups. Kerosene subsidy is prone to mis-utilisation with about half the subsidized kerosene supplies diverted and never reaching the intended groups. These arguments suggest that the LPG and kerosene subsidies are ineffective in serving the desired objectives. Therefore, the removal of LPG subsidy in a gradual manner, or at least a substantial reduction in the subsidy element, may be recommended. A more cautious approach may be justified in the reduction of kerosene subsidies since about a half of the rural households use kerosene primarily to light their homes.

Generally, it is assumed that clean fuels like kerosene, that are relatively environment-friendly compared to fuel wood, are not used as they are not affordable because of high prices and low purchasing power of the poor households. However, it is not affordability, but non-availability that may be restricting the use of clean fuels by poor rural households. Thus, the approach that may be sustainable in the long run for the purposes of expanding access and improving the quality of service is to create an open and competitive market with clearly defined and well-enforced rules and regulations for all participants.

Cash transfer to the poor to compensate for the reduction or elimination of subsidy does not appear to be a suitable strategy for inducing a shift toward hydrocarbons for use as cooking fuels. The urban poor and all rural households may use more wood with enhanced incomes from a modest cash transfer. An alternate approach may be to channel all sales of kerosene through the retail markets, and encourage small distributors of fuels. Coupons may be issued only to poor ration card holders with entitlement to purchase kerosene from a retailer at the subsidized price. This would discourage direct diversion of subsidized kerosene to other sectors.

To conclude, the domestic LPG and PDS kerosene subsidies seem to be ineffective in serving the desired objectives. Therefore, the domestic LPG subsidy may be gradually reduced or at least substantially restricted, while a more cautious approach should be pursued in the reduction of kerosene subsidies. About a half of the rural households use kerosene primarily to light their homes. Only state-owned oil companies have been permitted to market subsidized domestic LPG and PDS kerosene. This has stifled competition by curtailing the entry of private retailers. A market environment encouraging fair and healthy competition is the most effective way to expand the supply and availability of competitively priced kerosene and LPG.

24

Non-Conventional Energy Sources

Conventional Energy like coke, gas, wood etc. is limited on the earth. Every human being needs energy to satisfy his daily needs of food, transport etc. To solve the problem of exhausting conventional energy sources, an alternative has been found in Non Conventional Energy Sources. Major Non Conventional Energy sources are Biogas, animal Energy, Solar Energy, Hydro Power, Wind Power Generation Biomass Combustion/Cogeneration Power, Chemical Sources of Energy, Hydrogen Energy, Alternative Fuel for Surface Transportation, Tidal Energy etc. Government is providing various kind of assistance for development of non conventional energy sources. Government has started many programmes for this purpose.

24.1 National Project on Biogas Development (NPBD)

Introduction: Energy crisis is engulfing the world. The conventional sources of energy like oil, gas, good, etc. are depleting very fast. To solve this problem the use of non conventional energy resources like wind, solar and bio mass can be of great help. These resources are forever and never ending.

India is having the largest cattle population in the world with 22 crore cattle and 9.4 crore buffaloes as per recent Livestock Census spread over 5.75 lakh villages and thousands of the cities and towns. Cattle dung can be utilised as a source of energy, if dung is fermented in a closed place and gas is utilised for lighting, heating and motive power. Cattle owners are mainly using the cattle dung as firewood. In this manner, the country is deprived of good organic manure easily available with farmers. By installation of Gobar Gas plant, dung can be converted into gas, which can be used for fuel, lighting and motive power purpose and the slurry can be used as manure for various crops. One significant aspect of this programme is that the rural masses have accepted use of human night soil as feed material for the bio-gas plants in addition to other bio-degradable materials like animal dung, kitchen waste, water hyacinths etc.

National Project on Bio-gas Development was started in the year 1981-82 with a target of 4 lakh bio-gas plant during the Sixth Plan period.

Objectives: The objective of the project was to promote family type bio-gas plants which aim at providing clean and cheap source of energy in rural areas, producing enriched organic manure for supplementing the use of chemical fertilizers, improving sanitation and hygiene and removing the drudgery of women.

The objectives of the Bio Gas Plants are

- Production of methane gas by fermenting cattle dung or bio waste in a closed place and utilising the gas for the purpose of
  - lighting,
  - heating and
  - running the diesel engines and saving large amount of wood and diesel.
- Using the slurry coming out from the bio gas plants as manure in the fields and saving expenditure on costly fertilisers and encouraging organic farming by reducing/not using the chemical fertilisers.

The Ministry of Non Conventional Energy Sources was created in the year 1992 as the nodal agency of the Government of India. The programme is implemented by the State Government's and Union Territory Administrations, state corporate and registered bodies, the Khadi and Village Industries Commission and National Dairy Development Board, Anand, Gujarat.

When cattle dung alone is used in the gas plant, it may be called as Gobar Gas Plant and if any other organic material or biological waste like sugarcane baggase, cotton waste, other farm waste including cattle dung is used, it is called as Bio Gas plant.

The programme is sponsored by The Ministry of Non-Conventional Energy Sources (MNES), Government of India.

The programme is in operation all over India.

Technical Aspects of Bio Gas Plants: Gobar Gas consists of 55 per cent methane and 45 per cent carbon dioxide. For using it special type of burners and lamps are required. A special attachment is needed for using the gas in diesel engines. For deciding the capacity needed the following consumption requirements may be kept in mind.

For light	- 4.5 cft per 100 candle power lamp
For cooking	- 8 cft per day per head
For motive power	- 15 cft per hour per horse power

Approximate amount of dung available from per stable bound cattle is: Buffalo-15 kg, Cow/bullock- 10 kg and calves- 5 kg. 1.3 cft gas is produced from 1 kg of wet dung. One kg of gas is produced by the excreta of one person using the latrine. Khadi and Village Industries Boards may arrange for all the equipment required for installation.

KVIC Model Bio Gas Plant: After deciding the capacity of the plant and selection of the site, construction of the tank is started. Depending upon the capacity, a pit measuring 3 to 5 meter in depth and 2 to 4 meter in diameter is dug. Then cement concrete is spread to make the floor pucca. On this floor a round brick wall like well is constructed and plastered from inside. In the middle a partition wall is constructed up to the height of guide frame. At the height of about 60 cms from the floor of the pit, 2 slanting pipes (one inlet pipe and one outlet pipe) are fitted on both sides of the partition wall. These pipes have the opening on the ground. Thereafter a guide frame is fitted 1.25 to 1.5 meter below the upper level. Then the round wall is constructed up to 30 cm above the ground level. A central guide pipe is fitted with guide frame to guide the gas holder movements. On the sides two tanks, one for putting in the dung mixture and the other for slurry outlet are constructed on openings of the inlet and outlet pipes respectively. Opening of the inlet pipe is kept slight higher than the outlet pipe for easy outflow of slurry.

Janata Bio Gas Plant or Fixed Dome Type Bio Gas Plant: This type of plant has been designed after making few changes in KVIC Model. In the place of steel gas holder it has a permanent semi-circular dome built on digester with bricks fixed with cement, sand and mortar. The cost of such plant is less.

Working of the Bio Gas Plant: Dung and water are mixed in the ratio of 4:5 and filled up in the tank (digester). Thereafter the gas holder is put on the guide frame like cap. Thereafter anaerobic fermentation starts and gas is produced. This gas is accumulated in the gas holder. This gas pressurises the slurry in the digester tank and the level of slurry comes down.

Target Group: There is no specific target group for the scheme. Any person having the following eligibility criteria may be considered under the scheme.

Eligibility Criteria:

- Individuals/institutions are eligible for setting up of the Gobar Gas Plants for the benefit of the weaker sections.
- Applicant should have the required number of animals for the particular size of the plant for the purpose of getting sufficient amount of cattle dung.
- If the plant is for other type of bio waste, its regular availability should be ensured.
- There should be sufficient space for the plant.
- Arrangement for water, as the water is required to be mixed with the dung.

Other requirements:

1. State Government/corporate body will certify the technical feasibility of the plant.
2. The block/sponsoring agency provides technical guidance and supervision for erection of the plan.
3. Government body/corporate body arranges for fabrication of the gas holder and erection of the plant. After completion of the Plant, maintenance and service arrangements are also to be provided by them.
4. Farmers to be provided the training in maintenance and effective use of the plant by the sponsoring agency.
5. Training of the masons/technicians is also provided for construction of the plant by the Ministry of Rural Areas and

employment under TRYSEM scheme.

Financial Assistance: NABARD estimated unit cost might be considered for financial assistance.

Loan Amount: Unit cost less subsidy/margin may be provided as loan.

Margin: As the subsidy is available under the scheme, applicant need not deposit the margin money. If subsidy is not available, 15 to 25 per cent margin may be obtained.

Subsidy: To promote large scale use of the bio-gas technologies in rural India the Ministry of is providing financial subsidy and other financial support to the consumers and also to the entrepreneurs, corporate bodies and Non Government Organisations for the installation of bio-gas plants on turn-key basis with free service and maintenance warranty for the first 3 years. An additional subsidy is also provided to sanitary toilet linked bio-gas plants and use of bio-gas in diesel engines to save the diesel.

At present the subsidy for 1 to 10 cubic meter size of Biogas plant is Rs. 2,300 to Rs. 3,500 depending upon the target group. The project also provides for different types of financial incentives including central subsidy to users, turn key job fee to entrepreneurs, service charges to State Nodal Departments/ Agencies and support for training and publicity. The turnkey job fee for Private Trained Entrepreneur is Rs. 500 per Biogas plant in plain area and Rs. 700 per Biogas plant in difficult areas. There is god scope for employment of Private trained Workers for supervision of the installation of Biogas plants. It takes about 40 mandays to install a Biogas plant and other related works like feeding of plants, plumbing, fitting etc. There are fourteen manufacturers of ISI marked Biogas burners in the country. Quality Biogas lamps are also manufactured for use by the beneficiaries.

Interest Subsidy: Other than family size bio-gas plants, community, institutional and night soil based bio-gas plants are being installed for different type of applications. The scheme is [illegible] nted by the state government's nodal agencies and the non government organisations. The Indian Renewable Energy Development Agency has been providing interest subsidy for such projects.

Subsidy is provided by the Ministry of Non Conventional Energy Sources, Government of India. The Block arranges it.

Purpose of Loan: Loan is provided for the following purposes:

1. Purchase of bricks and other material
2. Purchase of steel dome, pipes, burner, lamps etc
3. Labour charges for digging of the pit and masonry work.

Coordinating Agency: Block Development Office coordinates the construction and completion of the plant. The State Governments and the implementing agencies are provided service charges linked with targets for organisational set up at different levels. Technical Back-up Units (TBUs) set up at 9 locations all over India are providing technical and training support in a decentralised manner. NABARD provides automatic refinance to banks for loans disbursed by banks for bio-gas plants.

Repayment Programme: Loan is repayable as follows:

- In 14 half yearly instalments for the plants with capacity up to 6 cubic meter.
- 10 half yearly instalments for the plants with capacity above 6 cubic meters.

The repayment period should coincide with the harvesting period. Wherever the loan has been granted to a dairy farmer, the repayment can be fixed in monthly instalments.

24.2 Solar Cookers

Up to a maximum of Rs.1.50 lakh, towards organization of promotional activities like publicity, cooking demonstrations, competitions, seminars, workshops, evaluation studies, development of improved models, etc. on solar cookers based on specific proposal received from them in the prescribed format. This support is also extended to SNAs for organizing workshops/ seminars/training programmes/business meets on solar cookers.

Support to manufacturers for taking Bureau of India Standards BIS approval: Reimbursement of BIS fee (including application and marking fee and test charges), directly by MNES on 100 per cent basis during 1st year and on 50 per cent basis during further years of 10th plan (subject to modification, if any), on submission of approval certificate and copies of necessary bills/receipts issued by BIS.

Solar Photovoltaic Programme: Financial assistance (central subsidy) is available for purchase of various solar PV systems to certain eligible categories of users. Under the PV water pumping programme a combination of soft loan and central subsidy can be availed.

Users of PV water pumping systems and intermediaries are eligible to avail a soft loan at the rate of 5 per cent/2.5 per cent per annum respectively for 90 per cent of the remaining unsubsidised part of the price of the SPV water pumping system. The loan can be repaid in maximum of 10 years in installments, beginning at the end of the first year.

24.3 Wind Power Programme

Following financial assistance is available for the Wind Power Programme:

- Fiscal and Promotional Incentives
- Concessional import duty on specified wind turbine parts
- 80 per cent accelerated depreciation in first year
- Sales tax, excise duty relief
- Loans through IREDA
- Income Tax holiday --States have introduced policies

Financial Assistance for Demonstration Projects: Land Based Demonstration Projects: 60 per cent of the cost of wind turbine equipment, maintenance spares, and erection commissioning, subject to eligibility and ceiling of Rs. 3.5 crore/MW for determination of CFA. However the ceiling in respect of all the Special Category States and Islands (excluding those that are Union Territories) would be Rs. 4 crore/MW.

Wind Hybrid Demonstration Projects: For wind hybrid projects, cost of wind turbine and control equipment, including spares and erection/commissioning subject to a ceiling of Rs. 70 lakh per 100 KW, would be provided. In addition, up to 90 per cent of the cost of laying new, or upgrading/ extension of existing lines for decentralized electrification in remote and inaccessible area such as Islands, remote and difficult areas would be provided. The cost of DG set(s) or its up-gradation and other local works would be met by the State Governments. All other costs are to be met by the State.

25

Transport

Transport is life line of any country. The development of rail, road, air and sea transport is must for socio-economic development of a country by moving goods as well as human beings from one place to another. Subsidies in transport sector are given on the basis of specified condition of the user and the utility of the goods for the public in general. Other than transport department other department also provides subsidize the transport of various kind of goods.

25.1 Air Travel

There are many airlines in our country and are offering competitive rates fir air travel. Special fares offered by Indian Airlines on Dollar tariff are Discover India fares, India Wonder fares, Youth fares and Ship crew fares. These fares are applicable for foreign nationals and Indians settled abroad.

Indian Airlines offers Special Fares for the following categories.

1. Armed forces and associated personnel discount

- Under this category, a discount of 50 per cent on economy class Indian Rupees fare is given to
- Armed Forces personnel belonging to Indian Army, Navy and Air Force
- Ex-Armed forces personnel, recipients of Bravery award
- Personnel from General Engineering Reserve Force
- War disabled officers
- War widows

2. Discounts offered on humanitarian grounds

- Blind persons
- Cancer persons

- Persons suffering from 80 per cent and above Locomotive disability
- Passengers on stretcher

3. Concessional fares are offered to

- Senior citizens
- Students
- Civilian citizens recipients of Gallantry awards
- Promotional fares are offered to Family travelling on Port Blair sector
- Return fares for Executive class passengers
- Night fares
- Excursion fares
- Visit Taj fares

25.2 Railways

Railways are major infrastructure requirement for development of any economy. The railways have to take care of the social responsibility of the countrymen. The concessions offered by Railways are innumerable keeping in view the size of the country. There are concessions in Ticket fare, freight charges etc. The railways grant concession in mail/express fares, and not in "ordinary" fares applicable on Passenger trains. Concession is granted in basic fares and all other charges like reservation fee, super fast surcharge, etc. are to be paid in full. Unless otherwise mentioned, concession is not admissible in Rajdhani/Shatabdi/Jan Shatabdi trains. Concession is granted from the booking counter at the stations/reservation offices and not in train. Concession is granted on production of prescribed documents.

Different Categories of Persons Eligible for Concession in Train Fares

1. Orthopaedically Handicapped/Paraplegic persons along with an escort travelling for any purpose.
2. Blind persons travelling alone or with an escort for any purpose.
3. Mentally retarded persons travelling with an escort for any purpose.

4. Deaf & Dumb persons (both afflictions together in the same person) travelling alone or with an escort for any purpose.
5. Cancer patients travelling alone or with an escort for treatment/periodic check-up.
6. T.B./Lupas Valgaris patients travelling alone or with an escort for treatment/periodic check-up.
7. Non-infectious Leprosy patients, for treatment/periodic check-up.
8. Heart patients travelling alone or with an escort for heart surgery.
9. Kidney patients travelling alone or with an escort for kidney transplant Operation/Dialysis.
10. Haemophilia Patients, suffering from severe & moderate form of disease, travelling alone or with an escort for treatment/periodical check-up.
11. Ostomy patients, travelling for any purpose.
12. Sr. Citizens of minimum 60 years, travelling for any purpose.
13. Recipients of President's Police Medal for Distinguished Service, after attaining the age of 60 years, travelling for any purpose.
14. Doctors, Allopathic, travelling for any purpose.
15. Shram Awardees, Industrial Workers awarded the Prime Minister's Shram Award for Productivity and Innovation-travelling for any purpose.
16. National Awardee Teachers, Teachers honoured with National Award by the President of India for exemplary service in the field of education, travelling for any purpose.
17. Either of parents accompanying the Child Recipients of National Bravery Award, travelling for any purpose.
18. War Widows - travelling for any purpose.
19. Widows of I.P.K.F. Personnel killed in action in Sri Lanka, travelling for any purpose.
20. Widows of Policemen & Paramilitary personnel killed in action against Terrorists and Extremists, travelling for any purpose.

21. Widows of defence personnel killed in action against terrorists & extremists, travelling for any purpose.
22. Widows of Martyrs of Operation Vijay in Kargil in 1999 travelling for any purpose.
23. Bonafide students.
24. Foreign students studying in India, travelling to attend camps/seminars organised by Govt. of India and also visit to places of historical & other importance during vacations.
25. Research scholars up to the age of 35 years, for journeys in connection with research work.
26. Youths attending National Integration Camps.
27. Students and non-students participating in Work Camps.
28. Unemployed youths.
29. Cadets and Marine Engineers apprentices undergoing Navigational/Engineering training for Mercantile Marine, for travel between home and training ship.
30. Bharat Scouts & Guides, for scouting duty.
31. Teachers of Primary, Secondary and Higher Secondary Schools, for educational tours
32. Kisans and Industrial Labourers, for visit to agricultural/ industrial exhibitions.
33. Kisans travelling by Govt. sponsored Special trains.
34. Delegates for attending Annual Conferences of: (i) Bharat Krishak Samaj and (ii) Sarvodaya Samaj, Wardha.
35. Delegates attending Annual Conferences of certain All India bodies of social/cultural/ educational importance
36. Nurses & Midwives, for leave and duty
37. Members of St. John Ambulance Brigade and Relief Welfare Ambulance Corps, Calcutta, for ambulance camps/ competitions.
38. Bharat Sewa Dal, Bangalore, for attending camps/meetings/rallies/trekking programmes
39. Volunteers of Service Civil International, for social service.
40. Artistes, for performance.
41. Sportsmen participating in: All India and State tournaments, National tournaments

42. Persons taking part in Mountaineering Expeditions organised by IMF
43. Press Correspondents accredited to the Headquarters of Government of India/State Governments/Union Territories/ Districts for press work.
44. Persons with income less than Rs. 400 p.m. working in unorganised sectors, for journeys up to maximum 100 Kms.(originally valid up to 31.12.2000 but extended till further orders)

Concession in Freight Charges: There are a number of concessions in freight charges depending upon the importance of that good for the economy of the country. Recently on November 29, 2005, the railways have offered 10 per cent concession on incremental loading in covered wagons for all commodities. Discretion has been provided to Zonal Railways to provide other concessions to freight customers.

25.3 Road or Surface Transport

Freight rates are also subsidized for various categories of persons and essential commodities, which vary state to state.

Part VII
Subsidies for Health and Education

26

Health and Family Welfare

26.1 Health Security in India

Health security is one of the major components of human development. Good health is not only an end product of development but also a necessary condition for economic development. Improved health contributes to economic growth by reducing production losses due to illness of workers. There is a significant relation between income growth and health.

Health care is one of the functions of the State. According to the Directive Principles of State Policy laid down in the Constitution, raising the level of nutrition, and the standard of living and the improvement of public health are among the primary duties of the State. Improvement in the health status of the population has been one of the major thrust areas for the social development programmes of the country.

The World Health Assembly held in 1977 adopted a resolution which said that the main social target in the coming decades should be the attainment by every citizen of the world of a level of health that will permit him to lead a socially and economically productive life. The Assembly had set the year 2000 as the target date for achieving the objective. Subsequently, the Conference on Primary Health Care held at Alma Ata declared that primary health care is the key to attaining this target as part of development, and in the spirit of social justice. Since then, many countries have adopted primary health care as the strategy for social security. India has also adopted primary health care as the main instrument for achieving the goal of *health for all.* A vast network of institutions at primary, secondary and tertiary levels has been established for this purpose. The provision of primary health care services constitutes one of the seven Basic Minimum Services included in the national agenda.

The primary health care infrastructure is intended to provide integrated promotive, curative and rehabilitative services to the population close to their residence. It is estimated that over 80 per cent of the health care needs of the population can be met by the primary health care infra-structure; only the rest may require referral to the secondary or tertiary health care institutions.

Nearly 30 per cent of India's population lives in urban areas. Due to the massive inflow of population to the towns and cities, the health status of urban slum dwellers is, at times, worse than that of the rural population. There has been a dearth of well planned and organised effort to provide primary health care services to the urban population within 2-3 kms of their residence and to link primary, secondary and tertiary care institutions in geographically defined areas. While an elaborate network of health services based on population norms has been established in the rural areas through group centres, primary health centres and community health centres, the services provided in these centres have, however, not been satisfactory.

The Planning Commission itself has admitted that the Primary Health Care System is facing the following problems:

- Persistent gaps in manpower and infrastructure especially at the primary health care level.
- Sub-optimal functioning of the infrastructure; poor referral services.
- Plethora of hospitals not having appropriate manpower, diagnostic and therapeutic services and drugs in government, voluntary and private sector.
- Massive inter-state and inter-district differences in performance, as assessed by health and demographic indices; availability and utilisation of services are poorest in the most needy states/districts.
- Sub-optimal inter-sectoral coordination.
- Increasing dual disease burden of communicable and non-communicable diseases because of ongoing transitions in demographic composition, lifestyle and environ-mental conditions.

- Technological advances which widen the spectrum of possible interventions.
- Increasing awareness and expectations of the population regarding health care services.
- Escalating costs of health care, ever widening gaps between what is possible and what the individual or the country can afford.
- In spite of these deficiencies, primary health care is regarded as the most appropriate strategy for attaining the goal of health for all, within a reasonable time frame.

As we have pointed out earlier, health care is also an important component of social security. Indeed medical care is widely regarded as the primary branch of social security since health is of concern to all age groups and all categories of employees. All comprehensive social security programmes, therefore, make provision for medical care. The ILO Convention No. 130 and Recommendation No. 69 contain guidelines for the provision of medical care under social security.

In this connection the following question arises: when the State is committed to a policy of health for all, and has built up, or is building up a huge health infrastructure to achieve that objective, is it necessary or desirable to set up a parallel system of health care under social security? If not, what is the role of social security in the field of health care?

Social security and public health had historically developed independently. This had led to the existence of different operational practices and models, centres of interest and pressure groups. To overcome the obstacles that might be created by vested interests, a consensus should be achieved on two fundamental principles applicable to health policy; the principle of equity and that of efficiency.

The need for equity is based on the fact that health could not be considered exclusively as an individual phenomenon, but has to be treated as a social problem.

It should be obvious that if a separate system of health care were to be established for providing medical care to the unorganised sector which covers practically the whole population except for the small number of persons in the organised sector, it will be more or less parallel to the existing system of public medical service and will amount to complete duplication. There is hardly any justification for it. Considering, however, that the public medical service has not been satisfactory, it is equally obvious that there cannot be a total reliance on that system. It has to be supplemented by other measures. This is the rationale for a variety of health insurance schemes that have come up, or are coming up. The ESI Scheme, the CGHS and the Mediclaim policies of the GIC are the most well known among the health insurance schemes.

It is evident that there is need as well as scope for extension of health insurance both for raising additional finances necessary to increase access to medical services and for enhancing quality. The need is for optimal utilisation of private and public resources and facilities. Although the 1983 National Health Policy reform encouraged health insurance services, there has been only a limited extension of such insurance through GIC-sponsored schemes since that time.

The available evidence is not clear on the health insurance priorities for workers in the unorganised sector. Most of them are more interested in ensuring the provision of primary, and some secondary health services, than to insure themselves against much less frequently occurring hospitalisation costs.

If workers prefer to contribute to primary and some secondary health services, one could use the new concept of managing and financing of health care, particularly in rural areas. Under the Community Health Centres (CHC) scheme, the provision and financing of health care will be undertaken by communities characterised by strong social bonds and mutual trust. The CHC would provide preventive services, immunisation, health promotion, family planning, maternal and childcare, and outpatient services to all its members, including drugs, for which a co-payment (part-payment) would be levied. Each community of about 1,000 people would have a health post serviced by one health worker paid by CHC, and a stock of generic drugs specified in the WHO essential drug list.

The CHC would also establish a primary health centre for a population of about 15,000 people, staffed by a doctor, a mid-wife, a clinical nurse, a primary care practitioner, a pharmacist, and an assistant. These centres would refer patients to the regional centres for tertiary care, possibly on the basis of a packaged foreign exchange or a capitation payment. Patients have the choice of obtaining free health services at the health posts and primary health centres or from private practitioners. When the service is obtained from a private practitioner, the CHC will only reimburse the patient 50 per cent of its costs.

This new organization would mean a significant improvement over services currently provided by the government, which finances one sub-centre for a minimum of only 5,000 people and one primary health centre for 30,000 people. If the preference of workers is for insurance to counter the cost of hospitalisation, then it may be advisable to follow the model developed by SEWA. It appears from their experience that the extension of worthwhile health coverage should be possible at affordable premium levels. In SEWA'S reckoning a satisfaction level of 50 per cent could be achieved towards reimbursement of a member's health expenses against a small annual premium of Rs. 15.

Thus, while basic health security has to be provided by the primary health care infrastructure, it may be supplemented by one or more of the various options indicated above. Considering the size and diversity of the population in India no one model would be adequate. It may be necessary to have a combination of schemes. As most of these schemes will be voluntary, development of such schemes may be left to the initiative of the people to form groups and to organise them according to their felt needs. Health insurance scheme of the ESI has an important role to play in supplementing the public medical service. It is, therefore, necessary to take all possible measures to improve its working and its expansion.

The expenditure on health comprises 5.2 per cent of GDP with public health investment at 0.9 per cent. Improvement in the health status of the population is a major thrust area under the social development programmes being undertaken in the country. This is sought to the achieved through improvement in the access to and utilization of health services in the country with special focus on under served and under privileged segments of the population. India has built up a vast health infrastructure and manpower at primary, secondary and tertiary care in government, voluntary and private sectors. Technological advances and improvement in access to health care technologies have resulted in a substantial improvement in health indices of the population and a steep decline in mortality. However, the extent of access to and utilization of health care has varied substantially between States, districts and different segments of society.

During the 1990s, the country has entered an era of dual disease burden. While communicable diseases have become more difficult to combat due to insecticide resistance among vectors, resistance to antibiotics in many bacteria and emergence of new diseases such as HIV increasing longevity and the changes in life style have resulted in the increasing prevalence of non-communicable diseases.

The Department of Health has formulated the National Health Policy (NHP), 2002 which was approved by the Cabinet in 2002. The National Health Policy, 2002 aims at achieving an acceptable standard of good health amongst the general population of the country and has set the goals for the next two decades.

Areas of attention in the Tenth Plan include the reorganization and restructuring of existing health care infrastructure at primary, secondary and tertiary levels so that they have the capacity to render health care services to the population residing in well defined geographical areas and have appropriate referral linkages with each other. Appropriate delegation of powers to Panchayati Raj institutions to ensure local accountability of public health care providers, horizontal integration of all aspects of the current vertical disease control programme, including supp-lies monitoring, IEC, training and administrative arrangements, development of appropriate two-way referral system utilizing information technology, exploring alternative systems of health care financing, and defining the role of various stakeholders – government, private and voluntary sectors – are the other focus areas.

The Plan outlay for the Central Health Sector Schemes during 2002-03 is Rs. 1550 crore which is an increase of 6.9 per cent over the outlay of Rs. 1450 crore made available in 2001-02. About 55 percent of the Central Plan outlay is spent on Centrally Sponsored Disease Control Programmes for the control of Malaria, Tuberculosis, Leprosy, AIDS, Blindness, etc.

26.2 Panchayati Raj Institutions and Health and Family Welfare Programmes

Panchayati Raj Institutions have been assigned several development activities including health and population stabilization. The National Population Policy 2000 and the National Health Policy, 2001, include decentralization and convergence of service delivery at village levels and recognize the Panchayati Raj Institutions as the agency responsible to ensure this. Now the Panchayati Raj Institutions coordinate the activities of the works of different departments such as: Health and Family Welfare, Social Welfare, and Education which are functioning at the Village and Block Levels".

26.3 National Rural Health Mission

Panchayats are seen as critical to the planning, implementation, and monitoring of the NRHM. Implementation of the NRHM in achieving its outcomes is significantly dependent on well functioning gram, block and district level panchayats.

The Mission was launched on April 12, 2005. It is proposed that more than 200,000 Associated Social Health Activists (ASHA) will be fully functional and over 1,000 block level community health centres will provide round the clock services in 2006-07. The allocation for NRHM has been increased from

Rs. 6,553 crore to Rs. 8,207 crore for the year 2006-07. The National Rural Health Mission (NRHM) is seen as a vehicle to ensure that preventive and promotive interventions reach the vulnerable and marginalized through expanding outreach and linking with local governance institutions.

26.4 Accredited Social Health Activist (ASHA)

ASHA is the mechanism to strengthen village level service delivery, will be a local resident and selected by the Gram Panchayat or the Village Health Committee. She will be supported in her work by the AWW, school teacher, community based organizations, such as SHGs, and the VHC. Her role would be to facilitate care seeking and serve as a depot holder for a package of basic medicines. She will be reimbursed by the panchayat on a performance based remuneration plan. The Village Health Committee (VHC) will form the link between the Gram Panchayat and the community, and will ensure that the health plan is in harmony with the overall local plan.

26.5 Drinking Water and Sanitation

The target for the current year for drinking water supply will be completed, and 56,270 habitations and 140,000 schools will be covered in the year 2006-07. Apart from non-coverage, there is the persistent problem of slippage. The strategy to tackle both includes conservation, better operational management, and water quality monitoring and capacity building at the village level. The Government will provide non-recurring assistance of Rs. 213 crore in 2006-07 for setting up district-level water testing laboratories and field-level water testing kits. I propose to increase the provision for the Rajiv Gandhi National Drinking Water Mission from Rs. 3,645 crore to Rs. 4,680 crore next year. The provision for the Rural Sanitation Campaign has been increased from Rs. 630 crore to Rs. 720 crore in 2006-07.

26.6 Elimination of Leprosy

The WHO standard defining 'elimination of leprosy' is one case per 10,000 populations. The goal of eliminating leprosy was reached in December, 2005. Continuing the vigorous immunization programme, it is we hoped that polio too will be eliminated from the country by December, 2007.

26.7 Integrated Child Development Services

The Integrated Child Development Services (ICDS) scheme has been extended and an additional 188,168 centres have been created. Supplementary nutrition is the most important component of the scheme. Beginning the year 2005-06, the Centre is assisting the States to the extent of 50 per cent of the actual expenditure incurred for supplementary nutrition or 50 per cent of the cost norms, whichever is less. The cost to the Centre this year is estimated at Rs. 1,500 crore, and this assistance is being increased to Rs. 1,700 crore for 2006-07. The total allocation for ICDS is being increased from Rs. 3,315 crore to Rs. 4,087 crore.

26.8 Special Health Schemes

Following Special Health Schemes are under operation for the benefit of the public.

26.8.1 All India Hospital Post Partum Programme: As per decision of the Planning Commission, the Post Partum Programme having an infrastructure of 550 District Level Post Partum Centres and 1012 Sub District Level Centres have been transferred to States/UTs Governments w.e.f. the year 2002-2003. Therefore, no budget provision has been made for the Tenth Five Year Plan.

26.8.2 Urban Family Welfare Centres: The scheme was launched during the first Five year Plan and subsequently expanded and established in a phased manner. At present there are 1083 centres functioning in various States under the scheme to provide outreach services, primary health care, MCH and distribution of contraceptives. There are three types i.e. I.II. III of these centres depending on the population covered by these centres i.e. Type I covers a population of 10000 to 25000, Type II covers 25000 to 50000 and Type III covers more than 50000 population. These are manned by 2 para-medical staff in Type I and II Centres and by 6 persons including Medical Officer in Type III Centres. The financial assistance under this component is given for the salary of staff, contingency and rent as per approved norms

26.8.3 Urban Revamping Scheme: This Scheme was introduced following the recommendation of the Krishnan Committee in 1983. The main focus was to provide services through setting up of Health Posts mainly in slum areas. The services provided are mainly outreach of RCH services, preventive services, First Aid and referral services including distribution of contraceptives. Four types of health posts were set up depending on the allotted population in the catchment's area of the Centre covered. For Type A, the criterion is less than 5000 population. For Type B it varies between 5-10 thousands whereas for Type C it is 10-20 thousands. For Type D the limit is 25-50 thousands population. Only Type D Health Posts have a post of Medical officer

26.8.4 Sterilization Beds Scheme: A Scheme for reservation of Sterilization beds in Hospitals run by Government, Local Bodies and Voluntary Organisations was introduced as early as in the year 1964 in order to provide immediate facilities for tubectomy operations in hospitals where such cases could not be admitted due to lack of beds etc. But later with the introduction of the Post Partum Programme some of the beds were transferred to Post Partum Programme and thereafter the beds were only sanctioned to hospitals run by Local Bodies and Voluntary Organisations.

As on date, Govt. of India is supporting 3299 sterilization beds throughout the country. Out of this 2769 beds are with NGOs, 458 beds with Local bodies 60 beds only with the State Governments and 12 beds with Autonomous Institutions.. At present 301 voluntary Organisations are participating in the scheme. The grant for maintenance of the sterilization beds has been raised from Rs. 4,500 to Rs. 6,000 per bed per annum with effect from 07.02.2001 for the institution/Local bodies/voluntary organizations participating under the scheme subject to the condition that a minimum of 60 tubectomies per bed per annum are achieved.

If the Local body/ Voluntary organization fails to achieve the above mentioned target but achieves a level of 45 tubectomies per bed per annum, the maintenance grant @ Rs. 4,000 per bed per annum is admissible. If the performance of an institution is below the target level of 45 tubectomies per bed per annum, proportionate grant at the norm of 45 tubectomies per bed per annum and at the rate of Rs. 4,000 per bed per annum would be admissible. In order to claim the grant under the scheme, it is mandatory for the Voluntary Organisation/Local body to maintain physically the bed sanctioned to it under the scheme.

26.9 Central Government Health Scheme

The Central Government Health Scheme provides free medical treatment to the following categories of people and their family members residing in CGHS covered cities:

1. All Central Govt. Servants paid from Civil Estimates (other than those employed in Railway Services and those employed under Delhi Administration except members of Delhi Police Force).
2. Pensioners drawing pension from Civil Estimates and their family members: (Pensioner residing in non- CGHS areas also may obtain CGHS Card from nearest CGHS covered City)
3. Hon'ble Members of Parliament
4. Hon'ble Judges of Supreme Court of India
5. Ex- Members of Parliament
6. Employees & Pensioners of Autonomous Bodies covered under CGHS (Delhi)
7. Ex- Governors and Ex-Vice Presidents
8. Former Prime Ministers
9. Former Judges of Hon'ble Supreme Court of India and Hon'ble High Courts
10. Freedom Fighters

CGHS provides service through Allopathic, Homeopathic, and Indian System of Medicines e.g. Ayurveda, Unani, Yoga and Sidha System

27

Education and Training

27.1 Education in India: An Introduction

Education is a critical input for investment in human capital. As against the goal of 6 percent of GDP, the total expenditure on education in India is currently 3.99 percent of GDP (2001-02). Plan expenditure on education has also increased rapidly since the First Five Year Plan. A high priority has been accorded to this sector in the Tenth Five Year Plan, with an allocation of Rs. 43,825 crore as against Rs. 24,908 crore made available in the Ninth Plan, representing an increase of 76 percent. During the Tenth Plan Rs. 28,750 crore has been allocated for Elementary Education.

The total Central Plan allocation for education has been enhanced from by 18.7 percent from Rs. 5,920 crore in 2001-02 (BE) to Rs. 7,025 crore in 2002-03 (BE). Out of this, Elementary Education has received the highest priority with the allocation increasing from Rs. 3,800 crore in 2001-02 to Rs. 4,302.30 crore (excluding Rs. 364.70 crore earmarked for North East region) has been provided in 2002-03 (BE) as against Rs. 200 crore made available the previous year. Rs. 2,125 crore have been allotted for secondary and Higher Education against Rs. 1,920 crore in 2001-02.

To enlist the support of all concerned and to mobilize extra budgetary resources for the education sector, Bharat Shiksha Kosh, a registered society has been set up for receiving contributions, donations or endowments from individuals, Central and State governments, NRIs and PIOs for various educational purposes.

The Constitutional (93rd Amendment) Bill has been passed by both Houses of Parliament and has received the President's Assent on December 12, 2002. This is a significant measure for achieving the goal of Education for All (EFA) by making free and compulsory elementary education a fundamental right for all children in the age group of 6-14 years. In order to fulfil this constitutional obligation, Sarva Shiksha Abhiyan has been launched in partnership with the States. The programme is an effort towards recognition of the need for improving the performance of the school system through a community owned approach and ensuring quality elementary education in a mission mode to all children in the age group of 6-14 years by 2010. It also seeks to bridge gender and social gaps. This programme will subsume all existing programmes (except *Mahila Samakhya* and Mid-day Meal Schemes) including externally aided programmes in due course with its overall framework with district as the unit of programmes implementation. For Annual Plan 2002-03, Rs. 1485 crore has been provided for the programme.

Over the decades, literacy rates have shown a substantial improvement. The total literacy rate which was only 18.33 per cent in 1951, rose to 52.21 per cent in 1991 and further increased to 65.4 per cent in 2001. According to the Census of India, 2001, the literacy rate has gone up to 75.85 per cent for males and 54.16 percent for females. During the last decade, female literacy rate has shown much higher growth, increasing by 14.87 percentage points as against 11.72 for males thus reducing the male-female differential in literacy rates from 24.84 in 1991 to 21.7 in 2001 (Table 27.1).

Table 27.1: Literacy Rates in India (1951– 2001)

Census Year	Persons	Males	Females	Male-Female gap in literacy rate
1951	18.33	27.16	8.66	18.30
1961	28.30	40.40	15.35	25.05
1971	34.45	45.96	21.97	23.98
1981	43.57	56.38	29.76	26.62
1991	52.21	64.13	39.29	24.84
2001	65.38	75.85	54.16	21.70

Source: Census of India.

The number of primary schools decreased from 642,000 in 1999-2000 to 638,738 in 2000-01. The number of upper primary schools increased from 198,000 in 1999-2000 to 206,269 in 2000-01. The ratio of upper primary schools to primary schools was 1:3.2 in 1999-2000 as against 1:3 in 2000-01. The total enrolment at the primary and upper primary school levels in India witnessed a steady increase. During 1999-2000 and 2000-01, the growth rate of enrolment for girls at the elementary levels was higher as compared to that for boys. Participation of girls at all levels of school education has improved appreciably over the years.

The Gross Enrolment Ratio (GER) at primary and upper primary levels improved perceptibly in 2000-01 over the previous year.

Out of the estimated population of 193 million in the age group of 6–14 years in 2000-01, nearly 81 per cent attended school. In 1999-00, nearly 79 per cent in the age group attended schools. The student retention rate at the primary school stage was about 58 per cent (1991-96). Drop-out rates at the primary and upper primary level have decreased over the years. At the primary level, the drop-out rate increased from 40.3 per cent in 1999-2000 to 40.7 per cent in 2000-01. At the upper primary level, the drop-out rate decreased marginally from 54.5 per cent in 1999-2000 to 53.7 per cent in 2000-01. Though drop-out rates at the elementary education stage have declined over the years, they are still relatively high especially in the case of girl students for whom the rates are 41.9 per cent and 57.7 per cent at the primary and upper primary stages respectively in 2000-01.

In absolute terms, the number of teachers registered at the elementary level was 3.2 million in 2000-01. The percentage share of female teachers to total teachers was 36.7 per cent in 2000-01. Despite the fact that the number of teachers has increased over the years, Pupil-Teacher Ratio (PTR) at the primary education level worsened to 43:1 in 2000-01, although that at the Upper Primary level increased to 38:1 in 2000-01.

Within the education sector, elementary education has been given the highest priority in terms of sub-sectoral allocations and a number of schemes launched by the Central Government to meet the needs of the educationally disadvantaged, viz.

- Operation Blackboard,
- District Primary Education Programme,
- Education Guarantee Scheme
- Alternative and Innovative Education,
- Mahila Samakhya,
- National Programmes of Nutritional Support to Primary Education,
- Lok Jumbish,
- Shiksh Karmi Project,
- Janashala Programme and
- Pradhan Mantri Gramodaya Yojana

Secondary Education sector prepares students in the age group of 14-18 years for entry into higher education as well as for the world of work. The number of secondary and senior secondary schools increased from 1,16,000 in 1999-2000 to 1,21,951 as on September 30, 2002, with a student enrolment of 28.8 million. The Kendriya Vidyalaya Sangathan manages 849 Kendriya Vidyalaya (as on December 31, 2001). The Navodaya Vidyalaya Samiti, through more than 451 institutions in predominantly rural areas, has taken up activities for extension of infrastructural facilities, introduction of vocational courses, training of teachers etc.

Technical and professional education in the country has played a significant role in economic and technical development by producing quality manpower. There are at present 1,203 approved engineering colleges at the degree and 1,195 colleges at the diploma level. Apart from this, 1,006 institutes impart courses on Master of Computer Application (MCA).

There are 930 approved Management Institutes imparting MBA courses. From the current academic year, All India Council for Technical Education (AICTE) has delegated the powers of approval of Diploma level technical institutes to the State Governments. Strong linkages have developed between technical institutions and the industry. For strengthening technical education and improving the quality of polytechnic pass outs, various steps have been taken through Technical Education Development programmes.

The National Literacy Mission (NLM) seeks to achieve full literacy i.e. a sustainable threshold level of 75 per cent literacy by 2005. The Total Literacy Campaign (TLC) has been the principal strategy of National Literacy Mission for eradication of illiteracy in the target group. These campaigns are area-specific, time-bound, volunteer-based, cost effective and outcome-oriented. They are implemented by Zila Saksharata Samities and district level literacy societies.

27.2 Selected Programmes at Elementary Education Stage

27.2.1 District Primary Education Programme: Launched in 1994 in 42 districts, this is a Centrally Sponsored scheme aiming at providing access to primary education for all children, reducing primary dropout rates to less than 10 percent, increasing learning achievement of primary school students by at least 25 per cent and reducing gender and social groups to less than 5 per cent. During 2001-02 the programme has been further expanded to 23 districts bringing the total coverage to 271 districts spread over 18 States. Rs. 1,330 crore have been allocated for 2002-03 as against Rs. 1,100 crore for 2001-02.

27.2.2 National Programme of Nutritional Support to Primary Education: Launched on August 15, 1995 with the objective to boost the Universalisation of Primary Education by impacting upon enrolment, attendance, retention and nutritional needs of children studying in class I–V. Under this programme more than 10 crore children are being targeted for coverage. At present, Gujarat, Kerala, Tamil Nadu, Madhya Pradesh, Chattisgarh, Orissa, Karnataka and Delhi are providing cooked meals. The remaining States and UTs are distributing foodgrains (wheat/rice). The Plan allocation for 2002-03 is Rs. 1,057 crore as against Rs. 930 crore in 2001-02.

27.2.3 Jumbish: This project started in 1992 and has completed in two phases up to June 1999. This programme is being implemented in Rajasthan and has shown a positive impact of micro-planning and school mapping process through community support. Year 2001-02 is the 3rd year of phase III of the project. The project is spread over 13 districts of the State, covering 101 blocks. Rs. 60 crore have been provided in the Annual Plan 2002-03.

27.2.4 Pradhan Mantri Gramodaya Yojana: This programme was launched during 2000-01 and envisages Additional Central Assistance for basic minimum services in certain priority areas. The scheme has six components covering elementary education, primary health, rural shelter, rural drinking water, nutrition and rural electrification. A minimum of 10 percent of ACA for all components except nutrition (for which it is 15 per cent) has been fixed. The allocation for the remaining 35 per cent of ACA would be decided by the States and UTs among the components of the Scheme, as per their priorities. Funds for elementary education sector under PMGY are utilized to further the goal of Universalisation of Elementary Education. During 2000-01, Rs. 398.06 crore was released by Department of Expenditure to States. For 2001-02, Rs. 486.16 crore has been provided out of which Rs. 271.41 crore has so far been released.

Keeping pace with its endeavours, campaigns and programmes, the NLM has strengthened and revitalized the States Literacy Missions. State Literacy Missions have been imparted greater autonomy. They now have the authority to plan, implement and monitor literacy programmes and sanction continuing education programmes at the State level. The NLM has also come to recognize the great potential that NGOs have in furthering its programmes and schemes. Given the major role, NGOs are now allowed to receive funds from *Zila Sakshara Samities* and actually run continuing education centres. The *Jan Shikshan Sansthans* have expanded their outreach and are also catering to the rural segment by offering around 225 vocational training courses.

Out of 600 districts in the country 587 have since been covered under Adult Education Programmes. At present 174 districts are in progress under Total Literacy Campaigns, 212 under Post Literacy Programmes and 201 under Continuing Education Programme. About 96.69 million persons have been made literate as on 31.3.2002. Out of the total clientele group under different Adult Education Schemes, about 60 percent of the beneficiaries are women, while 22 per cent and 12 per cent belong to scheduled castes and scheduled tribes respectively. Besides, 108 Jan Shikshan Sansthans and 25 State Resource Centres are functioning. The Directorate of Adult Education is functioning as National Resource Centre.

In education, the elementary sector is besieged by numerous systemic problems such as inadequate school infrastructure, presence of single-teacher schools, high teacher absenteeism (specially in rural areas), large-scale teacher vacancies, inadequate equipment, etc. This brings into focus the role of decentralization and people's participation in the provision of basic services. It is essential that control over schools and teachers should be transferred to local bodies, having a direct interest in teacher performance. This has also been highlighted as an area of emphasis in the Tenth Plan.

The National Policy on Education (NPE), 1986, as modified in 1992, emphasizes three aspects in relation to elementary education:

- universal access and enrolment,
- universal retention of children up to 14 years of age, and
- a substantial improvement in the quality of education to enable all children to achieve essential levels of learning.

NPE emphasises that education must play a positive and interventionist role in correcting social and regional imbalance, empowering women, and in securing a rightful place for the disadvantaged and the minorities. Government is firmly committed to providing education for all, the priority areas being free and compulsory elementary education, covering children with special needs, eradication of illiteracy, education for women's equality, and special focus on the education of SCs/STs and Minorities.

NPE 1986 had set a goal of expenditure on education of 6 per cent of the GDP. As against this target, the combined total expenditure on education by Central and State Governments was 3.49 per cent of GDP in 2004-05(BE). Central Plan Allocation for education was increased from Rs. 8,225 crore in 2004-05 (BE) to Rs. 15,244 crore in 2005-06 (BE), with Rs. 12,242 crore for elementary education, Rs. 290 crore for adult education and Rs. 2,712 crore for secondary and higher education.

27.2.5 Elementary Education: Allocation for elementary education in the Tenth Five Year Plan period (2002-07) at Rs. 28,750 crore is 75 per cent higher than the allocation in the Ninth Plan. Resources for elementary education have been augmented through imposition of the education cess at the rate of 2 per cent on direct and indirect Central taxes imposed through Finance (No.2) Act, 2004. With the imposition of the education cess, budgeted outlay for elementary and adult education more than doubled from Rs. 6,000 crore in 2004-05 to Rs. 12,532 crore in 2005-06.

Gross enrolment ratio (GER) indicates the proportion of children in the 6-14 years age group actually enrolled in elementary schools. It has increased progressively from 32.1 in 1950-51 to 84.91 in 2003-04. With the rate of increase in GER of girls higher than that of boys, the gender gap in enrolment is declining. Drop-out rate at the primary level (Classes I-V) declined from 39.0 per cent in 2001-02 to 31.4 per cent in 2003-04. As on October 2005, number of out-of-school children, as reported by States/UTs, was down to 95 lakh from 320 lakh in 2001.

27.2.6 Sarva Shiksha Abhiyan (SSA): The main vehicle for providing elementary education to all children is the ongoing comprehensive programme called Sarva Siksha Abhiyan (SSA) launched in 2001-02. The goals of SSA are:

- All children in School, Education Guarantee Centre, Alternate School, Back-to-School camp by 2005;
- Bridge all gender and social category gaps at the primary stage by 2007 and at elementary education level by 2010;

- Universal retention by 2010; and
- Focus on elementary education of satisfactory quality with emphasis on education for life.

SSA, implemented in partnership with the States, addresses the needs of 209 million children in the age group of 6-14 years. It covers 9.72 lakh existing primary and upper primary schools and 36.95 lakh teachers.

National Programme for Education of Girls at Elementary Level (NPEGEL) is an important component of SSA. NPEGEL provides additional support by way of girl-child friendly schools, stationery, uniforms, etc. for girls' education in educationally backward blocks (EBB), and in other areas for elementary education of under privileged and disadvantaged sections. EBBs are blocks with female literacy below, and gender gap above, the national average. Apart from EBBs, NPEGEL is also implemented in blocks of districts which are not covered under EBBs but have at least 5 per cent SC/ST population and where SC/ST female literacy is below 10 per cent, and also in select urban slums. In the Tenth Five Year Plan, an amount of Rs.1064.80 crore has been earmarked for this programme.

Another important component of SSA is the Education Guarantee Scheme and Alternative and Innovative Education (EGS&AIE). EGS&AIE is specially designed to provide access to elementary education to children in school-less habitations and out-of-school children. It supports flexible strategies for out-of-school children through bridge courses, residential camps, drop-in centres, summer camps, remedial coaching, etc., and helped to provide elementary education to 85.67 lakh children in 2004-05.

27.2.7 Mid-Day Meal Scheme: The Centrally-sponsored Mid-Day Meal Scheme was revised and universalized at primary level with effect from September, 2004 to make a provision for providing cooked meals to children studying in Government, Government-aided, and local body schools and EGS&AIE centres. Besides providing foodgrains free of cost to the States/UTs, and foodgrains transportation subsidy, the Central Government provides assistance for converting foodgrains into cooked meal at a rate of Re. 1 per child per day. The programme now covers nearly 12 crore children studying in over 9 lakh primary schools and EGS&AIE Centres. Budget provision for this scheme, which is the world's largest school feeding programme involving preparation of a hot meal everyday, for 2005-06 is Rs. 3345.26 crore.

27.2.8 Kasturba Gandhi Balika Vidyalaya (KGBV): The KGBV scheme was launched in August, 2004 to set up 750 residential schools at elementary level for girls belonging predominantly to the SC, ST, OBC and minorities, in EBBs. All 750 KGBVs have now been sanctioned by the Government of India, with 117 KGBVs (15.6 per cent) allocated to blocks with substantial minority population. Budget provision for the scheme for 2005-06 is Rs. 250 crore.

27.2.9 Prarambhik Shiksha Kosh (PSK): Department of Elementary Education and Literacy issued orders on November 14, 2005 constituting Prarambhik Shiksha Kosh (PSK) to receive the proceeds of the education cess imposed through Finance (No.2) Act, 2004. PSK is a separate, dedicated, non-lapsable fund to be maintained by the Ministry of Human Resource Development.

27.2.10 Adult education: Literacy rates in India have risen sharply from 18.3 per cent in 1951 to 64.8 per cent in 2001. Nevertheless, India continues to lag behind several other developing countries in the region such as China (86 per cent) and Sri Lanka (92 per cent). The National Literacy Mission (NLM) was launched on May 5, 1988 as a Technology Mission to impart functional literacy to non-literates in the country in the age group of 15-35 years in a time-bound manner. This age-group has been the focus of attention because they are in the productive and reproductive period of life. The NPE,1986, as modified in 1992, recognizes the NLM as one of the three instruments to eradicate illiteracy from the country, the other two being SSA and non-formal education.

NLM's objective is to attain a sustainable threshold literacy rate of 75 per cent by 2007. The Total Literacy Campaign (TLC) has been the principal strategy of National Literacy Mission for eradication of illiteracy in the target age-group. These campaigns implemented by Zilla Saksharata Samities (District Level Literacy Societies) are area-specific, time-bound, volunteer-based, cost effective and outcome-oriented.

At present, 137 districts are implementing TLCs, 165 districts Post Literacy Programmes and 295 districts Continuing Education Programmes. In addition, 157 Jan Shikshan Sansthan have been set up to provide vocational training to the neo-literates and backward sections of the society, and 25 State Resource Centres established for providing academic and technical resource support for the literacy programmes.

NLM has accorded priority for the promotion of female literacy. According to 2001 Census, 47 districts in the country have female literacy rate below 30 percent. Most of these districts are concentrated in Bihar, Jharkhand, Uttar Pradesh and Orissa. Special innovative projects have been taken up to raise the level of female literacy in these areas. Special efforts have been made to target female Panchayati Raj functionaries and make them literate.

27.2.11 Secondary and Higher Education: Secondary education prepares students in the age group of 14-18 years for entry into higher education and employment. The number of secondary and senior secondary schools increased from 1,07,140 in 1997-98 to 1,45,899 in 2003-04 with a total student enrolment of 35.01 million (Classes IX to XII). There has been an impressive growth in the area of higher education with an increase in annual student enrolment from 7.26 million in 1997-98 to 9.95 million in 2003-04. Enrolment of women students rose from 2.45 million in 1997-98 to 4.03 million in 2004-05, constituting 40.22 per cent of the total enrolment. As per NSSO survey (55th Round 1999-00), there were inequalities in enrolment in higher education across various social groups in rural and urban areas, and also in terms of gender. Women belonging to SC and ST and those living in rural areas are the most disadvantaged. A Constitution Amendment Bill has been passed by Parliament in December,

2005, which enables the State to make special provisions, by law, for admission of students belonging to SC, ST and socially and educationally backward classes to educational institutions, including aided and unaided private educational institutions, except minority institutions referred to in Article 30(1) of the Constitution.

27.2.12 Scheme of Assistance to Voluntary Agencies under Mahila Samakhya: Object of the scheme is to evolve a modality of planning involving government institutions and voluntary agencies reaching out to the women in villages in a continuous dialogue so that the educative principle is not subordinated to the desire for immediate results and to adopt an area intensive approach to integrate the existing efforts to provide formal and non-formal schooling, adult education upgradation of educational qualifications through condensed courses and vocational training.

Financial Assistance: 100 per cent assistance is provided for

- Taking up well-designed fields projects for women's empowerment and education;
- Developments of learning material, instruction/learning aids, and other aspects of technical resource development;
- Training;
- Creation of educational facilities for girls and women's education by taking up experimental/innovative programmes;
- Evaluation and research;
- Activities for dissemination of the outcome of experimental/innovative programmes and their adoption, including visits to experimental innovative projects, publications, documentation , etc;

Educational institutions, registered societies, public trusts and non-profit making companies which are working outside the Project Districts of Mahila Samakhya would be eligible for assistance under the Scheme.

27.2.13 Jan Shikshan Sansthans: District Repositories: The earlier scheme of Shramik Vidyapeeth will continue with a modified approach and the new nomenclature of Jan Shikshan Sansthan. Under the Ninth Plan, the activities of the Jan Shikshan

Sansthan have been enlarged and infrastructure strengthened to enable them to function as a district repository of vocational/ technical skills in both urban and rural areas. Jan Shikshan Sansthans, will be classified into three categories depending on the nature of the city/town and the quantum of work. The performance of the Jan Shikshan Sansthan will be appraised by reputed institutions and accordingly upgraded or downgraded on the basis of the evaluation reports.

The challenge of creating a learning society is a formidable one, more so for a nation of one billion people that began its nation-building efforts with such great disadvantages. The National Literacy Mission has been making a modest contribution to the whole process by involving the community in the educational advancement of the people.

27.2.14 Kasturba Gandhi Balika Vidyalaya Scheme: The Scheme was launched in 2004 and the results are encouraging. In the budget for 2006-07 Rs. 128 crore have been provided for opening of 1,000 new residential schools for girls from SC, ST, OBC and minority communities. An additional sum of Rs. 172 crore has been promised for the year 2006-07.

27.2.15 Incentive to the Girl Child for Education: As an incentive to the girl child who passes the VIII Standard Examination and enrolls in a secondary school, a sum of Rs. 3,000 will be deposited in her name, and she would be entitled to withdraw it on reaching 18 years of age.

27.2.16 Other Schemes: Union Department of Education has been implementing specific schemes to support various initiatives of the government in the field of adult Education:

- Scheme of Assistance to Voluntary Agencies in Adult Education is aimed at securing extensive involvement of Voluntary Agencies in adult literacy programmes of National Literacy Mission.
- Scheme of Jan Shiksha Sansthans in Adult Education is also aimed at securing extensive involvement of Voluntary Agencies.

The objectives of both the schemes are:

- To enrich the personal life of workers and their families by providing opportunities of adult education physical culture and recreation; and

To widen the range of workers knowledge and understanding of the social, economic and political systems in order to create in him critical awareness about the environment and his own predicament for better national integration and development.

Part VIII
Subsidies for Housing and Urban Development

28

Housing

Housing is one of the basic requirements for human survival. For a normal citizen owning a house provides significant economic and social security and status in society. For a shelter less person, a house brings about a profound social change in his existence, endowing him with an identity, thus integrating him with his immediate social milieu. A housing programme for the rehabilitation of refugees was taken up immediately after partition by the Ministry of Rehabilitation and this lasted till around 1960. Approximately 5 lakh families were housed in various centres mainly located in Northern India. A Village Housing Scheme was also launched as part of the Community Development Movement in 1957, in which loans to individuals and cooperatives were provided up to a maximum of Rs. 5,000 per house. However, only 67000 houses were built under this scheme by the end of the Fifth Plan (1980). In 1972-73, the Estimate Committee of the Lok Sabha in its 37th Report pointed out that "the Committee is distressed to note that although 83 per cent of India's population lives in villages and about 73 per cent of the rural population reside in unsatisfactory kutcha structures, the problem of rural housing has not received the close attention of the Government." Following this, certain initiatives were undertaken by Government including the launching of the House Sites-cum-Construction Assistance Scheme which began as a Central Scheme in the 4th Plan and was transferred to the State Sector with effect from 1.04.1974 on the recommendation of the National Development Council (NDC).

28.1 Indira Awaas Yojana

The scheme was launched during 1985-86 as a sub-scheme of Rural Employment Guarantee Programme. Thereafter it continued as a sub-scheme of Jawahar Rozgar Yojana (JRY) since its launching in April, 1989. 6 per cent of the total JRY funds were allocated for implementation of IAY. From the year 1993-94, the scope of IAY was extended to cover below the poverty line Non Scheduled Castes/Scheduled Tribes families in the rural areas. Simultaneously, the allocation of funds for implementing the scheme was raised from 6 per cent to 10 per cent of the total resources available under JRY at the national level, subject to the condition that the benefits to Non-Scheduled Castes/Scheduled Tribes poor should not exceed 4 per cent of the total JRY allocation. IAY was de-linked from JRY and made an independent scheme with effect from January 1, 1996.

The objective of the Indira Awaas Yojana is primarily to help construction/up gradation of dwelling units of members of Scheduled Castes/Scheduled Tribes, freed bonded labourers and other below the poverty line non-SC/ST rural house holds by providing them a lump sum financial assistance. The house is to be constructed by the beneficiary himself/herself. No contractor shall be involved in the construction of dwelling units under the scheme. The dwelling units should normally be built on individual plots in the main habitation of the village.

Funding Pattern: The Indira Awaas Yojana is a Centrally Sponsored Scheme funded on cost-sharing basis between the Government of India and the State Governments in the ratio of 75:25. In the case of Union Territories, the entire funds under this Scheme are provided by the Government of India.

The target groups for houses under the IAY are below poverty line households living in the rural areas belonging to Scheduled Castes/Scheduled Tribes, freed bonded labourers and non-SC/ST BPL rural households, widows and next of-kin to defence personnel/paramilitary forces killed in action residing in rural areas *(irrespective of their income criteria)*, ex-servicemen and retired member of paramilitary forces fulfilling the other conditions.

Funds Earmarking:

- At least 60 per cent of the total Indira Awaas Yojana allocation during a financial year should be utilized for construction/upgradation of dwelling units for SC/ST BPL households.

- A maximum 40 per cent for non-SC/ST BPL rural households.
- 3 per cent of the above categories for physically and mentally challenged persons.

If any particular category is exhausted or not available in a district, allocation can be utilized for other categories as per priorities given in the Guidelines after it has been certified to this effect by the Zilla Parishad/DRDA concerned.

Prioritization of beneficiaries will be as follows:

- Freed bonded labourers
- SC/ST household
    - SC/ST households who are victims of atrocity
    - SC/ST households, headed by widows and unmarried women
    - SC/ST households affected by flood, natural calamities like earthquake, cyclone and man-made calamities like riot.
    - Other SC/ST households
- Families, widows of personnel from defence services, paramilitary forces, killed in action.
- Non- SC/ST BPL households.
- Physically and mentally challenged persons.
- Ex-servicemen and retired members of the paramilitary forces.
- Displaced persons on account of developmental projects, nomadic/semi-nomadic, and de-notified tribals, families with physically/mentally challenged members.

The selection of the beneficiaries will be subject to the condition that the households of all the above categories except (iii) are Below Poverty Line (BPL). The District Panchayat/Zilla Panchayat/District Rural Development Agencies (DRDAs) on the basis of allocations made and targets fixed shall decide the number of houses to be constructed/upgraded Panchayat wise under IAY.

Involvement of Beneficiaries: The beneficiaries should be involved in the construction of the house. To this end, the beneficiaries may make their own arrangements for procurement of construction material, engage skilled workmen and also contribute family labour.

Unit Cost for Construction of IAY Houses and Upgradation: The ceiling on grant of assistance per unit cost under the Indira Awaas Yojana for construction of new house and upgradation of unserviceable kutcha house is given as under:

		Plain Areas	Hilly/Difficult Areas
a	Construction of house including Sanitary latrine and smokeless Chulha	Rs. 25,000	Rs. 27,500
b	Upgradation of unserviceable households	Rs. 12,500	Rs. 12,500

Credit-cum-Subsidy for Construction/upgradation of Rural Houses: Up to 20 per cent of the total funds can be utilized for up gradation of existing kutcha houses and toward subsidy for construction of houses with credit from Banks/Financial Institutions. Credit cum-subsidy will be provided subject to the following conditions:

- Rural households having an annual income of up to Rs. 32,000 only.
- Ceiling of subsidy under the Scheme Rs. 12,500 per household.
- The upper limit of construction loan under this scheme will be Rs. 50,000 only.

Criteria for Allocation of Resources: Central assistance under the IAY will be allocated to the States/UTs on the basis of poverty ratio and housing shortage, with each of these variables being given equal weightage. The proportions of rural SC/ST population and housing shortage in a district to the total rural SC/ST population and housing shortage in the State/UT are the criteria of inter-district allocation of the Indira Awaas Yojana funds within a State/UT. Both these variables are given equal weightage in the inter-districts allocation. The targets for the Blocks within a District will be decided on the same principles. Diversion of resources from one district to another is strictly prohibited. Up to 20 per cent of the total funds can be utilized for upgradation of existing kutcha houses and towards subsidy for construction of houses with credit.

A total of 5.86 lakh houses have been constructed during 2002-2003 up to November, 2002, of which 2.71 lakh houses for Scheduled Castes and 8.73 lakh houses for Scheduled tribes.

28.2 Housing Assistance by State Government

Various state governments have responded to the housing programme by placing it at the top end of their development priorities, thereby imparting great vigour to the implementation process. While the implementation lies with the DRDAs, the houses are constructed by the individual beneficiaries themselves, with absolute freedom of choice over the design. The scheme is closely monitored by an extensive network at the district, state and national level to ensure right selection and effectiveness in the implementation mechanism.

Punjab State Housing Corporative Federation has announced in April 2006 that the federation will construct 5000 flats or the poor in the 5 municipalities in the State. The Federations has already constructed the houses for the poor in Amritsar and Ludhiana.

28.3 Bharat Nirman Programme for Rural Houses

Under this Programme 870,000 houses have been constructed and a sum of Rs. 2,260 crore has been released till January, 2006. The scheme is to construct 60 lakh pucca houses.

28.4 Valmiki Ambedkar Awas Yojana (VAMBAY)

The VAMBAY was launched in December 2001 to ameliorate the conditions of the urban slum dwellers living below the poverty line without adequate shelter. The scheme ahs the primary objective of facilitating the construction and up-gradation of dwelling units for slum dwelling and providing a healthy and enabling urban environment through community toilets under Nirmal Bharat Abhiyan, a component of the scheme. The Central Government provides a subsidy of 50 per cent being arranged by the State Government. There are prescribed ceilings on costs both for dwelling units and community toilets. During 2003-04, Central subsidy to the extent of Rs. 239 crore has been released. Since inception up to May 2004, Rs. 522 crore have been released as Government of India subsidy for the construction/upgradation of 2,46,035 dwelling units and 29,263 toilets seats under the scheme.

29

Urban Development

29.1 Need for Urban Development

Over a third of India's population lives in urban areas. There are 35 urban agglomerations with population of more than one million, and about 37 per cent of the total urban population live in these million-plus cities. Urbanization in India is proceeding at a modest pace.

The likely increase in urban productivity and population due to the new economic policies of the Government of India will place a heavy demand on all kinds of urban infrastructure and services. The infrastructure bottlenecks in urban centres are likely to pose serious impediments in enhancing the productivity.

The 74th Constitutional Amendment Act, 1992 has given Constitutional status to municipal governments, has defined municipal responsibilities in broad terms and has left the individual State Finance Commissions, both the task of assigning the expenditures and revenues, and the task of defining the nature of financial relations between state and local governments. As a result, there has been considerable variation in the rigor and quality, across states, on the nature of State Finance Commissions recommendations and the extent to which they have been implemented.

In many states, the devolution of administrative powers related to planning, financing and managing municipal services has not yet become effective. The expected improvement in services, as an outcome of decentralization, is based on the notion that as expenditure responsibilities are devolved, local elected representatives would have decision making authority. However, the range of issues on which elected municipal representatives can take a decision is limited. There is a wide variation in availability of infrastructure and services in different cities. The larger cities have the ability to raise resources from the capital market, while smaller towns lag behind because of lack of resources and expertise. Urban Local Bodies (ULBs) and state development agencies have an important role to play in development of urban infrastructure. City Challenge Fund (CCF) was created in the budget 2001-02 to support Urban Local Bodies (ULBs) to undertake reforms. The CCF seeks to directly support the grass-root institutions like ULB, and partially finance the cost of developing a reform program and its implementation.

Programmes such as Mega City Project, Integrated Development for Small and Medium Towns (IDSMT), Accelerated Urban Water Supply Program (AUWSP) have shown some success in meeting the urban needs. IDSMT and Mega City schemes are being implemented in states to meet the requirements of water supply, sanitation, solid waste management, urban transport and development of new extensions like residential colonies and satellite towns to relieve congestion. The IDSMT was launched in 1979-80. 1,310 small and medium towns have so far been assisted under the scheme. Central assistance released under the scheme is Rs. 599.4 crore (up to January 31, 2003). Mega city scheme was introduced in 1993-94, covering five cities namely, Mumbai, Kolkata, Chennai, Hyderabad and Bangalore. The Central assistance released under the Scheme has been Rs. 809.3 crore (up to January 31, 2003). The Central assistance in these schemes has not been adequate in terms of amount and coverage of cities. Moreover, the implementation of the scheme has not been satisfactory in terms of timely completion of projects, augmentation of resources by ULBs, tie-ups of institutional finance etc.

29.2 Safe Drinking Water

As per 2001 Census of India estimates, approximately 20 percent of urban households do not have access to safe drinking water. Only 23.55 per cent had toilet facilities and up to March 1992, 52 per cent of the population was left uncovered by sanitation facilities. The coverage in terms of organised sewerage system ranged from 35 per cent in class IV to 75 per cent in class

I cities. The drainage system for rain water disposal covers only 66 percent of the urban population. The city roads are inadequate for traffic requirements, leading to congestion and fast deterioration in quality of roads due to excess loads.

Technological up-gradation and improved design can hike efficiency and rationalise consumption. Regularity in supply could mean lower project cost and greater willingness to pay on the part of the consumers. Micro-level systems need to be designed to recycle water at the household level. The supply should be metered to plug leakages.

Pricing is to be on cost-recovery basis in the long term or over the full life of the project. In the short term, since prices cannot be increased at one go, the government will have to continue to provide subsidies. The water tariff should be increased gradually to reach cost-recovery level. Part of the required increase may be capitalised and charged as connection charges or advance registration charges. Cost recovery may also be made by including water tax, water benefit tax, betterment charges or development charges.

Cross-subsidisation of domestic use of water by commercial and industrial use may prove self-defeating if the latter diversify their sources of water. Metering of water supply must be promoted. To improve monitoring of leakages, bulk metering should be adopted. A block tariff system may be adopted under which consumption of water is picked at a low initial rate up to a specified volume of use and at a higher rate per block thereafter. Differential pricing may also be related to time of use.

Differential treatment of water for different uses. Micro-level systems needs to be designed to recycle water at the household level. The supply should be metered to plug leakages.

29.3 Solid Waste Management (SWM)

The cost of collection, treatment and disposal of the solid water is to be reduced through various mechanisms. Technological innovation to improve the reusability of the recycled waste will increase returns and make projects viable.

Privatization of as many operations as is feasible in an urban area will improve efficiency and reduce costs.

- Greater attention to segregation of different kinds of waste at the collection point itself will reduce cost of disposal.
- Toxic waste should be collected and disposed of separately. The frequency of collection can be as low as once a month.
- Biodegradable waste should be tackled locally to avoid storage and transportation over longer distances. This waste can also be coupled with the local sewers and horticulture waste from streets in biodigesters. This will produce three important by-products — biogas, compost and recyclable water, which will improve the viability of disposal.
- Building debris (*Malba*) should be kept separately and used for filling building sites and low-lying areas.
- Remaining waste in each Indian city gets recycled by rag pickers. The small components left over can be disposed of through incineration or sanitary landfills.
- Wherever environmentally acceptable, disposal can be decentralised to save on transportation cost.
- Appropriate technologies should be used to improve the quality of processed waste. An improved quality of compost may fetch a higher price and reduce process time and mechanisation. Similarly RDF (Refuse-derived fuel) seems to have good scope for providing cooking fuel, process steam and power generation. These should be promoted. Converting waste management into biogas with fertiliser as the by-product is a commercially viable VD method. The small scale of operations and pricing structure have been the major constraints in this area. This may be tackled by providing supportive service to start operations on an economical scale. Landfills can be scientifically organised to minimise pollution from leaching. The biogas produced in a properly-designed landfill can be harnessed and utilised.

The 'polluter pays' principle should be applied. Operations which create waste may be charged a levy and the returns from the same may be used for financing waste disposal programmes.

The cost of collection, treatment and disposal of the solid waste should be reduced. Greater attention to segregation of different kinds of waste at the collection point itself will reduce cost of disposal. Wherever environmentally acceptable, disposal can be decentralised to save on transportation cost.

29.4 Sanitation

Use of low-cost technologies like that of Sulabh Shauchalayas must be promoted. SWD services can be unbundled and most functions entrusted to the private sector. This is one area where privatization has shown consistent productivity gains and cost reductions. Proper packaging – for instance, clubbing water supply and drainage projects together, can reduce project cost and improve viability. Similarly road development and storm-water drain management can be clubbed with commercial development of adjacent areas.

Cost of drainage and sewerage can be piggybacked on to the water tariff since these projects can be taken up as one package. The cost of storm-water drainage projects can be recovered by commercial use of adjacent lands. Taking up of integrated Area Development Schemes rather than isolated water supply or sanitation schemes should be given priority. Even in older areas, augmentation of water supply schemes and other facilities can be financed out of impact fees or valorisation charges or by a temporary surcharge on property tax.

The property tax base needs to be fed from the Rent Control Act. The Rent Control Act should be amended and pending that, the property tax should be made independent of the controlled rent. Resistance to tariff increases may be overcome by providing detailed and well-communicated information about cost of supply to the consumers.

29.5 Roads

Technological upgradation should be used to reduce maintenance costs. Better co-ordination with other departments like telecom/sewerage boards can reduce frequency and cost of levelling of dug-up roads.

Narrow earmarking of specific taxes and fees that are closely related to use of facilities help overcome resistance to taxes. Apart from taxation/user charges and impact fees, costs may be recovered by giving advertisement rights, limited development or license rights (like running kiosks), long lease for trees and the right to use their product.

In the roads sector, apart from taxation/user charges and impact fees, costs may be recovered by giving advertisement rights, limited development or license rights (like running kiosks), long lease for trees and the right to use their product.

29.6 Jawaharlal Nehru National Urban Renewal Mission (JNNURM)

JNNURM was launched by the Prime Minister on December 3, 2005 to encourage cities to initiate steps to bring about improvement in the existing service levels in a financially sustainable manner. The objectives of the mission, *inter alia*, include planned development of identified cities including semi-urban areas, outgrowths and urban corridors and improved provision of, basic services to the urban poor. The duration of the mission would be seven years beginning from 2005-06. The mission has subsumed the following on-going schemes of the Ministry:

- Infrastructure Development in Mega Cities,
- Integrated Development of Small and Medium Towns and
- Accelerated Urban Water Supply Programme.

Cities/Urban Agglomerations/Parastatals will be required to prepare detailed project reports for undertaking projects under identified areas. Funds for the identified cities would be released to the designated State Nodal Agency, which in turn would leverage, to the extent feasible, additional resources from the financial institutions/private sector/capital market. Private sector participation in development, management and financing of urban infrastructure would be clearly delineated.

The admissible components under the mission include urban renewal, water supply (including de-salination plants) and sanitation, sewerage and solid waste management, urban transport, development of heritage areas, preservation of water bodies etc. A provision of Rs.50,000 crore has been agreed to as Central Assistance for Jawaharlal Nehru National Urban Renewal Mission (JNNURM) for a period of 7 years beginning from 2005-06.

On completion of the mission period of seven years, it is expected that ULBs/Parastatals will achieve the following outcomes:

- Modern and transparent budgeting, accounting, and financial management systems designed and adopted for all urban services and governance functions.
- City-wide framework for planning and governance will be established and become operational.
- All urban residents will be able to obtain access to a basic level of urban services.
- Financially self-sustaining agencies for urban governance and service delivery will be established, through reforms to major revenue instruments.
- Local services and governance will be conducted in a manner that is transparent and accountable to citizens.

e-Governance applications will be introduced in core functions of ULBs/Para-statals resulting in reduced cost and time of service delivery processes.

29.7 Scheme for Urban Micro Enterprises (SUME)

Scheme for Urban Micro Enterprise (SUME) was implemented as a third component of Nehru Rozgar Yojana. The scheme was launched in the year 1989. This scheme was under Nehru Rozgar Yojana for the people living below poverty line.

The objective of the scheme is to encourage unemployed and under employed urban poor living below poverty line in metropolitan areas, cities and towns with population exceeding 10000 according to 1981 census, to take up self employment ventures with the help of subsidy and bank loan. The scheme commenced on October 11, 1989. The Urban Local Body will provide subsidy.

29.8 Prime Minister's Integrated Urban Poverty Eradication Programme (PM-IUPEP)

The scheme commenced on January 16, 1996 with the objectives of effective achievement of social sector goals, community empowerment, convergence through sustainable support systems and employment generation and skill upgradation. It provides for the following.

Self-Employment through Setting up Micro Enterprises and Skill Development: The maximum project cost should not be more than Rs. one lakh. The maximum loan amount is Rs. 95,000. Margin: The applicant has to bring Rs. 5,000 as margin in cash. Subsidy: A subsidy of 15 per cent with the maximum of Rs. 7,500 is available. The subsidy is to be provided by Town Poverty Eradication Cell. An allocation of Rs. 98.60 Crore was made under the programme for the year 1996-97 for 342 class II towns and 72 district towns.

Shelter Upgradation: A maximum of Rs. 7,500 or 75 per cent of the unit cost, whichever is lower can be sanctioned as loan. 25 per cent of the unit cost/repair/renovation cost is to be provided as subsidy with maximum of Rs. 2,500.

The loan is to be released in 2 installments on verifying the satisfactory progress of the project. Total training expenditure should not exceed Rs. 2,000 per trainee

29.9 Jawaharlal Nehru National Urban Renewal Mission

The Jawaharlal Nehru National Urban Renewal Mission was launched on December 3, 2005. For the next year, against the estimated outlay of Rs. 6,250 crore, I propose to provide a grant of Rs. 4,595 crore. Apart from the four projects, including Mumbai metro rail and Bangalore metro rail, mentioned in my Budget speech last year, the projects under active consideration include projects in Maharashtra, Madhya Pradesh and Gujarat.

Planned urbanization can act as a spur to growth, employment and a better quality of life. Government will actively promote the establishment of new towns, preferably focussed on a specific industry, for example Information Technology, or a specific theme, for example education or health. Some projects are on the anvil in West Bengal and Karnataka.

National Urban Renewal Mission has over Rs. 1989.62 crore with it unspent because of non implementation of many slum development projects for 2005-06. Ministry has surrendered Rs. 91.25 crore in 2001-02, Rs. 107.83 in 2002-03 and Rs. 40.25 crore in 2003-04.

29.10 Integrated Development of Small and Medium Towns (IDSMT)

The persons living in big cities are facing a lot of problems due to increasing population and under development of infrastructure. To improve the economic and physical infrastructure and also to provide essential facilities and service and also to slow down the growth of large cities by developing small and medium towns through increased investments in these towns the this scheme was started. This is a Centrally sponsored scheme initiated in the year 1979-80 and is continuing. The development of small urban centres would also help in reducing migration to large cities and support the growth of surrounding rural areas as well.

The scheme has the following objectives:

- Improving infrastructural facilities and helping in the creation of durable public assets in small and medium towns.
- Decentralising economic growth and employment opportunities and promoting dispersed Urbanisation.
- Increasing the availability of serviced sites for housing, commercial and industrial uses.
- Integrating spatial and socio-economic planning as envisaged in the Constitution (74th Amendment) Act, 1992.
- Promoting resource-generating schemes for the urban local bodies to improve their overall financial position.

Main Features of the Revised Scheme:

- Towns up to population of five lakh are eligible.
- The share of Central and State assistance has been increased and made available as grant.
- The State to prepare the urban strategy for the next 10 years and give justification for selecting priority towns to be included under IDSMT.
- In accordance with Constitution (74th) Amendment Act, 1992, IDSMT Scheme is applicable to those towns where elections to the local bodies are held and elected representatives are in position.
- The State Government to create State Urban Development fund at the State level and Municipal Revolving Fund at the Town level for continuous sustainable infrastructure development.
- A Sanctioning committee at the State level chaired by the Secretary Urban Development/Local Govt. (incharge of IDSMT Scheme) will approve the projects.
- Institutional finance is reduced to 20-40 per cent through HUDCO/Other Institutional Financing Agencies.
- The component of assistance are enlarged and made more flexible.

Central assistance in the from of grant-in-aid would be made available in the ratio of 60:40 (central & State) for the preparation of Project Reports/Urban Development (Investment plan) of IDSMT towns ranging from Rs. 3 to Rs. 6 lakh depending on the size of the town.

Selection of Towns:

- IDSMT Scheme will be applicable to town/cities with population up to 5 lakh subject to the stipulation that 1/3 of the total amount available each year, for the Scheme as a whole will be allocated to town with less than 50,000 population. While selecting the towns preference will be given to headquarter of districts followed by Mandy towns and Industrial growth centres, tourist places and pilgrim centres etc.

- The IDSMT Scheme will be applicable to only those towns where elections to the local bodies have been held and elected bodies are in position.

Components for Funding

The components for assistance under IDSMT will include works as per City/Town Development/Master Plans which may have city/townwide significance.

Strengthening of Master Plan road facilities including ring, arterial, bypass/link roads and small bridges, Sites and services, Development of bus/truck terminals, Construction/upgradation of Master Plan drains including Storm water channels, Solid waste management, Development of Market complexes/shopping centres, Provision of tourist facilities, Development of City/Town Parks, Street lighting for Master Plan roads, Slaughter houses, Major public amenities like Gardens, Playgrounds, Marriage halls, Pay-and-use toilets, etc. Cycle/Rickshaw stands, Traffic improvement and management schemes, Construction of retaining walls and slope stability measures in hill station towns, Social amenities, specially for the poorer sections.

29.11 Promotion of Non-Handicapping Environment for Disabled and Elderly Persons

At the meeting held at Beijing in December 1992, to launch the Asian and Pacific Decade of Disabled Persons 1993-2002, Economic and Social Commission for Asia and the Pacific (ESCAP) adopted the Proclamation on the Full Participation and Equality of People with Disabilities in the Asian and Pacific Region. India was a signatory to the said Proclamation. Ministry of Urban Development & Poverty Alleviation was designated as the nodal Ministry for implementation of barrier-free built environment for the disabled and elderly persons as envisaged in "The Persons with Disabilities (Equal Opportunities, Protection of Rights and Full Participation) Act, 1995.

Ministry of Urban Development & Poverty Alleviation also prepared Model Building Bye-Laws which contained a number of provisions for providing accessibilities to disabled persons to various public buildings. These Building Bye-Laws were sent to State Governments, Union Territories, Delhi Development Authority, Municipal Corporation of Delhi, New Delhi Municipal Committee etc. for adoption.

Part IX
Subsidies for Rural Infrastructure and Development

30. Rajiv Gandhi Grameen Vidyutikaran Yojana
31. Prime Ministers Gram Sadak Yojana (PMGSY)
32. Integrated Rural Development Programme (IRDP)
33. Scheme for Improved Tools to Rural Artisans (SITRA)

30

Rajiv Gandhi Grameen Vidyutikaran Yojana

The rural electrification programme is one of the important components in rural development and as important as rural drinking water supply, health, nutrition, primary education, shelter and rural connectivity. The availability of power in rural areas will lead to economic development and its attendant spin-off benefits like food security, better health, literacy, etc. With this in view, the Government has been focusing on village electrification since the beginning of the planning process. While this has resulted in the electrification of around 86 per cent of the country's villages, the use of electricity in villages for productive and subsistence needs is still very limited. About 70 per cent of the rural households are yet to get electric connections and power-based economic activities in the electrified villages are minimal. The actual benefits of the investments made in the rural electrification programme can only be realized if the people are in a position to use electricity for their day-to-day activities as well as for industrial and commercial activity. Therefore, the second phase of the rural electrification programme, apart from seeking 100 per cent electrification, must also ensure more widespread use of electricity by the rural people in a time-bound manner.

30.1 Main Features of the Scheme

The Prime Minister launched on April 4, 2005, the Rajiv Gandhi Grameen Vidyutikaran Yojana. This scheme is for rural electricity infrastructure and household electrification. The salient features of the scheme are:

In 5 years:

- Electrification of all villages and habitations
- Access to electricity for all households

- Electricity connection to Below Poverty Line (BPL) families free of charge

Through creation of:

- Rural Electricity Distribution Backbone (REDB)
- Village Electrification Infrastructure (VEI)
- Decentralised Distributed Generation (DDG) Systems

Accelerate rural development through:

- Irrigation pumpsets
- Village industries
- Cold chains
- Healthcare
- Education and IT

While full details of the scheme are awaited, State Governments have already started making requests for assistance under the scheme. Karnataka has sought Central assistance of Rs. 700 crore under the scheme to provide electricity to 16,000 hamlets in the State benefiting 5.5 lakh households.

31

Prime Ministers Gram Sadak Yojana (PMGSY)

31.1 Introduction

All-weather roads still do not connect about 40 per cent of the habitations in the country. In rural development, rural road connectivity is not only a key component by promoting access to economic and social services and thereby generating increased agricultural incomes and productive employment opportunities in India, it is also as a result, a key ingredient in ensuring any sustainable poverty reduction programme. With a view to redressing the situation, the Government launched the Pradhan Mantri Gram Sadak Yojana on December 25, 2000.

31.2 Objectives

The primary objective of the PMGSY is to provide connectivity, by way of an all-weather road (with necessary culverts and cross-drainage structures, which is operable throughout the year), to the unconnected habitations in the rural areas. It is to be done in such a way that habitations with a population of 1000 persons and above are covered in three years (2000-2003) and all unconnected habitations with a population of 500 persons and above by the end of the Tenth Plan Period (2007). The PMGSY will permit the upgradation of the existing roads in those districts where all the habitations of the designated population size have been provided all-weather road connectivity.

31.3 Planning for Rural Roads

The District Rural Roads Plan would indicate the existing road network system in the District and also clearly identify the proposed roads for providing connectivity to unconnected habitations, in an economic and efficient manner, in terms of cost and utility. The Core Network will identify the roads required to assure each eligible habitation with a basic access (single all-weather road connectivity) to essential social and economic services. Accordingly, the core network would consist of some of the existing roads as well as all the roads proposed for new connectivity under the PMGSY.

31.4 Funding and Allocation

The scheme is a 100 per cent Centrally Sponsored Scheme. 50 per cent of the Cess on High Speed Diesel (HSD) is earmarked for this Programme. Once the Core Network is prepared, it is possible to estimate the length of roads for New Connectivity as well as Upgradation for every District. States may, each year, distribute the State's Allocation among the Districts giving 80 per cent on the basis of road length required for providing connectivity to Unconnected Habitations and 20 per cent on the basis of road length requiring Upgradation under the PMGSY.

In making the District-wise allocation, the number of Habitations taken up under the PMGSY or any other Programme would be excluded from the total number of Unconnected Habitations (even if the road works are still under execution). The figures of connected as well as Unconnected Habitations in any District would keep on changing every year till such time as all Unconnected Habitations (of the stipulated population size) have been covered in the District.

31.5 Proposals

The list of road works to be taken up under the PMGSY will be finalised each year by the District Panchayat in accordance with the Allocation of Funds communicated to the District by the State Government. District Panchayat shall finalise the list through a consultative process involving lower level Panchayat institutions and elected representatives. It must be ensured that the proposed road works are part of the Core Network and that New Connectivity is given primacy. It must be noted that the PMGSY does not provide funds for Land Acquisition. The State

Government/District Panchayat will oversee that lands are available for taking up the proposed road works. A certificate that Land is available must accompany the proposal for each roadwork.

In drawing up the list of the road works, the District Panchayat shall ensure that primacy is accorded to providing New Connectivity to all Unconnected Habitations. The following Order of Priority shall be strictly followed.

- Providing New connectivity to Unconnected Habitations with a population of 1000 + (500 + in case of Hill States etc)
- Providing New connectivity to Unconnected Habitations with a population of 500-999 (250-499 in case of Hill States etc)
- Upgradation of Through Routes in the Core network (only Rural Roads to be covered)
- Upgradation of Link Routes

The only exception from will be in respect of those routes that include the Village Panchayat Headquarters or Market Centres or other educational or medical essential services or those, which are notified as places of tourist interest. In such cases, provision of new connectivity may be made irrespective of the population size. The proposals of the Members of Parliament are also required to be given full consideration.

31.6 Executing Agencies

Each State Government/UT Administration would identify one or two suitable Agencies (having a presence in all the Districts and with established competence in executing time-bound road construction works), to be designated as Executing Agencies. These could be the Public Works Department/Rural Engineering Service/Organisation/Rural Works Department/Zilla Parishad/Panchayati Raj Engineering Department etc. who have been in existence for a large number of years and have the necessary experience, expertise and manpower. The States for implementation of the programmes shall create no Agency. In States where the State Government has identified more than one Executing Agency, the distribution of work would be done with the District as a unit. The Executing Agency will have a Programme Implementation Unit (PIU) in the District, which should have an officer of the rank of Executive Engineer as its head.

The Responsibility for implementation of the PMGSY in every State/UT will be given to a nominated Department as the Nodal Department by The State Government/UT Administration. The Nodal Department will identify a State-level autonomous Agency (Society etc), with a distinct legal status, under its control for receiving the funds from the Ministry of Rural Development. If there is no such State-level Agency, the Nodal Department will take steps to register an Agency under the Registration of Societies Act, (there should not be more than one Agency), so as to be able to receive the funds. The Minister or the Chief Secretary and the Secretary in charge of the Nodal Department will head the Agency or a senior officer will be the Chief Executive. All the proposals will be vetted by the Agency before they are put up before the State-level Standing Committee and are sent to the NRRDA for clearance by the Ministry of Rural Development.

31.7 Preparation of Project Proposals and Their Clearance

After approval by the District Panchayat the proposals would be forwarded through the District PIU to the State-level Agency. The State-level Agency shall vet the proposals to ensure that they are in accordance with the Guidelines and shall place them before the State-level Standing Committee. The size of State project proposals as well as the time when they would be forwarded to the NRRDA will be as specified by the Ministry/NRRDA each year.

After scrutiny by the State Level Standing Committee, the Programme Implementation Units (PIUs) will prepare the Detailed Project Report (DPRs) for each proposed road work. The preparation of DPR requires collection and analysis of data required for the design of Pavement and Cross-Drainage works such as Inventory and Engineering surveys, Soil investigations,

Hydraulic data etc. The PIU will follow the given Guidelines in preparing the detailed project reports.

31.8 Empowered Committee

At the Central level, an Empowered Committee would consider the Project proposals received from the State Governments, to be chaired by Secretary, Department of Rural Development. The representatives of the State Government, whose projects are being considered by the Empowered Committee, may be invited to attend the Meetings, as and when required. The Recommendations of the Empowered Committee would, thereafter, be submitted to the Minister of Rural Development for clearance. The Ministry will communicate the clearance of the Proposals to the State Government. It may, however, be noted that clearance by the Ministry does not imply Administrative or Technical sanction of the proposals. The well established procedures of the Executing Agency/ies in this regard would continue to be followed.

Once approved, the alignment of the road should not be changed without obtaining the concurrence of the District Panchayat, the State Technical Agency and the State level Standing Committee.

31.9 Programme Implementation Units

At the District level, the Programme will be co-ordinated, and implemented through the Executing Agencies. While, for all the Districts, it is desirable that a dedicated Programme Implementation Unit (PIU) is set up, this is especially desirable for all States having an annual allocation of Rs. 75 crore or more per annum under the PMGSY, and all the participating States in the externally aided projects. An Engineer not below the rank of Executive Engineer may typically head the Programme Implementation Unit at the District Level. Competent technical personnel from amongst the available staff or through deputation will man all PIUs. All staff costs will be borne by the State Government. The Pradhan Mantri Gram Sadak Yojana does not provide for any staff costs.

31.10 Execution of Works

The relevant projects would be executed by the PIUs and completed within a period of 6 months, from the date of issue of the Work order. Delayed execution of projects, could adversely affect clearance of the proposals in subsequent years. PMGSY does not provide for any cost over-runs. Except for Hill States, the Road works under the PMGSY shall not be taken up in stages. Once road works are taken up, they should be completed to the requisite Technical Specifications in the prescribed time frame. In case of the Hill States about 18 months may be allowed to the Executing Agency to complete the projects. Any cost over-run, either due to time over-run or for any other reason whatsoever, would have to be borne by the State Government. An important principle of this scheme is the assured availability of funds, so as to facilitate timely completion of road works. Executing Agencies has to ensure timely payments to the contractors, subject to satisfactory execution of work. Delays, in payment due, should be avoided.

31.11 National Rural Roads Development Agency

The Ministry of Rural Development has set up the National Rural Roads Development Agency (NRRDA) to provide Operational and Management support to the Programme on the following aspects.

- Designs & Specifications and Cost norms.
- Principal Technical Agencies (PTAs) and State Technical Agencies (STAs)
- District Rural Roads Plans and Core Network.
- Scrutiny of Project Proposals
- ➢ National Quality Monitors
- ➢ Monitoring of progress of the PMGSY
- On-Line Management & Monitoring System
- Training, Workshops, Research, Pilot Projects and Literature.
- Human Resource Development

32

Integrated Rural Development Programme (IRDP)

32.1 Introduction

During 1980 it was estimated that 48 per cent of the India's population of 68.5 crore was living below poverty line. Hence it was thought necessary to provide them with the self-employment opportunities. This is the major poverty alleviation programme in our country. The programme commenced in April 1978 in 2300 selected blocks and was extended to all the 5011 blocks covering 5.64 lakh villages in the country since October 2, 1980. The programme involves the identification of thousands of families of the target group in each block, preparation of plan for assisting these families, arranging credit support for financing the plans, monitoring the progress of implementation of the scheme and follow up action to ensure that the beneficiary derive truly lasting benefits whereby they cross the poverty line. The target was to assist on an average 600 families in a block in a year thus assisting 3000 families during the Sixth Five-Year Plan period.
Thus a national target for assisting 15 million families was fixed.

An allocation of Rs. 5 lakh was given to each block on the basis of 50:50 share between Central and State Governments. The Programmes of Small Farmers Development Agency and Marginal Farmers Development agency were merged with the Integrated Rural Development Programme. The District Rural Development Agency created for implementation of IRDP will be responsible for implementation of all programmes viz. Drought Prone Area Programme, Dessert Development Programme, Special Livestock Production Programme, TRYSEM etc. The integration of all the programmes was done to reduce the expenditure on implementation of various programmes. With the extension of IRDP to entire country, the Scheme of Area Planning for Full Employment ceased to have separate identity from October 2, 1980.

The household cantered poverty alleviation strategy under IRD Programme should consist of not only the economic development but also the education of their children, health and welfare of the vulnerable members of the families. The implementation of National Rural Employment Programme works has also to be organised by the DRDA. It should be done in a manner so as to provide infrastructure support to IRDP and TRYSEM. This will reduce the need for creating infrastructural assets out of IRD funds.

The rural families selected under Lab to land Programme (launched by the Indian Council of Agricultural Research for transfer of technology to the farmers) were also assisted under IRDP subject to meeting the criteria for subsidy assistance.

On implementation of the New 20 Point Programme, the Integrated Rural Development Programme became part of it. The National Service Scheme (NSS) has been doing commendable work in the rural areas and has generated considerable enthusiasm and urge for social work amongst the youth. Under NSS the students are involved in social service work, sanitation drive, adult education programme, disaster relief, economic development programme, health nutrition etc. From 1976 onwards the main emphasis under NSS has been on rural reconstruction. Under NSS a large number of young, enthusiastic and motivated students are available, who could be intimately involved in planning and implementation of various rural development programmes. Keeping this in view the NSS students were involved in formulation, implementation, review and monitoring of IRD Programme. Integrated Tribal Development Agencies (ITDA) were also functioning in a concerted manner with DRDA for providing assistance under both these programmes.

Objectives of the programme are:

- To create self employment opportunities to the people living below poverty line by providing them permanent income generating assets to enable them to come up above the poverty line.

- To identify 600 families per year per block living below poverty line and providing them the bank loan and the subsidy depending upon the category of the beneficiary.

The aim of the programme is the emphasis on comprehensive development on family basis instead of conferring benefits in an isolated and sporadic manner. A cluster approach is advisable under the programme.

Under IRDP the priority was to be given to the women heads of the households, subject to their qualifying under the programme. It was also to ensure that the benefits in the form of loans and subsidies are directed towards women members of the households even where they are not heads of the households.

The Government of India sponsors the programme. The Centre and the State do the contribution of resources on 50:50 basis.

32.2 Commissionerate of Rural Development

From the inception of the Community development Programme, there was no separate Head of Department for the programme. In many States, the Development Commissioner, who was basically a secretariat officer, was expected to perform the role. In absence of effective field machinery, the operational aspects of implementation, review, monitoring etc. was not receiving adequate attention. Hence the State Governments created an administrative set up to deal with the programme as per the set up given below.

- Commissioner
- Joint/Deputy Commissioner
- Assistant Commissioner
- Deputy Conservator of Forests
- Deputy Director of Agriculture
- Executive Engineer
- Deputy Director (Statistics)
- Deputy Director of Animal Husbandry
- Deputy Director (Credit)

- Accounts Officer
- TDO (3)
- Accountant
- Deputy TDO (6)
- Research Assistant (5)
- Deputy Accountant (4)
- Clerk (12)
- Stenographer (6)
- Typists (6)
- Drivers (2)
- Peons (10)

Programme commenced in the year 1978 in 2300 blocks. 2000 of these blocks were selected from the blocks where various programmes were already running. 300 blocks were new. 300 blocks were added in 1979-80. The programme was extended in all the 5011 blocks since October 2, 1980.

32.3 Area of Operation

As the name denotes, the programme is in operation in all the rural areas.

32.4 Target Group

The target group of the IRDP is the families consisting 5 members and living below poverty line (at 1980-81 prices earning less than Rs. 3,500 per annum were treated as living below poverty line in Sixth Five year Plan). The same criteria were followed in the 1985-86 i.e. the first year of Seventh Five-Year Plan. In Seventh Five year Plan the poverty line was family income below Rs. 6,400 per year.

The target group of the programme at present is all the families living below poverty line (earning less than Rs. 11,000 per year) in rural areas. Earlier the categories were made among the poor people also to provide the benefits to poorer sections of the people among the poor people.

A growth centre or cluster approach was emphasised under IRDP. The intention of this approach is not to restrict the IRDP to few areas but to see that the spread of programme does not become so thin that the objective of helping families itself gets defeated. The following general criteria are laid down for selection of clusters in the operational guidelines for block level planning:

- Existence of specific infrastructure.
- Availability of credit institutions.
- Present level of development in the area and capacity to absorb credit to the desired extent.
- Concentration of scheduled castes and scheduled tribes and other weaker sections below poverty line.
- villages falling on milk route

32.5 Group Borrowings

A maximum of 25 per cent of the total allocation of funds to each DRDA was permitted to be utilised as subsidy under group ventures without any ceiling on the quantum of credit. The number of persons in a group may vary from 5 to 15. The group selected has to form a society, cooperative society, registered company or a partnership. It will be a voluntary group formed by the borrowers to be screened by the screening committee. NGO may also take part in formation of the Groups. The District Level Technical Committee will prepare project reports for the group. As the main objective of the group borrowing is to get the higher returns with higher investment, the project cost normally should not be of less than Rs. 1 lakh. The training is to be provided to the members of the selected groups by reputed institutions. Working capital loan is also to be considered. Subsidy will not exceed more than Rs. 1.25 lakh for each group.

32.6 Implementation

District Rural Development Agencies are having on their Governing Bodies a number of individuals representing Government Departments, banks, members of weaker sections Panchayat institutions etc. There are a number of other agencies and interest groups operating in the district, whose association with the functioning with the DRDA may be beneficial. These agencies like industrial and business houses, voluntary agencies, academic and scientific institutions, charitable organisations, organisations of scheduled castes and scheduled tribes. The benefit of their expertise should be taken by DRDA.

Integrated Rural Development Programme being a credit related programme, its success was largely to dependent upon flow of credit from the financial institution. To ensure proper availability of the credit, the following actions were to be taken:

- Simplification of forms and supporting documents.
- Posting of Credit Planning Officer at the district level.
- Branch expansion programme.
- Extension of lending operations of RRBs for IRDP.
- Strengthening of Bank branches.
- Formation of District and Block level Consultative Committees
- Commercial banks to be associated in selection of the borrowers from the beginning by the blocks.
- Monitoring of the credit to be done by the DRDA and Blocks about the applications received, sanctioned and the loan disbursed.
- Size of the units for various ventures should be viable and optimum.
- Expeditious disposal of loan applications.
- Resources of other agencies to be taken in to account while formulating the credit plan for IRDP.
- Practice of bunching of application to be discouraged
- Security should not be asked for up to the limit fixed by the Reserve Bank of India.
- DRDA and blocks may make available their jeep to bank officials where villages are far away. Joint tours could also be undertaken to effect economy.
- Adequate steps to be taken by DRDA to arrange supply of physical assets needed by the borrowers.
- Block officials should have regular coordination with bankers to ensure that the IRDP applications are receiving the

attention of the bankers.

- Incomplete applications returned by the banks should be processed quickly and returned to the bankers.
- DRDA should be associated with the market development for proper marketing of goods produced by the beneficiaries.
- Instead of a separate health certificate for animals financed under IRDP by a Veterinary Doctor, the minutes of the purchase committee which will include a veterinary doctor may contain a clause to certify the health of the animals. If required the format of the certificate of the purchase committee may be modified to include the clause relating to the health of the animals.

Banks have to make their own judgement if any particular scheme is viable in terms of infrastructure available and likely to be available.

For raising the incomes of the poor, it is necessary to improve the productivity of labour and provide them better access to improved tools, equipments etc. Hence the expertise of the local scientific and technical organisations was made available to help the beneficiaries in various ways. These organisations were:

- Research stations of Indian Council of Agricultural Research.
- Agricultural Universities
- Regional Research Stations of ICAR
- Krishi Vigyan Kendras
- Community Polytechnics
- Indian Institute of science and Technology

32.7 Other Features

Eligibility Criteria: The families having an annual income not more than Rs. 11,000 (living below poverty line) are covered under the programme.

Small farmers (owning irrigated land up to 2.5 acres or dry land up to 5 acres), marginal farmers (owning up to 1.25 acres of irrigated land or 2.5 acres of dry land), agricultural and non-agricultural labourers are eligible.

The selection of the beneficiaries is to be done by the Gram

Sabhas.

Financial Assistance: Loan Amount: There is no any limit for the loan amount. The unit cost less subsidy is to be financed.

Margin Money: As the subsidy is available to all the beneficiaries, the same is to be treated as the margin. No separate margin is to be brought by the beneficiaries.

Subsidy Administration: As per the recommendation of the Expert Committee on IRDP the system of back end subsidy is to be followed for adjustment of subsidy from the year 1996. As per the scheme the full project cost including subsidy would be disbursed to the borrowers as loan by banks. The subsidy admissible to the borrower under IRDP is to be kept in separate GL head (Subsidy Reserve Fund Account). A separate register is to be maintained to have the borrower wise details of the subsidy. There is no need to issue separate term deposit receipt in the name of the borrower. No interest should be applied on this account. Also for the purpose of charging interest on loan, subsidy amount should be excluded. The borrowers will not be entitled for subsidy if loan is fully repaid before the lock-in period. In case of repayment after lock-in period but before the currency of the loan, the borrower will be entitled for subsidy on a pro-rata basis only.

For the loans disbursed prior to introduction of back-end subsidy, the old procedure was to be followed. The old procedure was the adjustment of subsidy directly to the loan account. Or only net loan (project cost less subsidy) was released.

Purpose of Loan: Broadly any viable economic activity which is likely to raise the income level of the beneficiary above the poverty line on a lasting basis can be taken up for implementation under the programme. The following purposes may be considered for providing the loan.

- Agricultural Activities like work bullocks and bullock carts
- Allied activities like dairy, poultry, fisheries, piggery, sericulture, sheep and goat rearing etc.
- Industry likes carpentry, bee keeping, weaving, shoe making, cane and bamboo work etc.
- Services like tailoring shop barber shop, electrical appliances,

watch, cycle, TV, radio repairing shops etc.

- Businesses like tea, fruit, provisions, meat shop etc.

Loan Disbursement: The Government of India decided that the disbursement of loans under IRDP should be done in an open manner in the presence of a committee of non-officials. The committee should consist of at least 3 non-officials at the local level who should be invited to be present at the time of disbursement. The committee may include Panchayat Samiti Chairman as a member, if the bank branch is located in Block Headquarters. It could also include Panchayat Samiti Members and Village Pradhans and at least one elected women member, one scheduled caste and another schedule tribe member. A representative from a prominent NGO operating in the locality could also be co-opted. Borrowers are required to purchase assets from the dealers approved by DRDA.

District Rural Development Agency (DRDA) is the coordinating agency for the programme. District Collector is the Chairman of the DRDA.

Orientation Programme for IRDP Beneficiaries: Government of India has introduced a scheme of organising training programmes to create an awareness for the benefit of IRDP beneficiaries. The DRDA and Lead Banks will organise the programme, which will fulfil the following objectives:

- To increase the level of awareness of target group in regard to the programme content and the facilities provided under IRDP
- To encourage the participation of beneficiaries in the implementation of these programmes
- To promote cooperation and group action among the beneficiaries.
- To help them establish appropriate forum where a constant dialogue could take place between programme functionaries and beneficiaries group at the village level.
- To make the beneficiaries group self reliant to make them do things for themselves with guidance rather than expect others to do it for them.

For this the training camps of one-day duration will be

organised in a central village covering a cluster of villages. An awareness survey will also be conducted during the training.

Repayment Programme: The minimum repayment period for IRDP loans is fixed as 5 years. IRDP Loans are coupled with the subsidy and subsidy is now kept separately as sundry liability and is adjusted if the borrower maintains the account for a minimum lock-in period as follows:

Repayment period	Lock-in Period
5 years	36 months
6 years	42 months
7 years	48 months
8 years	52 months
9 years	56 months
10 years	60 months

Earlier there was no specific norm for the repayment programme. Due to this, the bank branches were fixing the repayment programme uniformly for 3 years for all the activities irrespective of the loan amount, type of activity, income generation capacity, life of the assets etc. It was the idea that repayment programme should be fixed in a realistic manner having regard to all factors and keeping in view the NABARD norms regarding gestation period and repayment programme for similar activities.

Recommendations of the Expert Committee on IRDP: Reserve Bank of India had appointed an expert committee under the Chairmanship of Shri D. R. Mehta, the then Deputy Governor of RBI to review IRDP and recommend suitable measures for its improvement.

The committee submitted its interim report. The RBI has accepted most of the recommendations of the committee, which are as follows:

Identification of Beneficiaries: The list of the people living below poverty line drawn by the Block authorities is to be approved by Panchayats. Bank officials, school teachers, village post masters, representatives of NGOs and prominent village elders should be invited by the Panchayats. Such list approved by the Panchayats should be approved by the Gram Sabha.

Identification of Investment Opportunities and preparation of Project Profiles: District Level Technical Groups Consisting of Lead District Officer of RBI, District Development Officer of NABARD, Lead Bank Manager, Technical Officials of State Government and non-government consultants are to be set up for preparation of project profiles. This cost to be borne by DRDAs. NABARD guidelines to be treated as suggestive for preparation of guidelines and not as outer limits.

Loan for Purchase of Land: Banks should provide loans under IRDP for acquisition of land together with short term credit. NABARD in consultation with revenue authorities may arrive at the cost of land at various places. NABARD has advised that the basis for valuation of land for the purpose of purchase under IRDP is 8 times of the net post developmental income from land or 80 per cent of the recorded price of land wherever record of sale prices of land is maintained by State Governments.

Infrastructure for Animal Husbandry: Adequate infrastructure for animal husbandry to be created for supply of feed, good quality of animal and marketing

Quantum of Investment under IRDP: Increasing both credit and subsidy should significantly enlarge per family/enterprise investment under IRDP. Government of India would examine the question of increasing the existing subsidy ceiling. RBI has suggested that without waiting for Government decision, Bank may advise controlling offices/branches to ensure that loan component are enhanced suitably to cover the project cost minus available subsidy. So that the project undertaken would be of adequate size to generate sufficient income to enable the beneficiaries to go above the poverty line in one go. RBI is also advising NABARD to consider revision of economic size of units in the light of the committee recommendations.

Working Capital Assistance: Working capital finance requirements should be fully taken into account while sanctioning loan to IRDP beneficiaries and suitable cash credit limit is sanctioned.

Security Norms: Limit for not obtaining mortgage should be uniformly fixed at Rs. 25,000 for all activities under IRDP. However for loans above Rs. 25,000 but up to Rs. 50,000 normal banking norms such as obtention of mortgage/margin etc. may be considered without however asking for any collateral security.

ISB Sector: Non farm, tiny/small enterprises and services sector should be further promoted for creating more employment opportunities.

Cash Disbursement under IRDP: Cash disbursement system may be extended throughout the country. Suitable instructions to DRDAs for dispensing with purchase committees will be issued by the Govt. FCP scheme formulated by NABARD should be encouraged. NABARD will further advise in the matter. The limit of cash disbursement was raised from Rs. 5000 to Rs. 10000 during February 1996 taking into account overall increase in prices of various articles subject to usual conditions like verification of assets etc.

Development of Infrastructure: DRDA must prepare a detailed perspective plan of infrastructure in consultation with DCC committees and BLBCs taking into account the availability of resources and the felt need of the rural population.

Provision of Training facilities: Banks may provide orientation training programme for IRDP beneficiaries.

Institutional/Organisational Support:

- Banks should fix realistic repayment schedules after taking in to account the level of income generation and economic life of the assets. The minimum repayment period for IRDP loans may be fixed as 5 years as against 3 years at present; initial moratorium may also be provided wherever required.
- Banks may provide group loans for various activities under IRDP; such group loans may also cover assistance required for infrastructure. The rate of interest and security requirements in such cases should however be related to per capita quantum of loan.

- The Lead Bank Officer should supervise the constitution and working of the Technical group referred to in point no. 2 besides maintaining liaison with controlling offices of other banks, State Govt. Officials, Panchayati Raj Institutions, VOs, and Self Help Groups. For reorganising DRDAs into compact teams of professionals and technical experts, credit Officer may be drawn from banks, RRBs and NABARD.
- In few districts on a pilot basis, instead of block authorities sponsoring applications, banks may be given freedom to select the beneficiaries out of BPL lists. Further instructions in this regards will be issued by RBI in consultation with Government of India who will also advise DRDAs suitably in the matter.
- In case of projects approved by CAPART, a few voluntary agencies at least on pilot basis can be given a list of BPL families for identification of borrowers for being sponsored by banks is the additional responsibility of ensuring backward/forward linkages and of verification of end use of credit. Government will issue necessary instructions to DRDA in the matter.
- Formation of Self Help Groups and their involvement in credit dispensation under IRDP should be encouraged.

Improving Recovery Performance: An analysis of recovery performance of IRDP scheme indicates that the recovery of loans constituted 33.1 per cent of credit as at end-March 1999 as against 32.9 per cent in the corresponding period last year. The following suggestions have been given to improve the recovery performance.

- Recovery Officers may be appointed by State Governments exclusively to recover bank dues. There may be one recovery officer in each district together with required complement of staff. The cost of such establishments may be borne by the DRDA and the Lead bank.
- Banks can utilise the services of utilisation reporter cum recovery facilitators on contract basis. They may be paid commission for reporting the maintenance of asset and

recovery.

- Group loans may be encouraged.
- Rescheduling of loans may be considered wherever necessary.
- More attention may be devoted to appraisal of loans.
- Wherever required, adequate gestation period or moratorium should be allowed in such a way that the commencement of recovery coincides with the income from the project.
- For projects where accrual of income is low in the beginning and goes up over a period of time, the instalment amount should be fixed up accordingly.
- Longer repayment period may be allowed to enable the borrower to utilise the higher percentage of incremental income for his own consumption.

While implementing the recommendations of the committee, the entire nature and content so also the general approach to IRDP may undergo substantial changes. Banks have therefore been expected to rise to the occasion by improving the quality of field level and other managerial staff by imparting adequate training so that they are better equipped to deal with the IRD programme.

Evaluation and Impact Studies: All programmes need the evaluation studies to enable the Government and all associated to know if the implementation of the programme is going on the right side or what are the changes to be made to make the programme more effective. During 1997-98, out of 16.97 lakh beneficiaries of IRDP, 46.13 per cent belong to SC/ST. The following specific areas were covered by the evaluation and impact studies of IRDP.

1. Is the DRDA, substantially following the methodology for preparing block level plans?
2. Are the beneficiaries being identified and assisted on the basis of criteria provided in the guidelines viz. The selection of poorest among the poor in the first instance?
3. In the selection of beneficiaries, are Gram Sabhas and other local institutions like Panchayats involved?
4. Are the beneficiaries provided substantial assistance for generating a sizeable incremental income and surplus for

them?

5. Have the beneficiaries been able to attain a substantially higher income level through the assistance provided to them under IRDP?
6. Are the beneficiaries repaying their loans within the stipulated time frame?
7. What is the proportion between the land-based activities and other activities in the projects funded under IRDP?
8. Are Scheduled Castes and Scheduled Tribes receiving the priority accorded to them in the guidelines?
9. Are Scheduled Castes and Scheduled Tribes beneficiaries receiving assistance of the same magnitude in terms of subsidies and loan, as other beneficiaries in the same block?
10. Are the banking institutions substantially complying with the instructions of Reserve Bank of India and other agencies in the matter of providing credit to the weaker sections? Are the arrangements of coordination with the banks are adequate and effective?
11. Is the implementation of IRD Programme properly linked and coordinated with implementation of other programmes, particularly for providing minimum needs and supporting infrastructure in terms of marketing facilities etc.?
12. What are the suggestions and recommendations for improving the quality of implementation of IRD Programme?

Findings of the sample study of IRDP by the Reserve Bank of India are as follows:

1. Out of 34668 applications submitted for loans up to Rs. 25,000, only 22959 (66.2 per cent) were sanctioned. The balance was rejected. Out of the sanctioned applications only 7698 (33.5 per cent) were sanctioned within a fortnight.
2. Application registers were not maintained properly.
3. Some private banks returned the applications on the plea of credit squeeze.
4. Disbursement was delayed due to non-availability of technical/field staff.
5. The procedure for implementation was not known to some of

the branch managers.

6. In some cases the loans were adjusted within a short period say within one year. This shows that the credit given was not need based.

4th Concurrent evaluation (September 1992 to February 1993) of the programme revealed the following.

Positive Points:

- The assets given to the beneficiaries in the 85 per cent of the cases were not of lower cost.
- A large percentage (96 per cent) of the beneficiaries informed that the type of assets provided to them were as per their choice.
- 69.2 per cent assets were found to be of good quality.
- The 51.5 per cent beneficiaries were selected by Gram Sabhas, 43 per cent by Local Officials and 5 per cent by Public Representatives.
- Roughly 34.1 per cent of the physically handicapped and 43.2 per cent of the assignees of surplus land were benefited under the programme.
- A large number (63 per cent) were provided assets under primary sector and among sub-sectors of the primary sectors, nearly 50 per cent of the assistance were given for milch animals.
- 56.58 per cent of the families assisted had a annual family income from assets of more than Rs. 2000.
- In 59 per cent cases no overdue was reported which shows that the recovery is satisfactory.
- Very high percentage (97 per cent) of the beneficiaries did not borrow from private moneylenders.
- Input and marketing facilities were available to a large extent in the primary sector.
- Overall per family investment (Credit + subsidy) was highest (Rs. 7,613) in tertiary sector, followed by Rs. 7,268 in the primary sector and Rs. 6,307 in secondary sector.
- 14.81 per cent of the old beneficiary families could cross the revised poverty line of Rs. 11,000 & 50.4 per cent of the

families were able to cross old poverty line of Rs. 6,400.

Areas of Concern:

- The extent of second dose of assistance to the old beneficiaries was very low (3.28 per cent).
- Annual family income of the assisted families was under estimated.
- 58 per cent of the beneficiaries were not aware about the Group Life Insurance Scheme.
- The claim settlement for perished assets remains unsettled in 56 per cent cases.
- Only 32 per cent of the beneficiaries were supplied with the Vikas Patrika.
- Only 2.13 per cent of the families reported that any of their members were assisted under DWCRA. This percentage was 3.88 for TRYSEM.

After review and restructuring of IRDP and allied programmes namely TRYSEM, DWCRA, SITRA, GKY and MWS, Swarnjayanti Gram Swarozgar Yojana (SGSY) was started with effect from 01.04.1999.

33

Scheme for Improved Tools to Rural Artisans (SITRA)

This scheme was launched to enhance the skill of the people working in various trades by providing them the improved tools in the area of their work.

This scheme was launched in July 1992 as a sub-scheme of IRDP in few selected district and became operative in all the districts later on.

The objectives of the scheme are

- To provide modern tools to artisans to enhance the quality of their products and to increase the productivity and income.
- This was also expected to help reduce their migration to urban areas.

All traditional rural artisans living below the poverty line except weavers, tailors needle workers and beedi workers are covered under the programme.

33.1 Progress under the Scheme

Since inception of the scheme 4.51 lakh tool kits have been distributed under the scheme. It was proposed to cover 2.22 lakh artisans with an outlay of Rs. 40 crore during the year 1996-97.

The target for 1998-99 was 327778 artisans with an outlay of Rs. 60 crore. The outlay for the year 1997-98 and 1999-2000 was Rs. 40 crore and Rs. 70 crore respectively.

The scheme envisages 10 per cent contribution from the artisan and 90 per cent subsidy from the Government of India for the average tool kit of Rs. 2,000.

33.2 Evaluation of the Scheme

1. The toolkits supplied and toolkits sanctioned to the beneficiaries showed large variations across states over the

period 1996-97, 1997-98 and 1998-99.

2. The value of the toolkits varied during the reference period due to the types and nature of the toolkits.
3. The highest per capita income earned by beneficiary households was recorded as Rs. 14,192 in Kerala, as against an earning of Rs. 2,664 in Bihar.
4. The study also traced the distribution of households under both beneficiary and non-beneficiary categories according to annual household income size groups.

   The income size groups are:

- less than Rs. 5,000;
- Rs. 5,000-Rs. 10,000;
- Rs. 10,000-Rs.15,000;
- Rs. 15,000-Rs. 20,000;
- Rs. 20,000-Rs. 30,000 and
- above Rs. 30,000.

It was found that at the all-India level, beneficiary households in the under Rs 20,000 categories comprised about 92.5 per cent of the total beneficiary households before the toolkits were received, while 7.5 per cent were in the above Rs 20,000 categories. Interestingly, by dint of hard work and with the help of the toolkits, some of them (about 14 per cent) upgraded their position to the above Rs 20,000 category. Besides, a number of households under the beneficiary category had acquired assets like ceiling fan, TV and three-wheeler. At the all-India, state and union territory levels, in contrast, about 94 per cent of the total households under the non-beneficiary category in all size groups were looking for indirect intervention to upgrade their economic position.

1. With everything else held constant, use of toolkits would enhance these households' income. Indeed, additional income from other sources may have increased overall income of households in this category, depending on the skill-specific jobs available in the market.
2. At the all-India level, about 50 per cent households under the beneficiary category felt that they received the toolkits simply

on the basis of their application, while 26 per cent felt that they got it due to their relationship with the sarpanch. About 2 per cent disclosed that they had paid (transaction cost) for it.

3. The study revealed that at the all-India level, 39 per cent beneficiaries of the total sample were able to get the benefit within a month, 37 per cent were able to procure it between two and four months and the rest in more than four months. About 2 per cent beneficiaries paid transaction costs, the highest incidence of such cases being found in Punjab (14 per cent) and the Andaman & Nicobar Islands (13 per cent). As regards the quality of the toolkits, 32 per cent of the total all-India level beneficiaries felt that some of the toolkits were good, 29 per cent found them 'all are in good condition', while 10 per cent felt that they were not good.
4. The study found that 34 per cent of the total households under the beneficiary category were using the entire toolkit, while a significant proportion of households (65 per cent) were using part of the toolkit. Strikingly, about 10 per cent were not able to use the toolkit because of its poor quality.
5. About 87 per cent of the beneficiaries felt that they benefited from SITRA, and this response was consistent across all states and UTs; for instance, product quality improved (77 per cent), total output went up (62 per cent), and earnings increased (64 per cent). However, in terms of savings, only 37 per cent beneficiaries at the all-India level felt that they were saving more. These beneficiaries also reported less borrowing (42 per cent). Finally, the beneficiaries on the whole (86 per cent) were happy with the programme and this perception was uniform across all states and UTs except Lakshadweep.
6. Only one beneficiary out of those interviewed reported owning a motorcycle. Strangely, no non-beneficiary was observed to possess any of these assets. Even here, only one non-beneficiary reported owning a three-wheeler.
7. The greatest concerns in India are poverty and not enough jobs (formal or informal) are available for its vast population. For any meaningful development it is imperative that policy-

makers adopt an integrated approach and not an exclusionary one.

8. Plentiful assistance does not necessarily mean less poverty, nor is it necessarily a satisfactory solution to the problems of rural artisans, given their uncertain outlays and incomes. Again, conventional practices may not always work for them either. Hence, it is the government's responsibility to facilitate the creation of a skilled workforce in the rural areas through technical support and training. Here it is crucial to adopt a local approach since there is no standard blueprint for training which is valid across all regions of the country. The institutional mechanism should allow local organisations to set their own rules. Training should be designed to meet market needs so that rural artisans can effectively produce and market their products and services.
9. Rural artisans are not always sufficiently aware of the government programmes as dissemination of information is usually less than adequate. Further, illiteracy makes bureaucratic machinery a daunting obstacle for them. Procedures should therefore be simplified and innovative mechanisms developed for rural artisans to make productive use of government support.

Part X
Subsidies for Welfare of Women, Children and Disadvantaged Groups

Part X

Schemes for Welfare of [illegible] and Disadvantaged Sections

14. [illegible]
15. Scheme for [illegible] (SLRS)
16. [illegible] (DWCRA)
17. [illegible] Programme
18. National Social Assistance Programme (NSAP)
19. [illegible]
20. [illegible]

34

Special Component Plan (SCP)

34.1 Objectives

Objective of this programme is that the financial assistance should be used for the development programmes of the scheduled castes persons, especially for the development of there business and to increase their productivity and income from their limited assets by taking up family oriented schemes. The population of Scheduled castes in our country is 13.82 crore as per 1991 census. Indian constitution provides for educational, economic and social development of SC/ST and other backward sections of the people.

Special Central Assistance (SCA) to Special Component Plan (SCP) of the States/Union Territories for scheduled caste people is linked to the Government of India's strategy for the socio-economic development of these people. The grant should be used to give an added thrust to the development programmes for the scheduled caste people with reference to their occupational patterns and the need for increasing the productivity of an income from their limited assets by taking up family oriented schemes for them. The SCA is used to fill the critical gap and vital missing inputs in family oriented income generating schemes so as to make the scheme more meaningful and effective.

Scheduled caste people are the target group under the Scheme. The State Governments and Union Territory Administrations are required to disburse Special Central Assistance to various sectors and agencies including State Development Corporations which are involved in the implementation of economic development programmes for scheduled castes.

Special Component Plan is a Central Government sponsored, most important poverty alleviation programme of the Ministry of Welfare for scheduled castes. States/Union Territories get 100 per cent subsidy for their assistance under Special Component Plan.

This special assistance is to be distributed by the administrations of the State Governments and the Union Territories to the organisations or agencies involved in the economic development of scheduled caste people. These agencies include Scheduled Caste Development Corporations.

34.2 Special Component Plan and Tribal Sub-Plan

The Ministry of Rural Development is implementing various Schemes/Programmes for providing avenues for employment to most disadvantaged sections of the society through special employment generation programmes and for improving the quality of life in rural areas. The Ministry has made specific provisions in the guidelines of the programmes being implemented to ensure adequate flow of resources to the Scheduled Castes and Scheduled Tribes.

In 1974, during the Fifth Five-Year Plan, Tribal Sub-Plan (TSP for Tribal Welfare and Development) was introduced, as an important Group Oriented Part of the Plan, with Special Central Assistance (SCA) as additive. During the Annual Plan of 1979-80, and subsequently from the Sixth Five-Year Plan, TSP was appropriately adopted as the Special Component Plan (SCP for the Scheduled Castes Development) with SCA as additive. This programme started in the year 1979-80 with an allocation of Rs. 5 crore only. In the year 1994-95, Rs. 273.85 crore and in the year 1995-96, Rs. 275 crore were released under the scheme. An amount of Rs. 308.27 crore was released under Special Central Assistance.

SC/ST Development Corporations in each state has been given the responsibility of preparing viable schemes for the socio-economic development of SC/ST persons. The corporations provide the subsidy and margin.

35

Scheme for Liberation and Rehabilitation of Scavengers (SLRS)

Scavengers are defined as "one who is partially or wholly engaged in the obnoxious and inhumane occupation of manually removing the night soil and filth". The dependent of a scavenger is one, who is member of his family or is dependent on him irrespective of the fact whether he is partially or wholly engaged in the said occupation. The scheme is centrally sponsored by the Ministry of Welfare and covers the areas all over the country.

Objective of the scheme is to liberate the scavengers from the degrading occupation of scavenging and assist them to start some gainful venture.

Eligibility: Scavengers in the age group of 18 to 50 years are eligible for assistance under this scheme. The most important aspect of this scheme is that each person in the above age group is a unit and is eligible for the assistance. The scheme would cover primarily all scavengers belonging to Scheduled Castes community. Scavengers belonging to other communities would also be covered. As the Government is committed to rehabilitation of the persons servicing dry latrines to eliminate the practice of manual scavenging, only such persons and their dependents are covered under the scheme.

Identification: The identification of the beneficiaries is to be done by the local body level committee. The corporations should adopt a cluster approach in training and rehabilitation programme. All Safai karmcharis eligible for the benefits under the scheme in a basti or locality should be rehabilitated together. At the time of selection of the beneficiaries for training and rehabilitation, the SCDCs would also intimate the Municipal Corporation, Municipal Council, Local Body and the Collector regarding the colonies serviced by the Scavengers, who are to be given training and financial assistance to ensure simultaneous action on conversion of dry latrines serviced by the scavengers and their rehabilitation.

The programme is sponsored by the Central Government.

The Government of India on March 22, 1992 launched the scheme.

The area of operation for the scheme is all over India.

The target group for the scheme is the scavengers living anywhere in India. The scheme would covers scavengers in urban/semi urban/rural or any other town or area including cantonment boards, colonies set up by public sector undertakings etc. where manual scavenging prevails.

Eligibility Criteria:

- Scavengers as per definition given above in the age group of 18 to 50 years are eligible under the scheme.
- Each member in the family in the above age group is eligible under then scheme.

Financial Assistance:

Loan Amount	The maximum Loan	Rs. 32,500
Margin	15 per cent of the project cost	Maxi. Rs.7,500
Subsidy	50 per cent of the project cost	Maxi. Rs. 10,000
Total project cost	Loan+Margin+Subsidy	Maxi. Rs. 50,000

S/C/ST development Corporation in the state will provide the margin under the scheme and hence no margin is to be contributed by the borrower.

50 per cent subsidy with a maximum of Rs. 10,000 is available under the scheme.

Subsidy is to be provided by the SC/ST Development Corporation of the state.

Hypothecation of the goods purchased out of loan amount is the security for the loan. No collateral security is to be taken for the loans under the scheme.

The slab rate of interest as prescribed by the Reserve Bank of India is to be charged. Differential Interest Rate (4 per cent) should be charged for the loan up to Rs. 6,500.

Purpose of Loan: The loan can be provided for services, business or agricultural purposes. The selection of trade for the beneficiaries should be carried out after detailed discussions with the beneficiaries keeping in view their preference, aptitude and competence for particular trades. The training provided and the trade should be the same. The market potential and the backward and forward linkages should also be kept in mind while formulating the projects.

Training: Training of the beneficiaries is an important input in this scheme and is to be arranged by the local body before disbursal of the loan. The training norms under this scheme would be the same as decided by the Ministry of Rural Development for TRYSEM on 5th may 1994. Any revision in TRYSEM training norms will also be applicable to SLRS. The State SC Development Corporation will take steps to constitute the State Level and District Level Coordination Committees on the TRYSEM pattern for various aspects of training. The existing TRYSEM set up could also be used.

Repayment Programme: The loans are repayable in 3 to 7 years. A repayment holiday up to 6 months may be granted.

Evaluation: In the report for the year 1995-96, the National Commission for Safai Karmacharis has given following recommendations to the banks for strict adherence by the Banks.

1. Branches should not ask for documents, guarantees etc. not envisaged in the scheme.
2. The beneficiaries should not be asked to deposit loan amount in the fixed deposit.
3. Banks should have transparent procedure to eliminate middlemen.
4. A joint committee of lead bank and SCDC should be set up to oversee the implementation of the scheme and remove bottlenecks.

A review of the implementation of the scheme was made in the year 1996 after 4 years of the implementation of the scheme. On the basis of the review several modifications were made in the scheme effective from 1.4.1996. The modifications have been included in the above paragraphs. Other observations are as follows:

1. It was observed that the banks and State SC Development Corporations have treated the maximum project cost as Rs. 20,000.
2. Applications are rejected on technical grounds by the banks.
3. Banks in some cases have asked for the collateral security.
4. The lower projects costs have lead to preponderance of non viable projects in which activity relating to piggery, poultry, and animal husbandry, small garment shop, basket weaving, small kirana/parchun shops, paan bidi shops are the main purposes. These projects do not provide sustainable income to the beneficiaries. Therefore the projects cost should be such that it is viable within the ceiling of Rs. 50,000.
5. It was observed that the women form a bulk of workforce engaged in manual scavenging. Even though the men folk have shifted to more dignified professions, women continue to do the scavenging. Hence women should be given the first priority for the rehabilitation. Post assistance support should be provided with special attention to the women beneficiaries.
6. Awareness should be created among the people regarding alcoholism and drug abuse.
7. Awareness is also to be created to break the stronghold of Jajmani system in which these women are trapped. These Jajmani rights are bought and sold and even registered in many states.
8. Other programmes like Minimum Needs Programme, Integrated Child Development Scheme etc. for overall development of the community should run simultaneously.

A quick study conducted by the Reserve Bank of India in January/February 1998 observed the following points.

1. Average size of loan is Rs. 25,000. The time taken for sanction is about 1½ months and for disbursal 3-4 months. No proper records of disposal of applications are kept.
2. Applications for SC/ST are to be rejected by the Divisional/Regional Manager. Many proposals were rejected on account of non-viability of proposals. Applications were rejected against the provision of the scheme/on flimsy grounds like:

- Applicants were employed by the Gram Panchayat/Municipal Bodies.
- Applicants have not submitted the affidavits as required.
- Not produced the caste certificates/ration card/photographs etc.
- Wife/Husband/mother/brothers were defaulters under the scheme or had already availed loan under other Government schemes like IRDP.
- Applicants do not belong to the service area of the branch.
- In case of female applicants, husbands approach for disbursal of loan.
- Targets are already achieved.

3. Loans are continued to be extended to the borrowers who are not actually engaged in manual scavenging/servicing dry latrines. As per revised guidelines of the Government, only those persons and their dependents who are servicing dry latrines should be rehabilitated.
4. Where the amount of loan was below Rs. 6,500, the normal rate of interest was charged instead of charging 4 per cent as per DRI scheme.
5. In some cases banks were insisting on third party guarantee or bank deposits.
6. Scheme has not percolated to the level of branches and the attitude is casual towards the scheme.
7. Approach is target oriented instead of employment oriented.
8. Group loans under the guidance and support of NGOs have not been encouraged.

9. In certain cases the repayments were regular but the units have not been established due to lack of supervision/post credit inspection.
10. Misutilisation of assistance in connivance with the supplier of goods, disposal of assets, low income generation, inadequacy of loan amount leading to abandonment of the project, diversion of funds etc. are some of the deficiencies that have been observed in the implementation.

On the basis of the study, the banks have been advised to improve their pre-sanction scrutiny and tighten post disbursement follow up and ensure proper asset creation.

36

Development of Women and Children in Rural Areas (DWCRA)

Involvement of women in rural development programmes was very less and was limited to only welfare programmes. It has been the experience in most of the beneficiary oriented rural development programmes that the individual poor are not in a position to retain benefit of the programme meant for them unless an institutional structure is created to help them do so. This scheme has been formulated as a specific response to these two needs of rural development programmes. There is an attempt to mould thinking patterns so that the rural poor especially women are given adequate importance in formulation of programmes and the top down approach is not perpetuated in their implementation. A large number of voluntary organisations, having the experience of running economic programmes for women are also to be involved.

The programme commenced in 1982. The program was launched as part of the Integrated Rural Development programme (IRDP).

This programme was started on a pilot basis in 51 selected districts.

Objectives: The objectives of the programme is to assist women to increase their income and become self reliant through group approach. The prime objective is the focussing attention on the women members living below poverty line. Total integrated approach to the development of the poorest families in rural areas will therefore necessarily require a greater emphasis on improving the quality of life of the women of those families.

Programme aims at empowering rural women living below the poverty line (BPL) by way of organizing them to create sustainable income generating activities through self-employment.

It was the first program of its kind that specifically focused on improving the quality of life of rural women. A unique feature of DWCRA, unlike other IRDP components, was that along with the improvement in income, it also focused on access to health, education, safe drinking water, sanitation, nutrition, etc. Thus it not only aimed at economic development, but also intended promoting social development. Another unique feature of the programme was that it emphasised group activity. It was thought that in the long run women's empowerment depends on creation of a movement that promotes awareness and self-reliance.

Target Group: The programme attempt to focus on women in poor families, which are being, assisted under various rural development programmes given the fact that most of women's earnings are spent on the essentials of daily consumption for their families. The group should comprise of 10 to 15 women. Earlier the number of group members was allowed as 15 to 20. But the experienced showed that in a large group, members do not know each other.

This is a sub programme of IRDP. Basic strategy adopted is a departure from strategy of rural development. It attempts to develop a receiving system to enable women to accept the benefits of various services and programmes which are focussed on them, but whose benefits they are not in a position to take. Under this programme group activities like pickles making, papad making, handicrafts etc. are also encouraged with an additional subsidy of Rs. 15,000 for the infrastructure facilities for the venture.

Revolving Fund: The amount of revolving fund received by the group will be deposited in savings bank account jointly operated by one member of the group and the Gram Sevika of the block. To make the group self-reliant the role of Gram Sevika was phased out in stages later on. The role of Gram Sevika was phased out after verifying that the group is:

- Purchasing raw material properly, or
- Utilising the raw material to produce finished products, or
- Selling the finished products, or

- Depositing the sales proceeds in full or in part as decided by the group, or
- Using this money as and when required, from 2 years from opening the joint bank account, the Gram Sevika may be withdrawn as one of the compulsory signatories to the joint account. She should be replaced by a group member who would sign the necessary documents/cheques along with group organiser.

Evaluation Study of DWCRA:

1. Overall, DWCRA was not able to meet the objectives that were set forth. The study showed that a large majority of beneficiaries could not utilise the programme to translate into substantial economic benefits. The average per day income of a beneficiary was reported to be only Rs. 42.
2. At the national level DWCRA programme was received well. There was wide spread knowledge about the various aspects of DWCRA. However, very small proportion of beneficiaries could tell the different components of program. Lack of commitment of officials, inability to mobilise NGOs for the benefit of program and high illiteracy of rural women were some of the reasons for this.
3. As women became more aware, there was a reduction in family size and time spent on household activities. More women were keen to spare some hours for productive work.
4. Eligible women, from both majority and minority communities, participated in DWCRA, in proportion of their overall population. However, since the programme was targeted at BPL families, a greater proportion of beneficiaries belonged to lower classes, and Scheduled Castes and Scheduled Tribes (SC& ST). The programme, as intended, also benefited disabled women. Analysis showed that 52.8 per cent of all beneficiaries were SC/STs, and 2.4 per cent were disabled.
5. DWCRA reached not only married women but it also benefited unmarried and widowed women, though their number was small.

6. As such, DWCRA beneficiaries had more number of children than others (non-beneficiaries), but the average age of beneficiaries was three years more than that of the later. This showed that more women, who had participated in DWCRA, had lower fertility.
7. Data showed that both literate and illiterate women participated in DWCRA. It had mobilized both educated and uneducated women, with better educated women often providing the leadership, as Adhyaksha or Treasurer.
8. DWCRA had no effect on schooling among children because all sections of society attached high significance to children's education.
9. DWCRA women had higher daily earnings than other women who had not participated in DWCRA. While the beneficiaries earned Rs. 42 a day, the non-beneficiaries earned Rs. 32.20. The annual family income of beneficiaries was Rs. 11,925 while that of the non-beneficiaries was Rs. 10,978.
10. Data on indicators such as kuccha-pucca house, toilet facilities in the house, and availability of drinking water indicated poor living condition of both beneficiaries of DWCRA and the non-beneficiaries. In both the categories, about 60 per cent lived in kuccha house and about 75 per cent lacked toilet facilities. Moreover, among the BPL families, few owned consumer durable or farm equipment, such as refrigerator, three- wheeler, tractor, power tiller, combined thrasher/harvester. Only 12.5 per cent had TV sets and 17.6 per cent had ceiling fans. Percentage of women whose family owned motorcycle or tractors was almost negligible.
11. Among the beneficiaries of DWCRA only 6.3 per cent read newspaper, 15.8 per cent listened to radio, and 12.8 per cent watched TV.
12. Under DWCRA different types of activities were chosen in different States. Yet more than half of them were related to the primary sector. Overall, 23.1 per cent groups chose agriculture related activities, and 20.9 per cent chose livestock

and fisheries activities. Another 11.6 per cent of the groups chose forest based activities.

13. One of the main goals of DWCRA was to promote group activities among the poor women. Observations showed that officials involved formed the groups only on paper. In actuality group members functioned as individuals. At the same time DWCRA had undoubtedly initiated group activities among women. They had come out of the boundaries of the household and learnt to interact with other women, village and block officials and consumers. Nearly half of the groups studied, maintained proper registers of DWCRA activities, which was not a mean achievement looking at the socio-economic milieu in which rural women operated. However, the auditing of records was poor.
14. In training respect the programme had not done well. Overall, only 26 per cent groups received any training.
15. According to the programme, those groups formed under DWCRA were to get interest free revolving fund and subsidised loan. The study showed that only 52.2 per cent of the groups had received the revolving fund. The percentage of groups that took loan was still less. The DWCRA groups were generally not interested in loan. Only 6 per cent of group leaders knew how much subsidy they were entitled for on bank credit. This reflects the low credit taking capacity of the rural poor.
16. DWCRA had a direct and significant impact on employment and group activities. The biggest achievement of DWCRA was that it raised desire for self-employment among poor, rural women and encouraged them to work in groups. 92.5 per cent beneficiaries reported that DWCRA has created a desire for self-employment. 88.8 per cent beneficiaries feel that DWCRA has raised their income. This may not immediately translate into income figures but in the long run it has a great transformative potential.
17. DWCRA had a visible impact on savings, economic conditions, and social prestige.

18. DWCRA had less impact on heath and sanitation, and drinking water, which are more of community services. It had no impact on schooling of children, as the demand for schooling was already very high.
19. There were significant regional variations in the implementation of DWCRA, number of groups formed per 1000 population, continuation of activity and impact on different indicators

At the end, it can be concluded that for the success of the DWCRA like programs:

1. There has to be a greater emphasis on participatory model, rather than the top down approach that was adopted.
2. The identification of beneficiaries should be left to Gram Panchayats.
3. Schemes should be made to achieve impact and not merely meet targets.
4. The model of micro lending through self help groups is a superior model, where in the groups get time to evolve over a period of time.
5. Project selection should involve groups, NGOs as well as bankers. Groups should be taking projects with adequate forward and backward linkages, avoiding overcrowding of projects in an area.
6. Capacity building of NGOs should be taken up at large scale.

36.1 Select Women Welfare Programmes

36.1.1 Support for Training and Employment (STEP): Under the programme of Support for Training and Employment (STEP) marginalized and asset less women are provided training in new technologies in agriculture, dairying, horticulture, fisheries, handicrafts, handlooms etc., organized into groups and provided with necessary infra-structure, managerial and marketing support for productive activities on a sustainable basis. Since the inception of the programme in 1987, 134 such projects have been implemented benefiting more than 6 lakh women throughout the country.

36.1.2 Women's Economic Programme: Under the Women's Economic Programme, now named Swavalamban, employment linked training is provided to women in various traditional and non-traditional trades. Annually more than a thousand projects are sanctioned to train about 50,000 women. During 2001-02, 1045 projects benefiting 53,050 women have been sanctioned.

36.1.3 Rashtriya Mahila Kosh (RMK): Since its inception in 1993 the Rashtriya Mahila Kosh (RMK) has sanctioned credit worth Rs. 113.50 crore (up to October 31, 2002) to benefit more than 4.28 lakh women through 1046 NGOs spread over the country. Government of India has approved an increase in lendable resources of RMK to Rs. 100 crore. Apart from its core activities, the RMK has been catalytic in the development of several new organizations dealing with micro-credit across the country both in the public sector and voluntary sector.

With a view to boosting its efforts to expand its outreach to hitherto uncovered/marginally covered states, the maximum amount of loan to an NGO has been raised from the present ceiling of Rs. 1 crore to Rs. 5 crore and the intermediate interest rate cap of 12 percent has been withdrawn, thereby giving necessary leverage to the prospective NGOs to fix interest rates for the ultimate beneficiaries between the range of 8 to 18 percent per annum. The objective of the above mentioned initiatives is to increase the outflow of RMK's funds to the needy women through the intervention of Women Self Help Groups.

36.1.4 Family Counseling Centres: The objective of the Family Counseling Centre is to provide preventive and rehabilitative services to women and children who are victims of atrocities and family maladjustments. The Scheme is being implemented since 1984 through voluntary agencies. During the year 2001-02 grants amounting to Rs. 374.06 lakh have been sanctioned for running 417 Family Counseling Centres benefiting 27,749 women.

36.1.5 Short Stay Homes: Under this scheme an amount of Rs. 603 lakh was released to 328 homes serving to 9,570 beneficiaries during 2001-02. The Department is also implementing a National Plan of Action for the rescue, rehabilitation and reintegration of women and girls trapped in commercial sex. The new scheme of *Swadhar* was launched last year for providing a comprehensive package of food, shelter, health cover, counseling and skill training to women and girls in difficult circumstances. Major States have formulated Action Plans and comprehensive project proposals synergising the efforts of the government and non-government organizations have been formulated for all the mega cities. 21 projects have so far been sanctioned for the rehabilitation of nearly 2913 women in difficult circum-stances.

36.1.6 Swa-shakti Project: After the success of the pilot project Swa-shakti under which more than 12000 self-help groups have been formed in 10 States, the Department launched a new scheme Swayamsidha on November 29, 2001. Under the programme, 53,100 Self-Help Groups comprising of 9,29,250 women beneficiaries shall be formed in 650 blocks (including 238 IMY blocks) throughout the country. The total estimated cost of the programme is Rs. 116.30 crore out of which Rs. 92.30 crore will be spent at the block level, Rs. 16 crore at the State level and Rs. 8 crore at the national level.

37

Antyodaya Programme

The philosophy of the Antyodaya is that the rich persons in the village should look after their poor neighbours not with the feeling of the gratitude but with the feeling of their utmost duty i.e. through self-motivated action. This is to obtain an egalitarian pattern in community life that is reflected by obtaining a living standard which in quantitative terms is neither too big to cause display of extravagance nor it is too small to cause deprivation of necessities for human existence. Due to the Government assuming the responsibility of the rich persons of the community, the meaning of Antyodaya has changed.

This programme was started in Rajasthan on October 2, 1977. The meaning of word "Antyodaya" is the last in the line. In other word we can say the poorest of the poor. Antyodaya Programme aimed at providing self-sustaining economic independence to the poorest of the poor persons.

Target Group: The poor people selected by the Gram Sabha were eligible for assistance under this scheme on the following basis:

- Families having no earning member between 15 to 50 years of age;
- Families having no economic assets have earning members but annual income of family does not exceed Rs. 1200.
- Families having some economic assets but annual income are less than Rs. 1,800.
- Other families having economic assets but living below poverty line.

The Rajasthan Government granted the relief for the following:

1. The allotment of land
2. Providing work under Food for Work programme

3. Allotment of House sites and financial assistance for construction of house
4. Loans for purchase of cattle
5. Land for village industries.

In some other states also this programme was started. This programme got appreciation even from the World Bank. Integrated Rural Development Programme has derived its roots from the Antyodaya Programme.

Target and Achievement: Initially the Rajasthan Government started the programme in 33000 villages and, identified 5 poorest families from each village. From these villages and other villages, 45700 families were benefited in the year 1977. In the year 1978, 160000 poor families were identified.

38

National Social Assistance Programme (NSAP)

The Programme introduces a national policy for social security assistance to the poor families and represents a significant step towards the fulfilment of the Directive Principles in Articles 41 and 42 of the Constitution recognising the concurrent responsibility of the Central and State Governments in the matter. The NSAP is a Centrally Sponsored Programme to extend 100 per cent Central assistance to the States/UTs to provide the benefits under it in accordance with the norms, guidelines and conditions laid down by the Central Government.

The NSAP provides opportunities for linking the social assistance package to schemes for poverty alleviation and the provision of basic needs. Specifically, old age pensions can be linked to medical care and other benefits for the old and the poor. Integrated Rural Development Programme (IRDP)/ Nehru Rozgar Yojana (NRY) assistance may be provided in addition to family benefits for the families of poor households on the loss of breadwinner. Maternity assistance can be linked to maternal and child care and provision of better diet to pregnant mothers. The NSAP shall be implemented by the Panchayats and Municipalities in the delivery of social assistance so as to make it responsive and cost-effective. In the process, the Panchayats and the Municipalities will be strengthened and it may be possible for them to mobilize local resources for supplementing benefits from the Government. Panchayats and Municipalities will be encouraged to involve voluntary agencies to the extent possible in taking these benefits to the poor households for whom they are intended. The responsibility for implementation shall, however, rest on the Panchayats and the Municipalities.

The scheme envisages that State/UT Governments will:

- Ensure wide and continuous publicity to the benefits under the NSAP and the procedures for claiming them through posters, brochures, media and other means. They shall ensure that application forms are widely available in local languages. Procedure for verification of applications should be prompt and simple. Sanctions should be expeditious. Delays and malpractices should be eliminated in disbursement. Adequate accounting arrangements should be instituted to enable proper post-audit. Every effort should be made through these means to ensure that only eligible persons obtain the benefits.
- Subject to these and other guidelines issued by the Government of India from time to time, suitable procedures may be instituted for the implementation of the Programme and Government of India kept informed. They may also comply with any modifications that Government of India may indicate, based on review. In the procedures so instituted, the nodal authority for the NSAP as well as the sanctioning authority for each scheme under the NSAP at the District level will also be prescribed.
- Intimate to the Government of India the number of beneficiaries under each component of the NSAP, district-wise. In order to facilitate smooth flow of funds to the implementing agencies and to ensure prompt disbursal of benefits under NSAP, the State/UT Governments would arrange for opening of separate accounts at the District level for the release of funds by the Central Government.
- Constitute State level and District level Committees for the purposes laid down in these guidelines in the implementation of the NSAP.

The State Level Committee will be headed by the Chief Secretary and will include:

- concerned Secretaries such as Finance, Rural Development, Municipal Affairs, Health and Welfare;
- a nominee of the Union Ministry of Rural Development;
- a nominee of the Ministry of Urban Development; and
- independent experts and representatives of NGOs.

This Committee will be responsible for monitoring and evaluation of the Programme and matters concerned therewith and to report to the Government of India.

The District Level Committee (DLC) will be headed by the Collector and will include:

1. concerned Members of Parliament;
2. about one-third of the Members of the State Legislative Assembly from the district, as far as possible representing all political parties;
3. Chairperson of the Zila Parishad and/or of its relevant Standing Committee;
4. Heads of the relevant Departments at the District level;
5. representatives from among chairpersons of Panchayat Samitis and Municipalities; and
6. independent experts and representatives of NGOs.

The District Level Committee will be responsible for monitoring and evaluating the Programme and for matters concerned therewith. The District Collector or any other officer given the nodal responsibility of implementing the NSAP at the District level, will be responsible for

- Efficient implementation of the NSAP in accordance with these guidelines and the procedures instituted;
- giving wide publicity to the NSAP and its procedures;
- for convening meetings regularly of the District level Committee.
- for monitoring and compiling information about the implementation of the scheme and furnishing it to the prescribed authorities;

The District Collector/Sanctioning Authority, in turn, will be responsible for arranging the payment of the benefit to the beneficiaries. Disbursement of this benefit to individual beneficiaries may take place preferably in the gram sabhas/ neighbourhood committees as the case may be.

The Panchayats/Municipalities will be responsible for implementing the schemes in their respective areas of operation and for:

- Disseminating information about the NSAP and the procedures for obtaining benefits under it. In this task, they should encourage and involve the cooperation of voluntary organisation.
- The Gram Panchayat/Municipalities are expected to play an active role in the identification of beneficiaries under the three schemes. The State Government may thus communicate targets for NOAPS, NFBS and NMBS to the Gram Panchayats/Municipalities so that identification can take place in the gram sabhas by the gram Panchayats and in neighbourhood/mohalla committee by the Municipalities in line with these targets. Further, central assistance under NOAPS, NFBS and NMBS may also be preferably disbursed in public meetings, such as gram sabha meetings in the rural areas and neighbourhood/mohalla committees in urban areas.
- Monitoring and following up delays, if any, in sanctions and disbursement.
- All benefit payments should preferably be payable to the bank account of the beneficiary in the Post office Savings Bank or in a commercial bank or through Postal Money Order. However, in the case of NOAP and NMBS cash disbursement may be permitted provided the payment is made in public meetings preferably of Gram Sabha in village and in neighbourhood/mohalla committees.

The Programme has come into effect from August 15, 1995. The Programme comprises three separate Schemes, namely:

- National Old Age Pension Scheme (NOAPS)
- National Family Benefit Scheme (NFBS) and
- National Maternity Benefit Scheme (NMBS)

38.1 National Old Age Pension Scheme (NOAPS)

The objective of the Programme is to extend financial assistance to old persons having little or no regular means of subsistence. Target group is the old persons who are destitutes in the sense of having no regular means of subsistence from their own sources of income or through financial support from family members or other sources.

Salient Features:

- Age of the applicant (male or female) should be 65 years or above
- The applicant must be a destitute in the sense of having little or no regular means of subsistence from his /her own sources of income or through financial support from family members or other sources
- The amount of pension is Rs.75 per month per beneficiary. The State Government may add to this amount from their own sources.

Upper ceiling on the number of beneficiaries for a State/UT is prescribed by the Central Government.

Village Panchayats and relevant Municipalities shall report every case of the death of a pensioner immediately after its occurrence to the appropriate sanctioning authority. The sanctioning authority shall ensure that payments are stopped thereafter.

The sanctioning authority shall have the right to stop/recover payments of any pension sanctioned on the basis of false or mistaken information about eligibility.

National Family Benefit Scheme (NFBS): The objective of the Programme is to extend financial assistance to households living below the poverty line in case of death of the primary breadwinner. Target group is households below the poverty line on the death of the primary breadwinner. The 'primary breadwinner' has been defined as the member of the family whose earnings contribute substantially to the total household income.

Salient Features:

- Central assistance for a lumpsum family benefit is available for the households below the poverty line on the death of the primary breadwinner in the bereaved family.
- The amount of assistance is Rs. 10,000.

- The primary breadwinner is a member of the family whose earnings contribute substantially to the total household income.
- The death of the primary breadwinner due to natural or accidental causes should have occurred while he or she is in the age group of 18 to 65 i.e. more than 18 years of age but less than 65 years of age.
- The maximum limit of the total number of beneficiaries of a State/UT is prescribed by the Central Government.
- The family benefit is paid to such surviving members of the households of the deceased who, after local inquiry, is determined to be the head of the household.

The family benefit will be paid to such surviving member of the household of the deceased who, after due local inquiry, is determined to be the head of the household. For the purpose of the Scheme, the term 'household' would include spouse, minor children, unmarried daughters and dependent parents. In case of death of an unmarried adult, the term "household" would include minor brothers/sisters.

The sanctioning authority shall have the right to recover payments made on the basis of false or mistaken information about eligibility.

38.2 National Maternity Benefit Scheme (NMBS)

The objective of the Programme is to extend financial assistance to pregnant women of households below the poverty line up to the first two live births. Target group is Pregnant women of the households living below the poverty line up to the first two live births.

Salient Features:

- A lumpsum cash assistance of Rs. 500 to the pregnant woman of the household living below the poverty line is given provided she is 19 years of age or above.
- The benefit is available up to the first two live births.

- The benefit is disbursed several weeks prior to the delivery. In case of delay, the benefit may be given even after the birth of the child.

The maternity benefit will be disbursed in one-instalment 12-8 weeks prior to the delivery. However, the benefit can be made even after the delivery of child subject to the sanctioning authority being satisfied about the genuineness of the case. It is desirable that the child receives one dose of oral polio and BCG vaccination at birth and the first dose of DPT and polio in the sixth week.

The sanctioning authority shall have the right to stop/recover payments made on the basis of false or mistaken information about eligibility.

Implementing Agency: The programme is implemented by the district level implementing authorities headed by the District Collector/Magistrate/Deputy Commissioner. It is implemented with the assistance of the Panchayats and Municipalities in the delivery of social assistance to make it more responsive and cost effective.

Achievement: The original budget provision for the National Social Assistance Programme during the year 1998-99 was Rs. 700 crore. However, the allocation was reduced to Rs. 620 crore at RE stage. The amount utilised against this RE is Rs. 620.20 crore during 1998-99. During the year 2001-2002, the amount allocated under NSAP is Rs. 635 crore.

Evaluation: The State level and District level Committees constituted as per the provisions of the NSAP guidelines meet from time to time to monitor and evaluate the performance of the schemes in their respective States/Districts. The Nodal Ministry at the Centre also monitors States' progress in implementing the schemes to evaluate performance of each one of them. An Evaluation Study on the Programme covering eight States has also been completed recently through a reputed Research Organisation. Another two such Studies are in progress in the States of Rajasthan and Uttar Pradesh.

Corrective Action Taken: Various aspects emerging from the periodical review meetings at the Centre, States and districts are taken note of and appropriate actions are taken accordingly for ensuring improvement in the implementation of the schemes. The findings of the Research Organisation which has since submitted its Report are being studied.

Evaluation of National Old Age Pension Scheme: National Old Age Pension Scheme is found to be extremely beneficial to the old destitutes. In general, it has succeeded in giving them a sense of security in life and has definitely improved their quality of life.

- A majority (81.22 per cent) of the NOAPS beneficiaries did not face any difficulty in availing the benefit. 82.12 per cent of the respondents got the approval from the authority concerned within 6 months and for a good percentage of them (49.76 per cent), the time lag between application and sanction has been only to the extent of 2 months
- Of the selected persons for the scheme, 81.16 per cent received the benefit within 2 months of sanction, of which 31.54 per cent received it within 15 days and another 30.35 per cent within 15-30 days' time.
- Nearly 96 per cent of the beneficiaries feel that the Scheme definitely made a perceptible change in the quality of their life at least to some extent.
- It is found that 72.79 per cent of the beneficiaries belong to the age group, 65-74 years. It is also noticed that only one person from a family is being provided with the benefit even if there are more than one eligible person in the family.
- Nearly sixty percent of the sample beneficiaries are found to be women. Socially backward communities like SC/ST/OBC constitute 83.79 per cent of the sample population. Of these, the SC/ST beneficiaries form 54.25 per cent.
- Majority (84.41 per cent) of the beneficiaries are illiterate and 53.82 per cent of their family members also belong to the same category.

- Most of the beneficiaries (68.20 per cent) are not engaged in any income generating activity. About 26.61 per cent are found to be unable to work while 41.59 per cent are currently not working.
- The beneficiary households are found to be earning income mainly from wages (38.42 per cent) and agriculture (26.11 per cent).
- Among the sample beneficiaries, 80.38 per cent are found to live in their own houses. However, of these, 79.27 per cent possess Kucha houses and 8.54 per cent live in houses with a plinth area of only 300 sq. ft. or less. Only 5.98 per cent live in houses of plinth area of 500 sq. ft. or more. About 36.42 per cent of the beneficiaries are found to possess landed property of their own.
- A vast majority of the beneficiaries (83.39 per cent). have reported that they do not incur any regular expenses in getting the benefit.

38.3 National Maternity Benefit Scheme

The following indicate that the benefit of the scheme is reaching the targeted women.

- Majority of the beneficiaries expressed satisfaction in the procedures for availing the benefit. As high as 82.13 per cent of the beneficiaries reported that they did not experience any difficulty in availing of the benefit.
- The most prevalent mode of payment of the benefit is cash. Also, 77.72 per cent of the payments in cash are received in a public meeting or in the presence of others, indicating transparency in the process.
- The major sources of household income are wages earned and agriculture. While 68.54 per cent of the beneficiary families earn income from wages, 41.14 per cent have reported income from agriculture. The annual household income is less than Rs. 20,000 in the case of 95.27 per cent of the beneficiaries, indicating that the benefits of the scheme are reaching the needy.

- Most of the beneficiaries (97.80) are aged above 19 years, which is the minimum age to qualify for availing the benefit under the scheme. Of these, as much as 83.78 per cent of the beneficiaries are young (aged between 19 to 29 years).
- Majority of the beneficiaries (85.64 per cent) belong to the socially and educationally backward communities. Of these, the SC, ST and OBC categories account for 34.50 per cent, 20.02 per cent and 30.94 per cent of the beneficiaries, respectively.
- 54.42 per cent beneficiaries are illiterate. Similar is the pattern with their family members.
- 90.15 per cent of the beneficiaries are found to live in kucha or semi-pucca houses. The sizes of the houses they live in are also small (less than 200 sq. ft. for 76.33 per cent of the beneficiaries).

The implementation of the scheme will be more effective if more care is taken in areas like selection of beneficiaries and timely disbursal of the benefits so that it can be better utilised for the benefits of the mother and the baby.

38.4 National Family Benefit Scheme

The scheme is definitely beneficial to the economically and socially backward as well as the weaker sections of the society. The following are some of the positive indicators of the scheme.

- Majority of the beneficiaries have expressed satisfaction over the benefit they have received. As many as 73.63 per cent are happy to some extent and 24.06 per cent are happy to a large extent. A majority (70.81 per cent) of beneficiaries report that they did not face difficulties in availing the benefits. Around 28.51 per cent beneficiaries received benefits within 2 weeks and 76.44 per cent got it within 2 months of sanction.
- Most of the beneficiaries (87.76 per cent) have reported that they have received benefits through cheque/money order/ demand draft. This reduces the incidence of the beneficiaries being cheated by paying lesser amounts as against the actual eligible amount.

- SC/ST/OBC categories constitute 85.12 per cent of the beneficiaries and 87.03 per cent of the sample beneficiaries are women. More than 20.27 per cent of the beneficiaries are aged above 50 years. 16.65 per cent of the beneficiaries are either unable to work or not currently working.
- 71.87 per cent of the sample beneficiaries are totally illiterate while 42.84 per cent of their family members also belong to the same category.
- Wages and agriculture are the major sources of income. The aggregate sample average annual household income works out to only Rs.7901.
- Only 45.72 per cent possess landed property. 76.82 per cent of the beneficiaries live in kucha houses and only 6.44 per cent own pucca houses and a majority of these houses are below 300 sq.ft. Only 6.25 per cent live in houses above 500 sq. ft. plinth area.
- Only 5.40 per cent beneficiaries own TV sets and 7.36 per cent own ceiling fan. Vehicles/refrigerators, etc. are owned by less than 1 per cent of the samples.

Areas for Improvement:

- Only 3.43 per cent of the total beneficiary samples feel that the scheme has in a way brought a sense of security to life. This figure is minimal and is to be improved.
- Only less than 4 per cent sample beneficiaries have responded to the question related to sources of information about the scheme. 75.73 per cent are not aware of the verification procedures and 68.62 per cent are not aware of the selection procedures. 42.26 per cent of the beneficiaries are not aware of the exact amount they are eligible for under NFBS. All these indicate that the general awareness of the scheme is on the lower side.
- Difficulties in obtaining death certificates (49.41 per cent) and non-co-operation of concerned officials (48.52 per cent) are the major stumbling blocks in availing NFBS benefits. Around 48.57 per cent of the beneficiaries availed NFBS

benefits without attaching a death certificate along with the application form.

- Delay in sanction is found to be high and extreme cases of over 2 yeas after submission of applications are also noticed. Since the bereaved families need immediate support, the procedures need to be toned up
- No uniformity is observed even within a state on application procedures like where the applications are available, where it is to be submitted, what are the certificates to be attached, etc.

39

Minimum Needs Programme (MNP)

Every human being has some minimum basic needs to lead a graceful life. To lead the graceful life certain basic amenities are must. Basic needs include two elements. First they include certain minimum requirements of a family for private consumption: adequate food, shelter and clothing are obviously included, as would be certain household equipment and furniture. Second they include essential services provided by and for community at large such as drinking water, sanitation, public transport, and health and educational facilities. Minimum Needs is the part of the dynamic basic needs concept and is therefore considered here in the context of the India's overall economic and social development. To secure essential infrastructure and social services, to the weaker sections of the society especially in rural areas within a reasonably time frame, the minimum needs programme was introduced.

The programme was also to create the unskilled labour due to having a large construction component in it. Elementary education, adult education, and nutrition programme of the revised Minimum Needs Programme is related to urban as well as rural areas. All other component of the programme is for rural areas. Programme has a large outlay for agricultural labourers and marginal farmers.

This programme was introduced in the year 1972. Keeping in view the changing situation, the programme was revised and new norms were to be achieved by the year 1988. To get the optimum benefit from the programme, all these programmes have to be taken a up a as package for specific areas and groups. For overall development of the area the sectoral approach of the departments will not bring desired result. The programmes are to integrate at implementation level so that the desired effects can be seen.

Date of Commencement: The Minimum Needs Programme commenced during the Fifth Five-Year Plan and it continued during the period of Sixth Five-Year Plan (1980-85).

Environmental Improvement of the Urban Slums: One fifth of the urban population was living in slums without basic amenities of life. For the Year 1988, such population was estimated at 3.6 crore. Water supply, sewerage, street paving, and provision of community latrines were the main improvement programme under these areas.

Nutrition: Supplementary nutrition and mid-day meals were two schemes under this programme. The scheme of supplementary nutrition was for the children less than 6 years of age (before going to school) and for expectant and nursing mothers from weaker sections of the society. Blocks with high concentration of SC and ST were to be covered. Supplementary nutrition of 200 to 300 calories and 8 to 12 Grams protein to school going children was to be provided for 300 days in a year. For each mother 500 calories and 25 grams of protein was to be provided. Special nutrition programme component of Integrated Child Development Services Programme was envisaged to cover one-fourth of the blocks with high concentration of SC and ST persons. Mid-day meal scheme was to attract the children to school and to avoid dropouts among the poor people. It was covering the children between the age of 6 to 11 years belonging to weaker section.

Rural Roads: All the village with a population of 1500 or more were to be linked with roads as per old MNP. And as per this estimate a road length of 76300 km was needed to complete the target till April 1, 1977. As per revised plan all the villages with population of 1000 and above were to be linked with roads by the year 1988. Thus 25690 additional villages are to be covered and this will need an additional road length of 77094 km @ 3 km per village. Thus total requirement was 153394 km. Half of this length was to be black topped. An outlay of Rs. 800 crore was kept under the plan.

Rural Electrification: As per revised MNP, 50 per cent of the villages were to be electrified compared to 36 per cent villages already electrified as on October 1977. The pattern of electrification was varying with 100 per cent in Punjab to only 3.9 per cent in Mizoram. Taking into account the electrification of 10698 villages @ Rs. 60,000 per village, total outlay required was Rs. 250 crore for the next 5 years.

Rural Water Supply: 1.52 lakh villages were having water problem (not having assured source of drinking water within reasonable distance of 1.6 km, water is having water borne diseases like cholera, guinea worms etc. and where water is having excessive salinity, fluorides content) as per 1972-73 survey. As per the estimates, the ongoing schemes would have covered at least 95693 villages by the period March 31, 1978. Some additional villages were also added as problematic villages making total villages to be covered 1.03 lakh. During the period 1978-83 all these villages were to be provided with safe drinking water. Keeping in view the varying cost of providing safe drinking water in various states. An estimate of Rs. 675 crore was made for the purpose.

Rural Health: For the purpose of providing better health services to rural areas, the coverage by a Primary Health Centre (PHC) was to be reduced from one lakh population to 50000 and of a Sub Centre (SC) from 10000 to 5000. 30 additional PHCs and 5000 additional SCs were to be established during 1978-83 Five Year Plan even as per the current norm. Other than that by the year 1988, 33000 more SCs were required to be established to achieve the revised norm. A target of upgrading 400 PHCs in to 30 bedded hospital for the 1978-83 Five Year Plan and 2000 PHCs for 1983-88 Five Year Plan was also envisaged. Community Health Worker Scheme was also started to strengthen the health System in the country by developing para medical staff on a large scale to provide elementary health assistance, preventive health care, covering a large area and lowering the cost of medical services. An amount of 490 crore was required for the purpose.

Elementary Education: Universalisation of elementary education for all the children in the country up to the age of 14 years is the commitment of the Government. With this in view all the children in the age group of 6 to 14 years were to be schooled by the end of 1990 decade and school going children in 1988 were projected tc be 7.2 crore higher than the enrolment at that stage. A teacher pupil ration of 1: 46 was worked out to know the teachers' requirement. At this ratio the teachers required were 1.59 lakh during 1978-83 and 1.98 lakh during 1983-88. It was decided that 50 per cent of the new enrolments might be given the education by the formal system and rest of the half through non-formal system. In fifth Plan 97 per cent coverage for the children in the age group of 6 to 11 years and 47 per cent coverage for the age group of 11 to 14 years was planned. This was enhanced to 90 per cent coverage for the age group of 6 to 14 years in 1983 and 100 per cent by the year 1988.

Adult Education: Adults play an important role in social, economic and cultural development of the country. They should be provided with full opportunities to play this role effectively by equipping them with the required tools like education. National Adult Literacy Programme was started for this purpose. All adults in the age group of 15 to 35 years were to be covered under the programme. The education should be oriented towards the needs and environment of the learners. For the adult literacy programme, the main responsibility was to be borne by the State Governments. Help from voluntary agencies, students, Yuvak Kendras, ex-servicemen and retired persons, block personnel, teachers, Government Functionaries, social workers may be engaged for the purpose on voluntary basis. A token honorarium was also proposed for them.

Homes for Landless Rural Labourers: Under this head the housing for the poorest among the rural population namely land less labourer was to be covered. At the beginning of the programme 1.7 crore land less rural labourers were in the need of the housing assistance. The assistance was to be provided for site development and repair work. This programme was of high priority.

40

Annapurna Scheme

In fact this is not a poverty alleviation programme, as it does not provide for any income generation. Objective of the scheme is to provide food security to meet the requirement of those senior citizens who, though eligible, have remained uncovered under the National Old Age Pension Scheme (NOAPS).

This scheme has been launched with effect from April 1, 2000.

Target Group: The Scheme is targeted to cover, 20 per cent (13.762 Lakh) of persons eligible to receive pension under NOAPS. The Central assistance under the Annapurna Scheme is, thus, provided to the beneficiaries on fulfilling the following criteria:

- The age of the applicant (male or female) should be 65 years or above.
- The applicant must be a destitute in the sense of having little or no regular means of substance from his/her own source of income or through financial support from family members or other sources. In order to determine destitution, the criteria, if any, in force in the States/UTs may also be followed.
- The applicant should not be in receipt of pension under the NOAPS or State Pension Scheme.

Part XI
Subsidies for Development of Special Problem Regions

41

Drought Prone Area Programme (DPAP)

Optimal rain is important for the growth of vegetation and the crops. Many parts of India are affected by drought frequently due to insufficient rains. Nearly 20 per cent of the cultivated land in India is under persistent drought. To provide adequate relief in such areas, this programme was launched. As per observation by The Irrigation Commission 1972, assuming that the areas which receive less than 75 per cent of rainfall per annum are liable to drought, 34 per cent area in 77 districts were covered under this category.

The programme was redesignated from Rural Works Programme, which was launched in 1970 for the integrated development of the areas affected by drought. An amount of Rs. 70 crore was allocated for the Rural Works Programme for the year 1970 to March 1974 in the 4th Plan.

Objectives: The objectives of the programme are as follows

1. To minimise the adverse effects of drought on production of crops and livestock and productivity of land, water and human resources through integrated development of the natural resources including rainfall for restoration of ecological balance in the long run.
2. To mitigate over a period of time the impact of the severity of drought.
3. To optimise the utilisation of all resources in areas with the primary emphasis on land, water, livestock and human resources.
4. To improve the economic and social condition of the rural poor who suffer most in times of scarcity and drought.
5. To promote the overall economic development and improve the socio-economic condition of the resource poor and disadvantaged sections inhabiting the programme areas.

6. To take up development works by watershed approach for land development, water resource development and afforestation/pasture development.

Date of Commencement: The programme commenced in 1973. The purposes of the programme are as follows:

- Development and management of water resources;
- Soil and moisture conservation measures.
- Afforestation with special emphasis on social forestry;
- Development of pasture lands and range management in conjunction with development of sheep husbandry.
- Livestock and dairy development
- Restructuring of cropping pattern and changes in agronomic practices and
- Development of subsidiary occupations.

Financial Allocation: During the Fifth Plan period an allocation of Rs. 181.5 crore was made under the programme. During 8th Five Year Plan total outlay under the programme was Rs. 1,000 crore. Since beginning of the programme till March 1995 an amount of Rs. 1,742 crore have been spent. The achievements of the programme are as follows.

S.No	Work undertaken	Area treated in thousand hectares
1.	Land shaping and development and soil moisture conservation	3000
2.	Development of water resources	946
3.	Forestry and pasture development	1784

Central share of allocation for the year 1995-96 and 1996-97 each was Rs. 125 crore. Under this programme more stress was laid on the development of the weaker sections, as they are the persons who suffer most during the drought period. This multi-pronged programme also provides opportunities for employment generation.

Coverage: Presently 961 blocks of 180 districts in 16 States namely Andhra Pradesh, Bihar, Chhatisgarh, Gujarat, Himachal

Pradesh, Jammu & Kashmir, Jharkhand, Karnataka, Madhya Pradesh, Maharashtra, Orissa, Rajasthan, Tamil Nadu, Uttar Pradesh, Uttaranchal and West Bengal are covered by the programme. The most recent identification of DPAP Blocks was made by the Hanumantha Rao Committee.

Funding Pattern: Until March 1999 the Centre and the State Governments were sharing the funding responsibility on a 50:50 basis. With effect from 1st April 1999, however, the allocation is shared on 75:25 basis between the Centre and State Government in respect of new projects sanctioned during 1999-2000. In respect of on-going projects that were sanctioned prior to April 1999, the old funding pattern continues. The cost norms adopted under DPAP for various eco-systems depending on the severity of the problem are as under:

Ecosystem Type	Per Ha Average Cost (Rs.)	Watershed Project Cost (Rs. lakh)
Semi-Arid Region	4,000	20.00
Dry-Sub-Humid Region	3,000	15.00
Dry Sub-Humid (Hill) Region	4,000	20.00

Physical and Financial Performance: Under DPAP, 6057 Watershed Projects were sanctioned in four different batches and taken up by the States up to 31.03.99. 2278 new watershed projects were sanctioned to the Programme States during 1999-2000 and 3371 new watershed projects were sanctioned during 2000-01.

Watershed Development: Since April 1, 1995, the programme is being implemented on watershed project basis as per the new guidelines for Watershed development. There is a target of developing 4995 watersheds during the period 1995-96 to 1998-99. A watershed of about 500 hectares is the field level unit for planning and development of the area and each project is to be developed in about 4 years. These projects are being implemented with the participation and involvement of the local people.

The responsibility for planning, executing and maintaining the watershed projects is entrusted to local peoples' organization specially constituted for the purpose. In view of the large area to be treated and the levels of available funding, the programme is taken up on a continuing basis for a period of about 5 years.

Watershed Committee is the executive committee for planning and development of the project consisting of 10-12 members from landowners, landless persons, 2-3 village panchayat members and one member of Watershed Development. There is a Watershed Association comprising of all adults residing within the watershed area. Watershed Committee receives and utilises the funds equal to 75 per cent of the sanctioned cost of watershed.

So far 6454 watershed projects have been sanctioned for implementation in 13 states through local communities. 5956 watershed projects are under implementation at various stages.

During the year 1995-96 an amount of Rs. 134.58 crore was spent against an allocation of Rs. 125 crore. The Central share of allocation during the year 1996-97 is Rs. 125 crore and during the year 1997-98 is Rs. 115 crore. This amount is to be spent mainly for the projects started during 1995-96.

Watershed Development Fund: NABARD has created a watershed development fund with a corpus of Rs. 200 Crore, as has been announced in the Union Budget for 1999-2000. The fund is expected to unify the multiplicity of watershed development programmes within the framework of a single national initiative to create a national movement of water shed development. The objective of the proposed fund is to spread the message of participatory watershed development through active involvement of local bodies like Gram Panchayats. This will create income generating opportunities for the land less and the poor, especially those belonging to the SC and ST and other backward classes. The programme would cover 100 priority districts in 14 states (Karnataka, Tamil Nadu, West Bengal, Himachal Pradesh, Jammu Kashmir, Uttar Pradesh, Andhra Pradesh, Gujarat, Madhya

Pradesh, Orissa, Bihar, Maharashtra, Rajasthan and Haryana) in 3 years. Tenth Plan allocation under the programme is Rs. 1,500 crore. Budget estimate for the year 2004-2005 is Rs. 300 crore.

Integrated Wasteland Development Projects: The Drought Prone Area Programme and Desert Development Programme adopted the watershed approach in 1987. The Integrated Wasteland Development Programme implemented by the National Wastelands Development Board in 1989 also aimed at developing wastelands on watershed basis. The Desert Development Programme focussed on re-afforestation to arrest the growth of hot and cold deserts.

The Drought Prone Area Programme concentrated on non-arable lands. Drainage lines for in-situ soil and moisture conservation, agro-forestry, pasture development; horticulture and alternate land use were its main components. The Integrated Wasteland Development Programme made silvi-culture and soil & moisture conservation in lands under government or community or private control as its predominant activity.

Evaluation: The Ministry of Rural Development appointed a Technical Committee on Drought Prone Area Programme and Desert Development Programme in 1994 under the chairmanship of Dr. C.H.H. Rao to evaluate the implementation and impact of these programmes. The Committee recommended that a common set of operational guidelines, objectives, strategies and expenditure norms for these three projects based on the watershed development approach should be evolved. The new guidelines, emphasising community participation in the programme and capacity building, were finalised as a follow up of the Technical Committee's recommendations. The focus of these programmes may differ but their common basic objective is land and water resource management for sustainable production.

Financial Performance: This quick evaluation exercise has revealed that in terms of utilisation of financial allocations, the performance under Integrated Wasteland Development Programme was comparatively better than under Drought Prone Area Programme. In the identified districts while financial allocations were utilised to the extent of 73.1 per cent under Integrated Wasteland Development Programme, the utilisation was 68.6 per cent in Drought Prone Area Programme. The performance under Desert Development Programme was 57.8 per cent. In overall terms, allocations were utilised to the extent of 61.7 per cent.

Increase in Irrigated Area: In the selected watersheds under Desert Development Programme the irrigated area increased by 60.4 per cent. The corresponding increase under Integrated Wasteland Development Programme and Drought Prone Area Programme was 49.1 and 31.6 per cent respectively. Provision of protective irrigation coverage in Drought Prone Area Programme areas needs higher emphasis.

Increase in Crop Productivity: The percentage increase realised in the yield of dominant crops in the selected watersheds has been analysed district-wise. In case of food crops i.e. paddy, wheat, jowar, bajra, arhar and gram the productivity increase was most impressive under Drought Prone Area Programme. In Kurnool district of Andhra Pradesh, for example, the increase in paddy yield of around 80 per cent was recorded compared to 29.8 per cent in Madhya Pradesh under Integrated Wasteland Development Programme. Similarly, in case of wheat yield increment of 82.2 per cent was realised in Gujarat (Bhavnagar) under Drought Prone Area Programme and 60 per cent in Haryana (Hisar) under Desert Development Programme.

Overall Impact: The impact of these programmes on the rural economy has been evaluated in terms of percentage increase in average income of household surveyed in the selected watersheds. These data indicate that the programme had a positive and significant impact on overall economic development in selected watersheds, except in Almora district.

Suggestions: In low fertility status soils covered by Drought Prone Area Programme and Desert Development Programme, cultivation of surface spreading crops (e.g. groundnut, soyabean, mung and urad) would help in checking soil erosion.

1. In non-arable lands 3 tier system of plantation (grasses,

bushes and trees) would provide adequate bio-mass to meet fodder, fuel and timber needs of the local population.

2. Contour vegetative hedges should be planted on sectional earthen bunds of small cross-section.
3. Sunken dugouts at suitable places need to be constructed for rainwater harvesting. Small stone and live checks across rills and gullies would stabilise soilscape and reduce erosion. Under DPAP, particularly, earthen and concrete water impounding structures should be constructed to collect maximum run off. Diversion drains in upper reaches of a watershed need to be provided for safe disposal of rainwater and prevention of soil erosion.
4. Crop cultivation alone cannot lead to viable farm enterprises. Although, the programme guidelines provide for developing alternative sources of farm income (e.g. livestock development, milk production, poultry & piggery, fisheries and bee-keeping etc.), in actual practice enough attention is not paid to such diversification. There is need for greater thrust to such programmes.

42

Backward Area Development Programme (BADP)

Some of the areas in the country were not going on the same platform as far as the question of development is concerned. Hence the concept of area oriented programmes started in 1970s focussing specific areas for various development purposes. The development of infrastructure was the major thrust in these programmes. Industrial growth in specific areas not only develops the area concerned but also provides employment to the people of the area. Thus that area gets a facelift due to development of various kind of infrastructure. Agricultural and allied activities alone can not provide all the year round employment to the labourer in the area. There has to be some alternative employment in the area other than agriculture and allied activities. The Backward Area Development Programme was a welcome move for providing the skilled employment to the youth of the area so that the pressure on agriculture can be reduced.

With the concept that the situation in backward areas cannot just be described as of comparatively less growth because in many areas the situation is worse than the stagnation due to negative growth, Backward Area Development Programme was launched in our country. The programme was to take care of these areas separately.

Area of Operation: There were 416 districts at that time in our country. Out of these, 273 industrially backward districts were covered under the programme in December 1982. The programme covers the following two industry-oriented schemes in these districts

- Special Scheme with Central outright grant/subsidy for setting up industrial estates/units in such areas.
- Concessional Finance Scheme for the projects in less

developed areas.

The programme was launched in the year 1971.

The Backward Area Development Programme brought some favourable results in providing employment to the unemployed youth and some people in local areas. Some development was noticed in the areas near industrial estates and units like some small eateries and small provision shops came up. But the industrial estates in backward areas could not succeed because of inadequacies of infrastructure and various other reasons. Hence the growth Centre strategy was adopted. However Backward Area Development Programme proved that for overall improvement of the economic situation of the country, industrial development is necessary.

43

Hill Area Development Programme (HADP)

Different approaches to area development were attempted in the Fifth Five-Year Plan. Under the Comprehensive Area Development Programmes a Comprehensive Plan for Hill and Tribal Area Development was devised. Under the programme two central sector hill area development programmes were taken up on a pilot basis one in Pauri Garhwal in Uttar Pradesh and the other one in Nungba in Manipur. Another Hill Area Development Project was set up in Tehri Garhwal. These projects were sanctioned entirely from domestic resources.

In the earlier plan periods, some special development projects were taken up in the area of hill development. These projects were launched under the Indo-German Assistance Programme in Himachal Pradesh (Mandi and Kangra Districts), Uttar Pradesh (Almora District) and Tamil Nadu (Nilgiri District).

Objectives: The programme has two objectives:

1. To maximize the agricultural production by integrated agricultural development and
2. To remove imbalances existing between the different sections of the community particularly in less endowed or disadvantaged areas and in different regions of the country.

Integrated development of agriculture, horticulture, animal husbandry, dairy, minor irrigation, soil conservation, drainage and provision of processing and marketing facilities were the aims of these projects.

This programme commenced in the Fourth Five-Year Plan and continued in further Plans.

Fifth Plan Period has an outlay of Rs. 2.10 crore for these projects.

The programmes were implemented through registered societies. The implementation of the programme resulted in agricultural demonstration, multiple cropping and use of high yielding varieties. Some of the Hill Area Development Programmes are given below to have an idea about various aspects of implementation.

Hill Area Development Programmes in Nilgiri Hills, Tamil Nadu: Under the Hill Area Development Programme implemented by the Government of Tamil Nadu, in 1993 on invitation from the Indo-German Bilateral Project to take up the community organization component on a pilot basis MYRADA entered in this area. This programme focused mainly on drainage line treatment. On completion of this project in 2000, MYRADA approached HOPE with a request to support initiatives in 3 micro-watersheds with the aims of soil conservation, water conservation and improving soil fertility on privately owned lands belonging to small and marginal farmers.

Watershed Management and Development: Sustaining Productivity' Project was approved by HOPE, Canada covering 3 MYRADA projects namely Talavadi, Kadiri and Kattery. The programme started in October 2000 and is for a period of 3 years, which will end in September 2003. The programme in Kattery covers 3 micro-watersheds with an area of around 1,070 hectares. There are 3 full time staff on the project, and 2 promoters support the programmes. The Project's main activities are the promotion of self help affinity groups of the poor and watershed development (including the promotion of community based institutions for watershed management). At present the project is implementing the following programmes:

Watershed Development: The Kattery Watershed Programme is funded by Hope International Development Agency, Canada, and covers 20 villages. Three micro-watersheds have been taken up for coverage, namely Muthinadu, Thambatty and Kattery. Self help affinity groups and micro-catchment associations have been formed in all three watersheds. During the year treatment works were taken up in the Thambatty and Kattery micro- watersheds on around 500 hectares. Activities such as bunding, land levelling, terracing, farm ponds, new tea plantations and re-plantations in existing small holders' gardens, and irrigation wells were taken up on privately owned lands. All these activities are taken up through the micro-catchment associations and are on a loan basis. Some treatment measures like check dams and gabion dams, stream lining and tree plantations were taken up on common lands with grants from the project and community contributions. Support was provided to establish a green house for floriculture, which is running well as an income generation programme for several families.

Programmes Funded by the Ministry of Planning and Development: The Shillahalla and Neeralipallam Watershed Project is funded by the Ministry of Planning and Development, Government of India, through the Hill Area Development Programme, Nilgiris. This programme covers 23 micro-watersheds, of which MYRADA partners the Government in 2 watersheds (i.e. Shillahalla and Neeralipallam). The role of the NGO is to organize the community into SAG/bs, Resource Management Committees. Watershed Associations, assist in capacity building of these CBOs, and assist in micro-planning along with the Government Line Departments like the Agriculture Engineering Department, Horticulture Department, Foresı Department, etc. The micro-plans are then consolidated, and based on the same, the programmes are then implemented by the watershed committees with the support of the Line Departments. In the current year, micro planning was completed in both the 2 micro-watersheds with which the Project is associated.

Tea Promotion Programme: Under the Tea Quality Upgradation Programme taken up by the Tea Board and funded by the Ministry of Industries and Commerce, the focus is on improving the quality of tea in Nilgiris District through village awareness, training, and mechanized pruning. 2 self help groups formed by the Project have been selected to participate in this programme. The members have been trained and inputs have been provided. Support to small growers also includes quality control and market linkages. In the current year, as a result of better garden management, plucking and marketing, the farmers were able to realise higher yields and were able to get 20 per cent to 40 per cent better prices.

Training Activities: All MYRADA-facilitated CBOs (*Community Based Organisations*) undergo a package of training to build their individual and institutional capabilities. During the year, 80 training programmes were conducted for self help groups, 12 training for federations, 13 training for micro-watershed associations and 7 training for the general category of farmers.

Future Plans: The HOPE-funded programme, which is the main programme of the Project came to an end in September 2003. As a follow-up, the Project will establish a Resource Centre to service the CBOs and provide necessary capacity building inputs and linkages.

In other hill areas also similar programmes are being implemented under Hill Area Development Programme.

44

Desert Development Programme (DDP)

The increase in human and livestock population in drought prone and desert areas has placed the natural resources of certain very arid areas under greater stress. The major problems are continuous depletion of vegetative cover, increase in soil erosion and fall in ground water table. All these factors account for diminishing productivity of land and loss of natural resources. The situation would have been worse but for the introduction of a highly focussed area-specific Dessert Development Programme in these regions. This is the sister programme of Drought Prone Area Programme.

The objectives of the programme are:

1. Controlling dessertification of desert areas through integrating and dovetailing other related Central/States programmes and to mitigate the adverse effects of desertification and adverse climatic conditions on crops, human and livestock population.
2. To conserve/develop and harness the land, water and other resources including restoration of ecological balance in the long run.

Though the main aim of the programme is to check desertification, the development of productivity and productive resources of the area is also being done under the programme. Afforestation, particularly forest and pasture development, water harvesting, animal husbandry and rural electrification are the areas receiving the attention.

The Desert Development Programme (DDP) was started in the year 1977-78. On the recommendations of the National Commission on Agriculture, in its Interim Report (1974), and the Final Report (1976), the programme was started both in the hot-desert areas of Rajasthan, Gujarat and Haryana, and the cold-desert areas of Jammu & Kashmir and Himachal Pradesh.

Area of Operation: In the beginning the programme covered 128 blocks in the following districts on the basis of variation in rainfall and temperature etc.

State	Districts Covered
(Hot Arid Regions)	
1. Rajasthan	All districts
2. Haryana	Hisar, Bhivani, Rohtak and Sirsa
3. Gujarat (Cold Arid Desert Areas)	Banaskantha, Mehsana and Kutch
4. Jammu and Kashmir	Ladakh Region
5. Himachal Pradesh	Lahaul and Spiti

From 1995-96, the coverage has been extended to a few districts in Andhra Pradesh and Karnataka. The programme is being implemented through Watershed Approach under the Guidelines for Watershed Development w.e.f. 1.4.1995. Prof. C.H. Hanumantha Rao Committee (1994) made the most recent identification of DDP Blocks. Presently 234 blocks of 40 districts in 7 States are covered under the programme as follows:

S. No.	State	No. of Districts	No. of Blocks	Area Covered in Sq Kms.
1.	Andhra Pradesh	1	16	19136
2.	Gujarat	6	52	55424
3.	Haryana	7	44	20542
4.	Himachal Pradesh	2	3	35107
5.	Jammu & Kashmir	2	12	96701
6.	Karnataka	6	22	32295
7.	Rajasthan	16	85	198744
	Total	40	234	457949

Funding Pattern: DDP is a Centrally Sponsored

Programme and funds are directly released to DRDAs/ZPs for implementation. Up to 31.3.1999 the Central share for different types of project area (based on the nature of the Eco-system) was as under:

S. No.	Type of Ecosystem	Central share
1.	Hot Arid (Non-Sandy) Areas	75 per cent
2.	Hot Arid (Sandy) Areas	100 per cent
3.	Cold Arid Areas	100 per cent

The ratio of sharing of funding, as between the Centre and the States, has been changed to 75:25 in all projects being sanctioned on or after 1.4.1999. Up to 31.3.2000, the project cost was Rs. 22.50 lakh per project in respect of the Hot Arid (non-sandy) areas, and Rs. 25 lakh in the other areas. However, for the projects sanctioned after 1.4.2000, the project cost has been enhanced to a uniform rate of Rs. 30 lakh per project.

From 1995-96 to 1998-99, 2194 watershed projects had been sanctioned in different batches and taken up by the Programme States under DDP. During 1999-2000, a total of 1500 watershed as well as special projects (Cost: about Rs. 325 crore, Area: 7.5 lakh ha.) were sanctioned.

Out of the 1500 new projects, sanctioned during the year 1999-2000, 614 were special projects sanctioned in 10 districts of Rajasthan, namely Churu, Nagaur, Jodhpur, Barmer, Sikar, Jhunjhunu, Pali, Jalore, Bikaner, and Jaisalmer to combat desertification.

These projects were specifically earmarked for afforestation, sand dunes stabilization and shelter belt plantation. It was decided by the Govt. that in these 10 districts, while 50 per cent of the funds allocated to a district may be used for normal watershed activities, the remaining 50 per cent should be earmarked for the aforementioned three activities.

During 2000-01, a total of 1659 projects were sanctioned at a total cost of about Rs. 497 crore. Out of these 293 special projects was sanctioned for the 10 districts of Rajasthan for afforestation, sand dune, stabilization and shelter belt plantation. In the year 2001-2002, 1359 new projects have been sanctioned at a cost of about Rs. 407 crore. This includes 264 special projects for 10 districts of Rajasthan.

Programme Implementation: In the beginning the programme had a budget of Rs. 15 lakh and the programme was being handled by the DRDA. The detail of the projects sanctioned and release from 1995-96 is given in the table below.

Projects Sanctioned and Releases Made under Desert Development Programme

S. No.	Year	Projects Sanctioned	Releases (Rs. crore)
1.	1995-1996	1693	101.00
2.	1996-1997	65	65.37
3.	1997-1998	36	70.01
4.	1998-1999	400	79.80
5.	1999-2000	1500	84.99
6.	2000-2001	1659	34.99
7.	2001-2002	1359	149.88
8.	2002-2003	1602	184.99
9.	2003-2004	1562	214.80
	Total	9876	1085.46
	2004-2005		215.00 (Budget Estimate)

Tenth Plan allocation is Rs. 1,100 crore under the programme.

45

Tribal Area Development Programme (TADP)

Government of India has specified 427 communities as Scheduled Tribes on the basis of their relative isolation in hills and forests, low level of technology and economic development, typical cultural ethos like language, beliefs, customs and institutions. In 1951 the tribal population of our country was 1.95 crore (4.29 per cent of the total population). In 1991 the tribal population increased to 6.77 crore (8.08 per cent of the total population). Majority (more than 60 per cent) of the population of Arunachal Pradesh, Meghalaya, Mizoram, Nagaland, Dadra and Nagar Haveli and Lakshdweep are tribals. 95 per cent of the tribal population live in rural areas. The all India literacy rate among the schedule tribes as per 1991 census is only 29.60 per cent against all India average of 52.21 per cent. And for tribal women the literacy rate is only 18.19 per cent against India average of 39.29 per cent. The position of majority of tribal population in respect of essential needs of the life like food, water, clothing, housing, sanitation is relatively much worse than other communities.

The need for a separate programme for tribals was recognized immediately after the independence. Hence special programme for the development of tribal people and tribal area was launched during the Second Plan period.

On the lines of Community Development Blocks, Tribal Development Blocks were established in predominantly tribal areas covering a population of 25000. 43 blocks were set up in the Second Plan, 415 in Third Plan and 4 blocks were set up in Fourth Plan. During the Fifth Five-Year Plan an Integrated Sub-Plan Approach for the tribal development was adopted for the first time. These sub-plans operated in 16 states and 2 Union Territories. It was estimated that about 66 per cent tribal population would be covered by these sub-plans. The tribals are living a primitive life on a subsistence economy living in the area and villages far from the modern society. One and all are exploiting them. They are also reluctant to any kind of change in their life style, rituals or the location. They were also dislocated from many areas due to coming up of Industrial Projects. As most of the tribal population remains in isolation from the main streams, their problems are also different and we need to cater to this category separately. The exploitation by middlemen and traders in procurement of forest produce and by moneylenders is common with tribal. Exploitation in sale of essential commodities, indebtedness, bondage etc. are some other common problems of tribal people.

To help tribals to come out of their miseries, the Large Sized Adivasi Multi-Purpose Societies (LAMPS) were formed. These societies were expected to provide production and consumption credit, supply of essential commodities and agricultural inputs and purchase of farm produce and forest produce from tribals. The societies were linked to District and State Cooperatives.

There are 194 Integrated Tribal Development Projects (ITDPs) functioning in the country at present, where the tribal population is more than 50 per cent of the total population of the blocks or the group of blocks. Under Modified Area Development Approach (MADA), during the Sixth Plan, pockets outside ITDP areas having a total population of 10000 with 5000 scheduled tribes were covered under the Tribal Sub Plan. So far 252 MADA pockets have been identified in the country. In addition to this 79 clusters with a population of 5000 having 50 per cent scheduled tribe population have been identified.

The programme broadly covers the following areas to improve the life of the tribal communities.

1. Communications
2. Education
3. Culture development of the tribal economy
4. Health
5. Housing and

6. Water supply.

Expenditure on Tribal Development was as given in the table below during various plans: (Rs. crore).

Expenditure on Tribal Development during Various Plans (Rs. crore)

S. No.	Plan	Period	Total Plan Outlay	Programme Expenditure on tribal development
1.	First Plan	1951-1956	1960	19.93
2.	Second Plan	1956-1961	4672	42.92
3.	Third Plan	1961-1966	8577	50.53
4.	Annual Plans -3	1966-1969	6625	32.32
5.	Fourth Plan	1969-1974	15779	75.00
6.	Fifth Plan	1974-1977	39303	1182
7.	Rolling Plans -2	1978-1980	24251	NA
8.	Sixth Plan	1980-1985	97500	3030
9.	Seventh Plan	1986-1990	180000	NA
10.	Annual Plans-2	1990-1992	173120	NA
11.	Eighth Plan	1992-1997	610000	NA
12.	Ninth Plan	1997-2002	875000	NA
13.	Tenth Plan	2002-2007		NA

The programmes have produced some favourable and beneficial results in tribal areas bringing in significant change in their thinking and attitude. These programmes have brought the tribal closer to the national main stream. The development was not spread over to all the areas and some areas got more benefits than other areas.

Special Central Assistance & Grants: Special Central Assistance is given to States/UTs to supplement their efforts in tribal development through Tribal Sub-Plan. This assistance is basically meant for family-oriented income-generating schemes in the sectors of agriculture, horticulture, minor irrigation, soil conservation, animal husbandry, forests, education, cooperatives, fisheries, village and small scale industries and for minimum needs programme.

National Scheduled Tribes Finance and Development Corporation: National Scheduled Tribes Finance and Development Corporation (NSTFDC) has been set up by the Government of India in April, 2001 as a Government company under Section 25 of the Companies Act by bifurcating the National Scheduled Castes and Scheduled Tribes Financial Development Corporation. NSTFDC is a fully owned Government of India undertaking with an authorised share capital of Rs. 500 crore. NSTFDC is an apex institution for financing economically viable projects to Scheduled Tribes. The corporation extends financial assistance to Scheduled Tribes at concessional rate for income generating schemes costing up to 10 lakh per unit, provides grants for skill development programme for STs and fill the critical gap by providing backward and forward linkages for activities undertaken by the target group. Members of the Scheduled Tribes whose annual family income does not exceed double the poverty line income limit, are eligible for financial assistance from the corporation, for economic activities in the fields of Agriculture and allied activities, manufacturing activities and service sector activities.

Efforts are directed to improve social and developmental indices of Scheduled Tribes and achieve better evaluation of the existing situation, bring about focussed attention on the felt needs of the Scheduled Tribes, and monitor the flow of funds to Tribal Sub-Plan from State Government/UTs, Central Ministries and Departments. Close monitoring of the implementation of the schemes/programmes for the welfare and development of STs has helped to improve better targeting of the beneficiaries and speed up the pace of expenditure on the schemes/programmes.

The strategy of Scheduled Tribe Development will continue to encompass protective as well as promotional measures. Protective measures include conservation of the existing land assets etc. with the Scheduled Tribes, Endeavour included arrangements to maintain land records showing the enjoyment of lands and to effectively implement the land reforms. However, effective steps are being taken for improving their lot and bringing them on par with others. They will get their due share in the fruits of over all development and feel a sense of participation in economic, social and political activities. The goal is to improve the quality of life and ensure them human dignity.

The Tribal Sub Plan (TSP) Strategy has been adopted for all round development of tribal areas throughout the country since Fifth Five-Year Plan. Under the TSP approach almost entire tribal inhabited area have been covered under one of the following, depending upon their population percentile:

- Integrated Area Development Project (ITDPs)
- Modified Area Development Approach (MADA)
- Clusters
- Primitive Tribal Groups

The TSP approach ensures allocation of fund for tribal areas from State Plan as well as Central Ministries. It is proportionate to population of tribals in the state (from state plan) and to the overall proportionate tribal population for the country from the budget of Central Ministries and Financial Institutions etc.

Part XII
Subsidies for Cinema, Art and Culture

46. Cinema, Art and Culture

46

Cinema, Art and Culture

Cinema, Art and Culture plays an important role in our society. Hence the development of these areas is very important. Some of the art forms are now becoming extinct because the people performing or creating that art are not able to earn sufficient money for their living from the art. Earlier the kings were the saviors of various art forms and the kings were providing the financial and other kind of assistance to artists. Now the Government is playing the role of kings. Hence various kinds of subsidies and assistance are being provided by the Government to save these art forms. Various Public Sector and Private Sector organizations are also encouraging the art and culture in India by providing various kinds of assistance.

Films gather good money. But they do also require the subsidy. As per U.P. Entertainment Tax Act 1979 section 11, the Government can make any film tax free, which it thinks that it has good utility for public and provides a good message subject to a maximum of 12 prints at a time are being shown in the State.. As per new policy, any film, which is shot at least 50 per cent in Uttar Pradesh, is eligible for subsidy from State Government. The Cabinet passed this on June 13, 2000 to give boost to the Film production in the state. U.P. Government gave exemption in entertainment tax to 31 films in last 17 months ending April 2005; out of this 11 films are in Bhojpuri and Regional Languages. Most of these films had got the assistance from the State Government. This resulted in loss of revenue in entertainment tax to the extent of Rs. 1.48 crore in the year 2003-04 and Rs. 2.45 crore in the year 2004-05.

Other States also provides various kinds of assistance and subsidy.

Multiplexes, which have many screens in one complex, are eligible for the concessions for 5 years. There was a loss of revenue to the extent of Rs.9 crore from the 5 Multiplexes in NOIDA and Ghaziabad alone. A subsidy of Rs.20.45 crore has also been provided to the 8 Multiplexes in the State.

Madhya Pradesh Government has decided to offer concession in entertainment tax to arrest dwindling cinema business in the State. Cinema halls have to pay the compounding duty payable weekly in advance @ 50 per cent in corporation areas and 40 per cent in other areas. The proposals for modernization and up-gradation of cinema halls will be considered by a committee subject to these halls are outside municipal limits and investment is above Rs. 5 lakh. Tax exemption will be available for three years.

The India Foundation for the Arts, a philanthropic group since 1993 is encouraging the local art. It provides grants to 14-15 artists every year. It has star-studded board e.g. Shyam Benegal, Chitra Vishveswaran, Simon Tata, Priya Paul etc. Grant is provided for Art Research and documentation, new performance, special grants for non-profit art organizations, art education etc. IFA has 125 projects in 17 States and has donated Rs. 6.2 crore so far.

The Kerala State Chalachithra Academy has submitted to the Government a `plan of action to tide over the present crisis faced by the film industry in Kerala' calling for urgent Government action on several issues and outlining various self-regulatory steps being taken by the film industry to overcome the crisis.

- Setting up of a `Film Fund' in the State to support and encourage the production of quality films in Malayalam and the overall well-being of the film industry. While quality films from the State get national and State recognition, there is little help forthcoming to distribute such films, the report says.
- Request is there that the best five films could be subsidised to the tune of Rs.5 lakh each. Presently subsidy is granted only to those films produced in Chithranjali studios, the report suggests that the Government grant subsidy to all Malayalam films produced in Kerala.

- An entertainment tax holiday is also demanded for all Malayalam films for the first 30 days from the date of release, exemption from entertainment tax for award winning films and children's films and a reduction of entertainment tax so that it becomes 25 per cent in corporation areas and 15 per cent in rural areas. It also calls for abolishing shooting fee in public places. special power tariff for theatres
- Providing tax exemption to theatres for the first three years are also suggested.
- Withdrawal of the turnover tax that is being reimposed on some distributors for 1993-1999 and sought exemption for 15 deemed HT' theatres from conversion to HT theatres.

Ministry of Culture takes care of various art and dance formed of our country. Here are many schemes in these areas. Some of the schemes are given below:

46.1 Schemes of Financial Assistance to persons Distinguished in Letters and Arts

The objective of the scheme is to assist the persons distinguished in letters, arts and such other walks of life who may be in indigent circumstances and their dependents. The Scheme cover the existing beneficiaries under the 1961 Scheme and fresh cases of writers, artists, etc. who are eligible for a grant under the Scheme.

To be eligible for assistance under the Scheme, a person's contribution to art and letter, etc must be of significance. Traditional scholars who have made significant contribution in their fields would also be eligible notwithstanding the absence of any published works. The personal income of the applicant (including income of the spouse) must not exceed Rs. 2,000 per month. Besides this the applicant should not be less than 58 years of age (This does not apply in the case of dependents).

Assistance from the Government may be in the form of monthly allowance. Such allowance given to artists recommended under the Center State Quota will be shared by the Centre and State Government/UT Administration concerned in the ratio of

3.1. However, the monthly allowance contributed by the Central Government in such cases shall not exceed Rs. 1,500 per month per beneficiary and in cases of those categories under Central Quota the assistance shall not exceed Rs. 2,000 per month.

46.2 Scheme for Financial Assistance for the Guru Shishya Parampara

Indian culture has great tradition of Gurukul. The Guru Shishya Parampara envisages great masters to impact knowledge to their disciples in the true traditions of "Guru Shishya Parampara. The Department of culture has noted the important of the great cultural traditions of India and started the Guru Shishya Parampara in 1990-91. The objective of this scheme was to preserve and a lot of rich cultural traditions. There are lot of rare and vanishing art forms in India, Which need to be encouraged through this scheme. It is essential that young talents should be nurtured to acquire skills in their chosen field of art under the guidance of experts and masters (Gurus). The various art fields where Guru Shishya Parampara can be implemented include traditional folk and classical art forms.

The Guru Shishya Parampara scheme in the identified art fields could be for a period of two years, subject to further extension of one year at the maximum. There will be one expert as guru with one accompanies and 4 pupils in each identified art form.

The honorarium/scholarship is to be paid to the guru, one accompanist and to the disciples after receiving the quarterly progress report from the guru. Their daily attendance is to be verified by the Guru.

The financial assistance for the guru could be Rs. 2,000 per month and accompanist could be offered Rs. 900 per month. The selected pupils would be given scholarship of Rs. 500 per month.

46.3 Cultural Talent Search Scholarship Scheme (CTSS)

Objective of the scheme is to provide financial assistance to outstanding young children selected in the age group of 10 to 14 years studying either in recognised schools or belonging to families of practicing traditional performing artists for developing their talent in various cultural fields such as traditional forms of music, dance drama, as well as painting sculpture and crafts laying special emphasis on rare forms which are in process of becoming extinct. Total Number of Scholarships available are 350.

The areas of scholarships are:

- Indian Classical Music: Classical Hindustani Music (Vocal and Instrumental), Classical Carnatic Music (Vocal and Instrumental)
- Light Classical Music: Rabindra Sangeet, Nazrul Geeti, Atulprasad, Qawali, Ghazal, Thumri and Dadra.
- Indian Classical Dance/Music: Bharatnatyam, Kathak, Manipuri Dance/Music, Odissi Dance/Music, Kathakali, Kuchipudi, Thangta, Mohiniattam, Sattriya, Gaudiya, Chhau Dance/Music,
- Theatre: Drama/Mime
- Folk/Traditional and Indigenous Art: Puppetry/Folk Theatre/Folk Dances/Folk Music/Others
- Visual Arts: Painting, Sculpture, Traditional Craft Form

46.4 Scheme for Financial Assistance for Journal Work

This scheme provides grants to Grants to universities institutions etc by Archaeological Survey of India under grant-in-aid and financial assistance for the work of publication of the report/journal etc. Grant -in-aid may be sanctioned to universities, education institution research bodies for the promotion of the Archeology; Ancient Indian history; Excavations and explorations, Publication of reports pertaining to different monuments and antiquates, conservation preservation of ancient monuments.

Universities/Research institutions may be granted financial assistance for publication their reports on exploration/excavation and their journals on archaeological research by the director general of the survey on the following conditions:

- The financial assistance shall not exceed Rs. 25,000 or the actual cost of publication whichever is less in each case.
- The expenditure on the salaries of the staff of the university institution attached to the work of publication of the report/journal shall not be taken into account while calculating the actual cost of publication and shall be restricted to the actual cost of publication and shall be restricted to the actual cost of paper printing block making and binding.
- All case of financial assistance in excess of Rs 25,000 shall be referred by the director general to the IFD of the department of culture for their prior concurrence.

46.5 Scheme for Financial Assistance to Professional Groups and Individuals for Specified Performing Art Projects

Under this scheme financial assistance will be provided to dramatic groups, theatre groups, music ensembles, children theatre, solo artists and for all genres of performing arts activities for following major components:

Salary Grant: Salary grant will be given to a maximum number of 20 artists and salaries to be decided by the Expert Committee. Amount of grant is Rs. 3,000 per month for Artist and Rs. 5,000 per month for One Guru/ Director.

Production Grant: A maximum of Rs. 1 lakh per year shall be given to the Organisation/Individual depending upon the project. However, in case of larger Productions meeting specific requirements in tune with the scheme the upper limit of grant could be relaxed with approval of the Minister

46.6 Celebrating History and Heritage

Country will celebrate the 150th anniversary of the First War of Indian Independence in the year 2007, an event that shaped the destiny of the nation. To ensure that the event is observed in a befitting manner, a provision of Rs.10 crore has been made in the budget for preparatory activities.

The two Gandhian institutions, the National Gandhi Museum, Rajghat and the Kasturba Gandhi National Memorial Fund, Indore have been provided Rs.5 crore each to the corpus of these institutions in 2006-07.

Kuttiyattam, Vedic Chanting and Ramlila have been declared 'Oral and Intangible Heritage of Humanity' by the UNESCO. These old art forms and oral traditions need to be safeguarded. An initial provision of Rs.5 crore has been made for the year 2006-07.

Union Cabinet has sanctioned an amount of Rs. 46.33 crore for completion of the Khalsa Heritage Project in Punjab. The Project would provide an insight in to Sikh Faith and showcase its history.

Appendices

Appendix 1

Estimates of Poverty in India

Poverty is a widespread social evil in underdeveloped countries of the world, particularly in Asia and Africa. There is no standard definition of poverty for all the countries of the world. Being a relative concept, the meaning of poverty differs from country to country. The concept, incidence and causes of poverty in India are examined below. Government measures to deal with this national problem are also described.

How is Poverty Line Drawn?

In India, poverty is defined in terms of a minimum (subsistence) level of living rather than a reasonable level of living. Thus, minimum physical quantities of cereals, pulses, clothing etc. are determined for a subsistence level. These physical quantities are multiplied by their prices and converted into monetary terms, determining the per capita consumption/income for subsistence level. Persons whose income/consumption is below this determined figure are considered to be below the poverty line.

Hence, poverty line is based on the definition of a norm which takes nutritional requirements into account and all persons below the norm are classified as poor. The present basis of the estimation of poverty line is based on the desired requirements of calories of 2,400 per person per day in the rural areas and 2100 per person per day in the urban areas. The monetary expenditure per capita needed for meeting these calorie requirements is revised upward periodically taking into consideration the rise in the prices of consumption goods.

Based on the foregoing procedure, the poverty line for a household worked out to Rs. 6,400 per annum for the rural sector and Rs. 7,300 per annum for the urban sector in 1984-85 at 1984-85 prices. In other words, poverty line for a household worked out to Rs. 533.5 per month for the rural areas and Rs. 611 per month for the urban areas. Or Rs. 17.70 per day for rural households and Rs. 20.36 per day for urban households. Assuming that an average household consists of five members, the figures turned out to be Rs. 3.55 per capita per day for rural areas and Rs. 4.07 per capita per day for urban areas. According to this definition, nearly 37 per cent of the people in the country were living below the poverty line in 1984-85. [1]

The Government increased the annual household income/expenditure for computing poverty line to Rs. 11,060 at 1991-92 prices during the Eighth Five Year Plan (1992-97). [2] Earlier, the income for the purpose was Rs. 6,400 at 1984-85 prices. In this connection, the Eighth Plan observed, "Views vary on the concept of poverty line and the method of estimating poverty. However, irrespective of the concept and measurement, there is evidence that poverty is on decline since the middle of the seventies. In 1987-88, as per the official methodology, around 30 per cent of the population was poor. Assuming that by 1991 poverty proportion declined to 27 per cent, even then about 230 million people were poor and not capable of providing bare essentials of existence....The target is to eliminate poverty by the turn of the century." [3]

cidence of Poverty

Widespread poverty in India has attracted the attention of a nber of economists and organisations. Leading studies on rty have been conducted by Dandekar and Rath, B.S. Minhas, Bardhan, World Bank and the Planning Commission of .

. **Estimates of Dandekar and Rath:** In their book *Poverty ia* (1971), Dandekar and Rath made a path-breaking study poverty phenomenon in India. Using the NSS data on nption, they concluded that in 1960-61, about 40 per cent of l population and about 50 per cent of the urban population low the poverty line.

B. Estimates of Planning Commission: The Ninth Five Year Plan (1997-2002) gave estimates of incidence of poverty for the year 1993-94. These were based on the National Sample Survey (NSS) consumer expenditure data of 50th Round (July 1993 to June 1994). Table A1.1 presents poverty ratios and the number of poor at the all-India level for different years. With reference to Table 8.1, the Ninth Plan remarked, "The incidence of poverty expressed as percentage of people below the poverty line is observed to have declined from 56.4 per cent in 1973-74 to 37.3 in 1993-94 in rural areas and from 49.0 per cent in 1973-74 to 32.4 per cent in 1993-94 in urban areas. For the country as a whole, the percentage of people below the poverty line declined from 54.9 per cent in 1973-74 to 36 per cent in 1993-94. However, the number of poor in the country remained more or less stable at around 320 million due to the rise in population. This fact should not over-shadow the 300 million persons who joined the non-poor group during the twenty year period between 1973-74 and 1993-94, but underlines the need for containment of the growth rate of population." [4]

Table A.1.1: Percentage and the Number of Poor in India

Year	Poverty ratio			Number of poor (in million)		
	Rural	Urban	Combined	Rural	Urban	Combined
1973-74	56.4	49.0	54.9	261.3	60.0	321.3
1977-78	53.1	45.2	51.3	264.3	64.6	328.9
1983	45.7	40.8	44.5	252.0	70.9	322.9
1987-88	39.1	38.2	38.9	231.9	75.2	307.1
1993-94	37.3	32.4	36.0	244.0	76.3	320.3

Note: The estimates are based on the methodology recommended by the Expert Group on Estimation of Proportion and Number of Poor as adopted by the Planning Commission.
Source: Government of India, Planning Commission, *Ninth Five Year Plan, 1997-2002*, Vol. I, p. 27, Table 1-9.

The latest estimates of poverty incidence in India are available in *Economic Survey, 2002-03*. These are reproduced in

Table A.1.2. To quote, "The success of the anti-poverty strategy is reflected in the decline in the combined poverty ratio from 54.9 per cent in 1973-74 to 36.0 per cent in 1993-94. The poverty ratio declined by nearly 10 percentage points in the 5 year period between 1993-94 to reach 26.1 per cent in 1999-2000. While the proportion of poor in the rural areas declined from 56.4 per cent in 1973-74 to 27.1 per cent in 1999-2000, the decline in urban areas has been from 49 per cent to 23.6 per cent during this period. The poverty reduction target set by the Planning Commission for the Tenth Five Year Plan aims at achieving a poverty ratio of 19.3 per cent for the country as a whole by 2007, 21.1 per cent for the rural and 15.1 per cent for the urban areas." [5]

Table A.1.2 Estimates of Incidence of Poverty in India

Year	Poverty ratio (%)		
	Rural	Urban	Combined
1973-74	56.4	49.0	54.9
1993-94	37.3	32.4	36.0
1999-00	27.1	23.6	26.1
2007*	21.1	15.1	19.3
*Projection			

Source: Government of India, *Economic Survey, 2002-03*, p. 213, Table 10.6 (excerpted)

The conclusions of various studies are different because they have adopted different methodologies to arrive at their estimates. However, there is a consensus on some points. Firstly, poverty in urban areas is largely the overflow of rural poor into the urban areas. Secondly, the incidence of poverty is the greatest among small farmers and landless workers in rural areas.

Causes of Poverty

Widespread poverty in India is attributable to a host of factors, viz. population explosion, lack of industrialisation, failure of land reforms and failure of fiscal policy to narrow the gap between the rich and the poor.

Industrial development of the country has neither been on desirable lines nor at expected rate. Undue emphasis on capital-intensive industries has failed to generate sufficient jobs for the labour force.

Land reforms programme was started with great fanfare soon after Independence. However, it has failed to achieve the desired results. The incidence of poverty in rural areas is mainly due to the failure of land reforms.

Similarly, taxation and expenditure policies of the government have not been used effectively to bridge the gap between the rich and the poor.

Government Measures to Remove Poverty

Poverty eradication may either be left to the automatic mechanism of growth process and/or to programmes aimed at direct assault on poverty. The initial thinking of the Government relied on the automatic benefits of growth coupled with a progressive taxation policy. However, this strategy did not work on desired lines. As the Eighth Five Year Plan (1992-97) observed, "The equity objective was sought to be pursued through redistribution of assets. But, land reforms could not be implemented effectively. The problem of poverty could not be tackled through growth, which itself was slow over a long period of time. Hence, direct intervention through poverty alleviation programmes became necessary." [6] Lately, the Government has increasingly resorted to direct attack on poverty through rural development and rural employment schemes.

Some major anti-poverty programmes of the Government of India are the following:

- Integrated Rural Development Programme (IRDP) was launched in 1978-79 as a programme of total rural development.
- The National Rural Employment Programme (NREP) was started as a part of the Sixth Five Year Plan to help those who

depended largely on wage employment in the agricultural sector.

- Rural Landless Employment Guarantee Programme (RLEGP) was launched on August 15, 1983 with a view to expanding the employment opportunities for the rural landless.

In February 1989, Government announced a new scheme called Jawahar Lal Nehru Rozgar Yojna for employment creation in 120 backward districts of the country. On April 1, 1989, the three employment schemes, viz. NREP, RLEGP and Jawahar Lal Nehru Rozgar Yojna were merged into a single rural employment programme named Jawahar Rozgar Yojna.

Tenth Plan on Poverty

Presenting the future scenario of poverty in India, the Tenth Five Year Plan (2002-07) remarked, "...the mandated reductions in the poverty rate of 5 percentage points during the Tenth Plan and another 10 percentage points during the Eleventh Plan, as stipulated in the Approach Paper, will still leave more than 11 per cent of the population, or about 130 million people, below the poverty line in 2012. Every effort, therefore, needs to be made to reduce the poverty rate even faster. It is estimated that with a proper sectoral and regional focus, it may be possible to reduce the poverty rate by nearly 7 percentage points over the Tenth Plan period if the growth target of 8 per cent is achieved through the state-wise break down that has been drawn up in consultation with the States." [7]

Notes

1. Statement of the Minister of State for Planning in the Rajya Sabha, November 28, 1985.
2. Statement of the Minister of State for Planning in the Rajya Sabha, March 9, 1992.
3. Government of India, Planning Commission, *Eighth Five Year Plan* (1992-97), Vol. I, p. 31.
4. Government of India, Planning Commission, *Ninth Five Year Plan* (1997-2002), Vol. I, p. 27.
5. Government of India, *Economic Survey, 2002-03*, p. 213.

6. *Eighth Five Year Plan* (1992-97), op cit., p. 7.

7. Government of India, Planning Commission, *Tenth Five Year Plan (2002-07),* Volume I, p. 7.

Appendix 2

Centrally Sponsored Schemes

A contentious issue related to Plan assistance pertains to Centrally Sponsored Schemes. In view of their national importance, these schemes are launched by the Centre and implemented by the State Governments with Central assistance. The Central Ministries concerned propose and formulate these schemes which are approved by the Planning Commission. The States execute these schemes under the technical guidance and supervision of the Centre which also issues guidelines regarding the contents, coverage, expenditure pattern, and staffing of such schemes. The assistance given for these schemes on a matching basis is over and above the assistance given for State Plans and the provision for it is made in the budgets of the Central Ministries. For example, in the agricultural sector, these schemes pertain to propagation of research and improved technology, disease control, preserving ecological balance, support to specific crops like pulses, cotton, jute etc.

The States are generally unhappy with their inadequate involvement in the formulation of Centrally sponsored schemes which mainly pertain to subjects included in the State List. Sponsoring of these schemes by the Centre is also considered an intrusion into subjects reserved for States. In this connection, the Administrative Reforms Commission opined, "The intrusion is not, technically, unconstitutional for it is protected by Article 282 but it is a question whether, with the help of financial carrot such intrusion is desirable and conducive to the growth of healthy federal relationship." [1]

The States have also complained against Centrally sponsored schemes on the ground that the system of matching grants involved in the schemes favours the richer States because they are better placed to provide matching funds to avail Central assistance. Such schemes induce the States to divert their limited resources to areas which may occupy low priority in the investment scheme of a State. As regards the magnitude of Centrally sponsored schemes, the Ninth Finance Commission observed, "Centrally sponsored schemes have grown in volume and number over the years. As of April 1985, the schemes under implementation were as many as 262. The outlay of Rs. 18,000 crore approximately of these schemes accounted for about 80 per cent of Central assistance provided for the State Plans during the Seventh Five Year Plan. This has happened despite States' objection to their proliferation and the decision of NDC in 1979 to roll them back to the level of 1/6th of the Central assistance for States' Plans by hacking away schemes costing a total of Rs. 2,000 crore. More recently, the NDC after considering the Ramamurti Committee Report in November 1985 had set up a Committee headed by the then Union Minister for Human Resources Development to go into this matter. This Committee had in turn constituted a group of officials whose recommendations favour retention of most of the schemes." [2]

The confrontation between the Centre and the States on this issue was considerably reduced when at the December 23-24, 1991 meeting of the NDC, it was decided to transfer 113 sponsored schemes to the States along with the allocations being made for these schemes.

Government's policy regarding Centrally sponsored schemes was made clear in the 1996-97 budget speech of the Finance Minister, "...it is our desire that most Centrally-sponsored schemes should be transferred to the control of the State Governments. In the meantime, States will be given greater flexibility in the implementation of these programmes. Provisions available under all other schemes will be pooled and the basic entitlement ratio will be worked out for each State. The States will be free to select for implementation, within their annual entitlement, such schemes that are more suited to their needs." [3]

Notes

1. Administrative Reforms Commission, *Report of the Study Team on Centre-State Relation-ships*, Vol. I, 1968, op. cit., p. 122.

2. *First Report of the Ninth Finance Commission*, 1988, p. 24.

3. Government of India, *Budget papers 1996-97: Speech of the Finance Minister*, Part I, p. 16.

Appendix 3

Highlights of the National Common Minimum Programme (CMP) of the United Progressive Alliance (UPA) announced on May 27, 2004

Fiscal Policy

- Revenue deficit to be eliminated by 2009
- VAT to be introduced
- Special scheme to unearth black money
- Revenue administration to be updated
- A cess to be levied on all central taxes
- Subsidies to be made explicit and provided through the Budget
- States to get more funds

Financial Sector

- PSU banks to have autonomy

Social Sectors

- Employment Guarantee Act to be enacted
- Public spending on education to be raised to 6% of GDP
- A national cooked midday meal scheme to be funded by the Centre
- A Reservation Act to codify reservations
- Spending on health to be 2-3% of GDP
- Labour laws to be streamlined

Industry and Infrastructure

- FDI-friendly industry policy to be brought
- Review of the Electricity Act, 2003

Agriculture

- Agriculture to get high priority
- Flow of rural credit to be doubled

External Sector

- Misuse of DTAA to be stopped